Organizations and Activism

Series Editors: **Daniel King**, Nottingham Trent
University and **Martin Parker**, University of Bristol

From co-operatives to corporations, Occupy to Facebook, organizations
shape our lives. They engage in politics as well as shaping the possible
futures of policy making and social change. This series publishes books that
explore how politics happens within and because of organizations, how
activism is organized, and how activists change organizations.

Scan the code below to discover new and forthcoming titles in the series, or visit:

bristoluniversitypress.co.uk/
organizations-and-activism

STUDYING
POLITICAL PARTIES
AS ORGANIZATIONS

STUDYING POLITICAL PARTIES AS ORGANIZATIONS

Four Perspectives on Denmark's Alternative Party

Emil Husted

BRISTOL
UNIVERSITY
PRESS

First published in Great Britain in 2024 by

Bristol University Press
University of Bristol
1-9 Old Park Hill
Bristol
BS2 8BB
UK
t: +44 (0)117 374 6645
e: bup-info@bristol.ac.uk

Details of international sales and distribution partners are available at bristoluniversitypress.co.uk

British Library Cataloguing in Publication Data
A catalogue record for this book is available from the British Library

ISBN 978-1-5292-1137-5 hardcover
ISBN 978-1-5292-1139-9 ePub
ISBN 978-1-5292-1138-2 ePdf

Cover design: blu inc
Front cover image: iStock/Mlenny

For my dad, Kristian Fabricius Husted,
who passed away while I finished this book.
I will always love you.

Contents

Series Editors' Preface

Daniel King and Martin Parker

Organizing is politics made durable. From cooperatives to corporations, Occupy to Meta, states and NGOs, organizations shape our lives. They shape the possible futures of governance, policy making and social change, and hence are central to understanding how human beings can deal with the challenges that face us, whether that be pandemics, populism or climate change. This book series publishes works that explore how politics happens within and because of organizations and organizing. We want to explore how activism is organized and how activists change organizations. We are also interested in the forms of resistance to activism, in the ways that powerful interests contest and reframe demands for change. These are questions of huge relevance to scholars in sociology, politics, geography, management and beyond, and are becoming ever more important as demands for impact and engagement change the way that academics imagine their work. They are also important to anyone who wants to understand more about the theory and practice of organizing, not just the abstracted ideologies of capitalism taught in business schools.

Our books offer critical examinations of organizations as sites of or targets for activism, and we will also assume that our authors, and hopefully our readers, are themselves agents of change. Titles may focus on specific industries or fields, or they may be arranged around particular themes or challenges. Our topics might include the alternative economy; surveillance, whistleblowing and human rights; digital politics; religious groups; social movements; NGOs; feminism and anarchist organization; action research and co-production; activism and the neoliberal university; and any other subjects that are relevant and topical.

'Organizations and Activism' is also a multidisciplinary series. Contributions from all and any relevant academic fields will be welcomed. The series is international in outlook, and proposals from outside the English-speaking global North are particularly welcome.

This book, the eighth in our series so far, is an extended discussion of one organization, a Danish political party called Alternativet. It might be seen to sit oddly within this series since we have tended to publish work about social movements and alternative organizations, and didn't really imagine political parties as being in the same category. We failed, for example, to mention them in our indicative list of topics for this series. This is rather odd, because most people would happily talk about activists within political parties, and it is clear enough that parties have been credited with many progressive social changes – whether by occupying the high ground of the state or having a significant influence on those who do. Finally, as Emil Husted states clearly at the beginning of this lucid book, political parties are organizations. They have employees, strategies, budgets, premises and all the managerial and socio-digital infrastructure of the modern organization.

Nonetheless, Alternativet is rather a different political party. It was launched in 2013, and gained its first political delegates in 2015. Refusing to situate itself on the left–right axis, this 'Nordic Green' party distinguished itself by a radical approach to policy formation. Using what it described as 'political laboratories' – a version of a 'citizen's assembly' – it built a political platform democratically from the grassroots up. Rather than announcing a manifesto in advance, either based on a particular political framing or the use of engineered focus groups to establish policies and language that would play well, Alternativet decided to begin with what its members wanted to achieve. This was a combination of political education with policy formulation which claimed to be based on 'values' (courage, generosity, transparency, humility, humour and empathy) not ideology, and which, in 2015, produced a remarkable crowdsourced manifesto with many sophisticated ideas and commitments.

Emil Husted knows Danish politics well, and this book is based on a great deal of close access to Alternativet. It's a fascinating story, but it's not always easy (particularly perhaps for non-Danes) to understand its implications more widely, which is why the author frames four different views of what this organization is and does. Distinguishing between the classical perspective, the configurational perspective, the comparative perspective and the cultural perspective, he shows us what is at stake in different accounts of focus, assumptions and blind spots. Depending on how we understand the organization, we get a different view of what it is that matters about The Alternative, and Husted encourages the reader to see his object of enquiry by using a multiplicity of perspectives. One view will not do, because organizations and the world are too complicated to be seen from one place, from one paradigm.

It seems to us that there has been an awful lot of interest in social movement politics in radical circles over the last few decades, and that this has taken place in the context of a widespread sense that the vertical needs to be replaced by the horizontal, the ends by the means, vanguardism by prefiguration and so on. It was as if all the exciting action, both politically and academically, was taking place outside 'the party', and indeed that 'the party' was increasingly connoting hierarchical, masculine and tribalist politics. We think that this book begins to challenge this common sense in two ways: first, by exploring the idea that the political party can be practised in different ways, perhaps becoming more inclusive, more democratic, and less electorally motivated in its policy proposals; second, by beginning to dissolve the distinction between party and movement, which itself relies on some old distinctions that organization theorists have inherited from Weber, between the formal and the informal, structure and culture, as if either side of those dualisms could be imagined on their own. This is the story of a political party as an *activist organization*, and it will hopefully build some long overdue connections between political science and organization theory.

We hope you enjoy this book. If you want to discuss a proposal yourself, then email the series editors. We look forward to hearing from you.

List of Figures and Tables

Figures

Tables

Acknowledgements

Some sections of this book include short passages from previously published journal articles. More specifically, Chapter 1 includes passages from the editorial 'Welcome to the party' (Husted et al, 2021), published in *ephemera*, and the article 'Political parties and organization studies: The party as a critical case of organizing' (Husted et al, 2022), published in *Organization Studies*. Chapter 8 includes passages from the article 'Alternative organization and neo–normative control: Notes on a British town council' (Husted, 2021), published in *Culture and Organization*, and Chapter 9 includes passages from the article 'Some have ideologies, we have values: The relationship between organizational values and commitment in a political party' (Husted, 2020), also published in *Culture and Organization*. Permission to reuse selected passages has been granted by all three journals.

1

Introduction

> Most contemporary analyses resist studying parties for what they
> obviously are: *organizations*. This resistance is partly due to the
> objective difficulties in an organizational analysis of parties. But
> it is also the result of widespread prejudices and attitudes in the
> literature on parties that create barriers between the observer
> and the object observed.
>
> Angelo Panebianco (1988: 3): *Political Parties*

Is the party over?

Not too long ago, the renowned political theorist Simon Tormey (2015)
published a short and punchy book, entitled *The End of Representative Politics*.
One might have expected a question mark at the end of the title, but the
book's name is phrased as a bold proposition rather than a question to be
debated – this is the end. On the cover, a diverse group of stick figures turn
their backs on a sign saying 'vote here', while marching towards some kind
of unknown destination, presumably beyond the formal political system.
The book's main thesis is simple: people across the world are increasingly
abandoning representative politics in favour of extra-parliamentarian modes
of political organization such as social movements, activist networks or
online communities. According to Tormey, politics is gradually becoming an
individualized activity that may concern common causes but is performed by
discrete and heterogeneous individuals rather than unified and homogeneous
groups. This development is very much driven by the emergence of new
information and communication technologies that afford what W Lance
Bennett and Alexandra Segerberg (2012) call 'connective action', but it
is also fuelled by a more general desire for speaking and acting on one's
own behalf instead of being governed by representatives (Beck and Beck-
Gernsheim, 2001).

Hence, we are moving towards an 'immediate or non-mediated' kind of politics (Tormey, 2015: 2), where individuals have realized that *democratic* politics is not the same as *representative* politics; and the first casualty of that realization is obviously the political party, with its supposedly myopic ideologies and hierarchical lines of command. As Tormey puts it (pp 90–91):

> So what, then, is the fate of the mass party? Decline, so it would seem, to a point where they become withered imitations of the once great organizations they used to be. What is left, as political commentators often note, are post-ideological 'brands' with vague connotations that help them to differentiate themselves from other offerings in the political supermarket. ... Political parties are now much less bearers of distinct visions than vehicles for rival leadership groups seeking power.

Plenty of signs in the present seem to support Tormey's thesis. For instance, party membership is approaching rock bottom in most corners of the world, particularly in countries like the UK and France where fewer than 2 per cent of the population are registered as rank and file (van Biezen et al, 2012), although the UK has experienced a slight overall increase in recent years (see Seyd, 2020). Similarly, voter turnout has plummeted worldwide since the middle of the 20th century, currently at a level well below 70 per cent in many countries (Solijonov, 2016). Voters' tendency to identify with specific parties is likewise declining due to the reconfiguration of class-consciousness and the emergence of 'liquid loyalties' in the electorate (Ignazi, 2017: 201). Finally, people's trust in political parties is at an all-time low, with politicians deemed less trustworthy than complete strangers and more dishonest than second-hand car dealers (Newton et al, 2018). As such, it seems fair to conclude, as many have recently done, that the party is – or, perhaps, should be – over (for example Holloway, 2002; Day, 2005; Rosanvallon, 2008; Keane, 2009; Castells, 2012; della Porta, 2013; Hardt and Negri, 2017).

To paraphrase Mark Twain, however, the reports of the party's pending death are greatly exaggerated. Financially at least, political parties have never been stronger. Owing particularly to a significant increase in public funding since the 1980s, parties are today more resourceful than ever before. In fact, most European parties receive more than two thirds of their income from state subsidies alone, and some are almost exclusively funded by public resources (Falguera et al, 2014). This tendency has given rise to the much-debated 'cartel party thesis', which extends the seminal work of Robert Michels (1915) by suggesting that party organizations are becoming increasingly dependent on the state – not their members – for survival (Katz and Mair, 1995 and 2009). On top of this, a range of countries across the world are currently going through a process of 'constitutionalizing' political parties, thereby acknowledging them legally as 'desirable and procedurally necessary for the effective functioning of democracy' (van Biezen, 2012: 187). The combination of growing public discontent and widespread state consolidation has thus created a paradoxical situation in which political parties are as powerful as ever, yet increasingly seen as illegitimate representatives of common interests (Ignazi, 2017).

At the same time, new 'challenger parties' (De Vries and Hobolt, 2020) have recently emerged across the political spectrum and created a much-needed sense of party revitalization in Europe and elsewhere. Podemos in Spain, Movimento 5 Stelle in Italy, Syriza in Greece, Feminist Initiative in Sweden, France Insoumise, the Momentum faction of Labour in Britain, the International Pirate Party, the pan-European Diem25, and many other radical contenders have contributed to this development. With inspiration from the inclusive and democratic spirit of 'square protests' such as Occupy Wall Street and 15M (Prentoulis and Thomassen, 2013), these parties have sought to translate the conventional approach to party organization by introducing social movement principles and practices to the electoral arena (della Porta et al, 2017). For instance, Podemos initially structured its organization around 'circles' where members and non-members could meet and discuss political issues in the absence of formal hierarchies (Pavía et al, 2016). Similarly, Movimento 5 Stelle successfully exploited the mobilizing affordances of digital platforms to become one of the most popular formations in Italian politics (Deseriis, 2020), and the international Pirate Parties generally created their success on the basis of bottom-up policy making (Almqvist, 2016). Towards the other end of the political spectrum, parties like the far-right Alternative Für Deutschland have similarly reconfigured German politics by relying heavily on social media for generating support and coordinating events, whereas the Dutch anti-Islam PVV has gone the opposite direction by creating a party with only one member (Mazzoleni and Voerman, 2017).

Such innovations within the formal political system point directly to the need for a deeper understanding of how these new contenders orchestrate their internal affairs, and how their novel modes of operation challenge conventional practices and procedures. However, the established literature on party organization tends to focus exclusively on topics that tell us very little about what Katarina Barrling (2013) calls 'the inner life of the party'. While we currently know quite a bit about things such as voter demographics, membership modalities, income sources, campaign strategies and methods for candidate selection, we know surprisingly little about what actually goes on beneath the glossy surface of party organizations (Borz and Janda, 2020; Heidar, 2020; Faucher, 2021; Gauja and Kosiara-Pedersen, 2021). In fact, the literature on party organization has even been characterized as empirically unsophisticated, precisely because it often fails to account for what is going on inside the party machine (for example Noel, 2010).

This is why, as Kaare Strøm and Wolfgang Müller (1999: 12) suggest, we need to find ways of opening the 'black box' of party organization. Fortunately, one breed of researchers is particularly skilled in this regard: organization scholars. The problem is, however, that organization scholars – particularly the 'critical' kind – seem to have very little interest in political parties. In a sense, organization scholars closely mirror the general public's tendency to disregard parties as important and relevant objects of interest, preferring instead to focus on 'alternative' and extra-parliamentarian modes of organizing (Husted et al, 2021 and 2022; Parker, 2021). The overall ambition of this book is to convince organization scholars and academics with similar proclivities that this is a mistake and to show them that there is much to be gained from studying *parties as organizations*.

The politics of organization and the organization of politics

Organization scholars have always been interested in politics. Not only does the discipline that today calls itself Organization and Management Studies (or OMS) often trace its century-old pedigree back to the work of political sociologists like Karl Marx, Max Weber and Mary Parker Follett (for example, Adler, 2009), some of the first research projects that openly claimed to be concerned with *organizational* issues centred on political organizations such as trade unions, social movements and political parties. Weber, for instance, derived a great deal of his insights on charismatic leadership and bureaucratic authority from first-hand experiences with the German Social Democratic Party and the National Liberal Party (Lassman and Spiers, 1994). Similarly, Follett used her own personal engagement with activist neighbourhood groups in the Boston area as a foundation for her visionary theses on organizational democracy and creativity (Ansell, 2009). Other pioneers of organization theory, such as Alexis de Tocqueville, Moisei Ostrogorski and Robert Michels, wrote explicitly about political parties but formulated their contributions to the discipline in more general terms (see Lipset, 1964; Swedberg, 2009; Diefenbach, 2019). In fact, one might even view OMS as a splinter-discipline that grew out of early political sociology.

For decades, the foundational interest in politics heavily influenced the work of organization scholars. However, towards the end of the 20th century, the focus on what might be called the *organization of politics* (the internal orchestration of collectives that openly engage with political issues) gradually gave way to a more general focus on the *politics of organization*, understood as intra-organizational struggles about means and ends in seemingly non-political enterprises (Mayes and Allen, 1977; Drory and Romm, 1990; Fleming and Spicer, 2007). The interest in the politics of organization intensified in the early 1990s with the emergence of the sub-field known as Critical Management Studies (see Adler et al, 2007) and is particularly visible in academic literature on the 'micropolitics' of various organizational phenomena (Contu and Willmott, 2003; Swan and Scarbrough, 2005; Wright et al, 2012).

Recently, however, a renewed interest in the organization of politics has emerged within organization studies. This has resulted in refreshing empirical work on different kinds of political organizations, such as worker collectives (for example Kokkinidis, 2015), NGOs (for example Dyck and Silvestre, 2019), activist networks (for example Sutherland et al, 2014), alternative organizations (for example Reedy et al, 2016) and large-scale social movements (for example Reinecke, 2018). However, one type of political organization has been almost entirely neglected: the *political party*. Considering the important role that parties play in contemporary society (Rosenblum, 2008), it is surprising how little attention has been paid to these political behemoths within organization studies. A quick search through some of the most well-read journals in the field shows that, save for a few exceptions (such as Moufahim et al, 2015; Husted and Plesner, 2017; Ringel, 2019; Sinha et al, 2021), hardly any studies investigate parties from a truly organizational point of view. Even independent journals that focus explicitly on the intersection of politics and organization, such as *ephemera* or *Tamara*, had, until very recently, only published one or two pieces on topics related to parties (for an exception, see issue 21(2) of *ephemera*).

One can only speculate about the reasoning behind organization scholars' lack of interest in political parties. In my view, there are two apparent reasons, both of which are highlighted by Angelo Panebianco (1988: 3) in the opening epigraph of this chapter. The first has to do with 'the objective difficulties in an organizational analysis of parties'. Compared with so many other organizations, political parties are difficult study objects. Not only are they, due to their heavy reliance on public support, incredibly sensitive about their public image and therefore not particularly inclined to give researchers access to their internal affairs, they are also relatively difficult to anonymize for purposes of confidentiality, especially in two-party systems. Moreover, political parties have porous boundaries, which makes it difficult for researchers to establish where the organization begins and ends (who are members of the organization, and who can speak on its behalf?). Finally, given the highly politicized nature of electoral politics, research on political parties can easily be read as partisan or biased, particularly if it is based on qualitative data such as interviews and observations rather than hard numbers or 'official' material produced by the parties themselves (see Katz and Mair, 1992).

Taken together, these things make political parties unattractive study objects for organization scholars, many of whom are used to studying cases that are relatively accessible, demarcatable and presumably non-political. However, there is another reason why organization scholars might prefer not to study political parties. It has to do with those 'widespread prejudices and attitudes in the literature on parties that create barriers between the observer and the object observed' (Panebianco, 1988: 3). To fully appreciate the extent of these attitudes and prejudices, we need briefly to consider the history of political parties as an unpopular yet prevalent mode of political organization.

A crude history of parties

Save for a few 'golden' decades after the Second World War (Mair, 1994: 2), political parties have always had a bad name. The first signs of partisanship arguably appeared in ancient Greece around 400 AD (Osborne, 2010), although the currently dominant understanding of a political party as a 'team of men [sic!] seeking to control the governing apparatus by gaining office in a duly constituted election' (Downs, 1957: 25) is clearly the product of a 'modernising topos' (Anastasiadis, 1999). Back then, political leaders did indeed form small groups among themselves, but, since ancient Greek city-states were direct democracies and not representative democracies, modern conceptions of parties sit uneasily with ancient understandings of *dēmokratia* (Hansen, 2014). As George Tridimas (2019: 988) puts it:

> There was no party alteration in government the way it is understood in modern democracies. Contrary to representative democracies where the government typically initiates legislation, in Athens citizens brought issues for discussion to the Council and the Assembly. Political leaders did not propose legislation in any official capacity, but as private citizens.

Hence, if members of assemblies formed partisanships, 'they did so on an *ad hoc* basis and readily dissolved them' (Hammond, 1988: 521). One reason why ancient Greeks were quick to dissolve any kind of political groupings is that notions of factionalism, later engrained in the word party (from the Latin verb *partire*, meaning to divide), was almost unanimously criticized by leading figures of ancient Greece for corrupting 'holist' understandings of the common good (Rosenblum, 2008). Plato, for instance, was adamant about the need for the Republic to act as a 'unified, harmonious and stable *polis*, with no source of dissension or rivalry' (Brown, 1998: 13–14). Parties, by their very nature, create dissension and rivalry. In fact, they have 'partiality and opposition *as their aim*' (Rosenblum, 2008: 11). As such, parties were frowned upon – or, rather, unthinkable – in ancient Greece.

The negative connotations associated with parties or factions were later solidified by Roman thinkers such as Cicero and Sallust who, perhaps even more forcefully, underscored the problems of promoting *partial* interests at the expense of society as a *whole*. Cicero, for instance, repeatedly argued that 'only harmony among the parts sets the conditions for the best government, just as the complementary functioning of bodily organs keeps a person healthy' (Ignazi, 2017: 12). Such conceptions of *Res Publica* laid the foundation for a profound scepticism towards all kinds of partisan expression, which came to dominate political thinking for almost two millennia and shape the common understanding of state-building in the early modern period, with Thomas Hobbes' notion of Leviathan as the most obvious example. As David Hume (1742: 33) later put it in his polemic essay 'Of parties in general': 'As much as legislators and founders of states ought to be honoured and respected among men, as much ought the founders of sects and factions to be detested and hated.'

The contours of modern party politics emerged in the middle of the 17th century when English politicians cautiously began forming groups in Westminster, according to the old Tory-Whig rivalry (Ostrogorski, 1902). However, political parties with actual members 'on the ground' (outside parliament) did not appear in Europe until the immediate aftermath of the French Revolution, where the Jacobin Clubs proliferated across France. What makes the Jacobins the first example of a proper party is that they not only managed to organize members of the National Assembly around a common strategy of protecting the outcome of the revolution from the aristocracy, they also subjugated these parliamentarians to 'one of the most effective party machines in history' (Brinton, 1961: 18). Although the Jacobin Clubs were later disbanded due to the combined pressures of anti-association laws and the Reign of Terror, the seeds for the emergence of the political party as the dominant template for political organization had been sown.

The resurgence of European democracies after the Second World War further confirmed the (pluralist) party system's role in guaranteeing democracy. At this point, mass parties gained legitimacy by manifesting a way to channel the political demands of previously excluded parts of the electorate along a left/right scale based on class distinctions spawned by industrialization (Neumann, 1956). This meant that 'the party' became the main object of class-based identification, with some parts of the electorate (most notably trade union members) automatically enrolled as rank and file (Wilson, 1974). In Denmark, for instance, almost 30 per cent of the electorate were members of political parties in 1950 (Kosiara-Pedersen, 2017: 29) and similar numbers can be identified in most other European countries (Kölln, 2016). However, with the post-industrial turn of the 1970s and 1980s, this logic became less evident. As children of the industrial revolution, mass parties had problems reflecting postmodern concerns over gender, ethnicity and environmentalism, and even greater difficulties responding to the increasing demands for intra-party democratization (Ignazi, 2017). On top of this, 'the party' became associated with atrocities of the 20th century, committed by fascist regimes in Europe and elsewhere, and therefore seen by many (at least on the political left) as an organizational model that led more or less directly to the concentration camp (Parker, 2021).

As popular support for mass parties once again declined, they transformed into what has been described as 'cartel parties' (Katz and Mair, 1995). Significant for the cartel party is that it forms stronger bonds with the state and collects more state funding, thereby becoming less dependent on the recruitment of members (see Chapter 4). The cartel party is thus less of a popular movement and more of a career route for politicians and functionaries. This development has arguably contributed to the current disillusionment with parties unfolded earlier: low party membership, low voter-turnout and low trust in politicians. The perceived decline of political parties goes hand in hand with the rise of 'new' social movements since the late 1960s and the subsequent proliferation of digital activism in the early 2000s. As Tormey (2015) shows, these movements resist not only the stifling ideological messages that are so characteristic of political parties but also their hierarchical mode of organization, preferring instead to organize according to 'subactivist' (Bakardjieva, 2009) principles that prefigure a more democratic, inclusive and individuating society (Monticelli, 2022).

In short, the party has fallen out of fashion, in the wider public and in the academic literature (see Dean, 2016). Holism, understood as the idea that 'political society should be a unity and that divisions are morally unwholesome and politically fatal' (Rosenblum, 2008: 25), is back on the agenda. The result is that researchers today increasingly prefer to study super-inclusive social movements and super-democratic activist networks rather than political parties (du Plessis and Husted, 2022). As argued earlier, this tendency is perhaps nowhere as visible as within organization studies.

Why study parties as organizations?

The argument advanced earlier is a simplification. There might be many different reasons why organization scholars disregard political parties as interesting and relevant study objects. I maintain, however, that the two causes highlighted by Panebiaco (1988) continue to hold validity: *parties are not only difficult to study, they are also difficult to love.* If we accept the argument that we, as organization scholars and social scientists more broadly, should try to overcome these two challenges and start studying parties as organizations, one important question begs an answer: *why?* There are many things that are difficult to study and difficult to love but lack genuine scientific value. So, what makes parties interesting, besides the fact that they are hegemonic characters in contemporary Western society? Or, more precisely, what makes parties interesting study objects for organization scholars?

A few years ago, I published an article in the journal *Organization Studies* with Mona Moufahim and Martin Fredriksson (Husted et al, 2022). In the article, we highlight five reasons why organization scholars should take an interest in political parties. Based on these five reasons, we maintain that organization scholars can use parties as 'critical cases' (Flyvbjerg, 2006) that allow us to zoom in on dynamics that may be concealed or even suppressed in seemingly non-political organizations such as traditional business firms and public agencies, or even in other voluntary organizations. This does not mean that these characteristics are unique to parties. It merely means that they are more visible and therefore potentially more rewarding to study in party organizations. What follows is an overview of these main points.

First, political parties are interesting study objects for organization scholars because they, more than most other organizations, have to engage actively with strategies of *exclusion and inclusion*. While in-group and out-group dynamics clearly exist in all organizations (Luhmann, 2018), and perhaps particularly so in membership associations (Solebello et al, 2016), political parties rely much more explicitly on the exclusion of ideological dissidents to define and demarcate themselves from competing actors in the political landscape (Karthikeyan et al, 2016). For instance, while few business firms would admit to discriminating against certain groups in terms of recruitment or promotion (such as women or immigrants), several parties on the far-right openly commit such exclusionary practices. So, political parties exemplify how constructions of organizational identities are never ethically or politically neutral as they always rely on the exclusion of certain interests and identities. Even parties that might be considered inclusive or progressive rely on exclusions to bolster their own organizational identity (Husted, 2018). Although this is perhaps not an entirely novel observation, the detailed examination of exclusion and inclusion processes within political parties could help organization scholars illustrate more vividly the political constitution of any given organization (see Moufahim et al, 2015).

Second, political parties tend to conduct their *infighting in the open*. While most organizations go to great lengths to hide internal conflicts (Contu, 2019), parties are often inclined – perhaps even forced – to display and act out their internal conflicts in public. Sometimes, this reflects a commitment to transparency and democracy (Ringel, 2019); in other cases, competing fractions use public attention for strategic purposes (Kelly, 1990). Additionally, since parties typically represent a highly formalized mode of organization, their structural configuration is often geared to address internal conflicts, providing spaces such as annual conferences and political rallies where internal struggles can unfold and be observed in real time (Faucher-King, 2005; Faucher, 2021). This habit of openly displaying internal conflicts makes political parties particularly suited for studying how such struggles unfold in practice, and how they produce certain organizational effects that would otherwise be hidden from public view (see Sinha et al, 2021).

Third, political parties rely heavily on active members who are *committed without being contracted* in any meaningful sense. Since the vast majority of party workers are not employed or salaried, their willingness to sacrifice time and money to work voluntarily for a political party reflects a strong normative and affective commitment to the organization (Husted, 2020). In fact, unlike social movements and activist networks, political parties usually charge members with subscription fees, thereby rendering the entry barriers extremely high and the exit barriers equally low. Recalling the perhaps most recognized definition of organizational commitment as a 'partisan' and 'affective' attachment to the goals and values of an organization beyond its 'purely instrumental worth' (Buchanan, 1974: 533), political parties provide good case studies for investigating more closely how such commitment is forged and maintained in voluntary associations. They also allow scholars to theorize what technologies are conducive in terms of building strong commitment to certain progressive values such as democracy and democratic participation.

Fourth, as they are created and maintained by committed volunteers, political parties must rely on *other modes of discipline* compared with most conventional organizations. The fact that very few active members are employed or contracted also means that parties have weaker formal means to control their members than employee-based organizations have (such as legal sanctions or material incentives). Political parties are thus forced to rely primarily on normative control mechanisms to ensure that members stay 'on board' and 'in line' (Rye, 2015). As such, what is sometimes described as 'party discipline' may be seen as an intensified version of traditional normative control, as observed in other kinds of organization (Willmott, 1993), which is why it makes sense to think of parties more generally as critical cases of normative control regimes. As such, parties can help us understand these mechanisms in general and the political dimension of normative control in particular.

Finally, political parties are currently involved in a transition *from bureaucracies to platforms* that is fundamentally reshaping many parts of society and its organizations (Deseriis and Vittori, 2019). Hence, the present represents a particularly interesting time to engage more closely with parties as organizations, since contemporary parties have been forced to reconsider their modus operandi in light of recent technological developments (Ignazi, 2017). The rise of social media platforms as a dominant means of interaction reshapes how political parties communicate with followers and foes and is beginning to affect their very organizational structures (Almqvist, 2016). A new generation of 'digital parties' are increasingly employing platform technologies and logics to enhance internal communication and democracy (Gerbaudo, 2019). Such new party models are relevant for organization scholars because they draw inspiration from the world of business and their success represents an example of profound institutional change.

Taken together, these five characteristics make political parties interesting and relevant study objects that organization scholars should not neglect (nor leave to political scientists). One of the many merits of organization scholars is their ability to penetrate the glossy surface of organizations and uncover the informal dynamics that help constitute social systems. Leveraging this ability in relation to political parties would undoubtedly bring many valuable insights about parties in particular and organizations in general. To make such contributions, organization scholars must of course familiarize themselves with the established literature on party organization. A secondary aim of this book, besides convincing organization scholars that parties are indeed interesting, is to assist them in this endeavour. The following section, therefore, reviews four waves of literature on political parties. Coincidentally, these four waves also represent four more or less distinct perspectives on party organization. The remaining chapters in this book are structured according to these four perspectives, and what follows is therefore a short summary of what is to come.

Four waves, four perspectives

The four perspectives considered in this book can all be given names that begin with C (perhaps this makes them easier to remember): the *classical* perspective, the *configurational* perspective, the *comparative* perspective and the *cultural* perspective. While the first three are well established in the conventional literature on party organization, the fourth is still in its infancy. In a way, the cultural perspective represents my own attempt to assemble the relatively small amount of work that has been done on parties within organization studies, in an attempt to give it a common name and therefore an honest chance of competing with the three original perspectives. As always, categorizations rest on simplifications. Some might argue that the configurational and the comparative perspectives overlap too much, or that a fifth perspective should be added. At the end of the day, this is my reading of the literature. Hopefully, it provides some clarity and helps organization scholars embark on a quest to study parties as organizations.

First wave: the classical perspective

As already shown, parties or factions have been at the centre of intellectual debates about politics at least since classical antiquity, although their democratic legitimacy remained in short supply until the late 19th century, where the rise of mass parties successfully challenged holist ideas about harmony and consensus (Ignazi, 2017). The acceptance of parties as integral to electoral politics thus coincides with the birth of political sociology as a hybrid discipline that overlaps with early organization studies (Adler, 2009) in its focus on issues that previously had been neglected by political scientists and classical sociologists (Sartori, 1969). This newfound interest for hitherto black-boxed phenomena is, in many ways, what fuelled the first wave of party organization studies. One example is Michels' (1915) canonical exposé of oligarchic tendencies in European socialist parties and trade unions. Having personally experienced how these otherwise democratic organizations slowly grew into bureaucratic machines and eventually succumbed to elite rule, Michels formulated his 'iron law of oligarchy', which would come to dominate studies of political parties for decades and has influenced research well beyond political sociology (Tolbert and Hiatt, 2009). As Michels (1915: 365) famously put it: 'It is organization which gives birth to the domination of the elected over the electors, of the mandataries over the mandators, of the delegates over the delegators. Who says organization says oligarchy.'

Michels' explanation for this seemingly inevitable drift towards elite rule is that, whenever a party gains maturity and influence, it becomes dependent on the state for survival. Its leaders then acquire an interest in preserving their own position in the formal political system and seek to defend their hard-won privileges. Hence, instead of trying to overthrow the established system and realize its own radical aspirations, the party's attention settles on the aggregation of members and the consolidation of power *within* the system. As such, it is no longer interested in fighting political opponents in the name of the greater good, only in outbidding them for personal and political gains. Rather than a means to achieve 'definite ends', the organization suddenly becomes an end in itself. According to Michels (1915: 333), there is thus a certain conservatism embedded in the 'nature of organization', which means that oligarchy is not unique to a certain type of party (socialist parties), but can potentially be found in any organization that pursues power and influence (Diefenbach, 2019).

This way of thinking about 'democratic aristocracy' (Michels, 1915: 43) as a phenomenon inherent to political organizations is likewise reflected in other founding texts within political sociology such as Follett's (1918) work on group organizations and Weber's (1919) writings on 'politics as a vocation'. However, the strong anti-party sentiment that undergirds Michels' analysis of oligarchy is perhaps most visibly expressed in one of the first texts to contemplate issues pertaining to party organization, namely Ostrogorski's (1902) seminal two-volume treatise, *Democracy and the Organization of Political Parties*. Committed to unravelling the historical circumstances leading to the rise of parties in America and Great Britain, Ostrogorski's work is perhaps best described as an inquiry into the pathologies of party-based government in general. The thesis that drives the text is that the formal inclusion of the masses in representative democracy spawned an unprecedented need for political association, which was accommodated by party organizations. In this sense, parties serve a perfectly legitimate function by ensuring the smooth workings of the governmental machinery. What makes them pathological, according to Ostrogorski (1902: 539), is that they fail 'miserably' in 'upholding the paramount power of the citizen' because party organizations tend to curb individuality and silence independent thinking. To remedy these shortcomings, Ostrogorski famously proposed an abolition of all 'permanent' parties.

Anticipating the work of Michels and Follett in particular, Ostrogorski thus identifies 'organization' as the main problem with party-based democracy. To these writers, the process of uniting citizens in hierarchical chains of command has a disciplining effect on the group, which limits individual freedom and undermines the revolutionary potential of democracy. Besides the shared disdain for political parties and their self-preserving nature, what characterizes the classical perspective on party organization is its inductive line of reasoning, whereby in-depth studies of a few selected cases provide the basis for formulating general social laws. A final characteristic of the classical perspective is the essayistic style of writing that allows the authors to blend sociological descriptions with moral judgements and to infuse their arguments with passion and indignation. Perhaps this is one reason why their work has had such lasting effects on political science and sociology.

Second wave: the configurational perspective

The second wave of party organization literature begins with Maurice Duverger's (1954) efforts to reinvigorate the scientific programme, initially announced by the above-mentioned writers, with the title of his most famous book *Political Parties* revealing a clear intertextual link to Michels' work in particular (also called *Political Parties*). Unlike these authors, however, Duverger introduces a completely new level of systematism. Instead of merely pointing to certain tendencies in electoral politics, his aim is to develop a 'general theory of parties' in order to show how 'present-day parties are distinguished far less by their programme or the class of their members than by the nature of their organization' (Duverger, 1954: xiii–xv). Duverger pursues this task through a three-fold focus on structure, membership and leadership. While all three themes are approached in genuinely new ways, his framework for analysing party structures marks the most solid milestone in the literature on party organization. Duverger starts by separating 'direct' parties (established and driven by members) from 'indirect' parties (established and driven by outside organizations such as unions or the Catholic Church). He then proceeds to the argument that all parties consist of a number of 'basic elements', four of which are prevalent: caucuses, branches, cells and militias (Duverger, 1954: 17).

Whereas caucuses (small elite units) are the basic elements of conservative parties as well as US parties in general, branches (large mass units) function as building blocks in labour parties and Catholic parties; and, while cells (clandestine occupational groups) are the *sine qua non* of communist parties, militias (highly disciplined private armies) constitute the backbone of fascist parties. This typology sets the scene for the rest of the book. Duverger consistently uses it to confirm his initial proposition about organizational configurations being the defining factor in distinguishing one party from another. For instance, caucus-based parties (also called 'cadre parties') are characterized as having a very small but active membership base, while branch-based parties ('mass parties') are described as operating with a large but more passive pool of members. Similarly, although most parties are said to exhibit some degree of oligarchy, the means for achieving and legitimizing elite rule varies, with militia-based parties openly embracing it due to the 'divinity' of their leaders, and cell-based parties disguising it through an elaborate system of 'indirect representation' (Duverger, 1954: 138).

Several of Duverger's contemporaries embraced his systematic approach and shared his focus on organizational structure as the primary unit of analysis (including Neumann, 1956; Eldersveld, 1964; Epstein, 1967). Many also continued the scientific programme of synthesizing; that is, of developing ideal types and categorizing parties accordingly. One noteworthy example is Otto Kirchheimer's (1966) account of the transformation of Western European party systems, caused by the gradual emergence of what he famously dubbed the 'catch-all party'. To some extent, catch-all parties resemble mass parties organizationally, in the sense that enrolling and coordinating large numbers of rank and file is a key ambition. Unlike mass parties, however, catch-all parties are characterized by a watering down of their ideological stance. A weak ideological position allows the parties to cater for the 'median voter' – the mass of citizens at the middle of the political spectrum (Downs, 1957) – and to secure political power by 'catching all'. The effectiveness of the catch-all strategy has, according to Kirchheimer, resulted in parties imitating each other politically as well as organizationally, thereby causing significant changes in party systems across Western Europe.

What sets Duverger's and Kirchheimer's contributions apart from those of Ostrogorski and Michels is their systematism, their focus on organizational configurations and their efforts to group rather different parties into homogeneous categories (caucus, mass, catch-all and so on). Common themes across both waves of literature include a preference for inductive lines of reasoning, where selected cases provide the empirical basis for widespread generalizations and the conviction that parties are only minimally impacted by their societal context. Kirchheimer's (1966) catch-all thesis is telling in both regards. However, both characteristics are challenged by the rise of the third wave of party organization literature and the emergence of a properly comparative perspective.

Third wave: the comparative perspective

The third wave of party organization literature is inaugurated by yet another book entitled *Political Parties* (Panebianco, 1988). While the exact reason for this case of title isomorphism remains unknown, the work of Panebianco is certainly indebted to Michels' *Political Parties* and Duverger's *Political Parties*, in the sense that all three books share a persistent focus on the organization as the primary unit of analysis. What sets parties apart is thus not so much their political programme or voter demographic, but their organizational dynamics. Panebianco's contribution to this research agenda is to turn Michels' interest in the internal organization of parties and Duverger's preoccupation with organizational structures into a framework for empirical analysis. The purpose of creating such a framework is, for Panebianco, to advance an approach he calls 'comparative-historical analysis', which enables researchers to move beyond single-case studies and 'isolate similarities and differences between the various cases' of political parties (Panebianco, 1988: xiv). To aid him in this endeavour, Panebianco turns to one of the most dominant organization theories of all times, namely contingency theory.

Panebianco's contingency theory of party organization begins with the proposition that political parties can be distinguished based on two factors: their history and their environment. In terms of history, parties tend to uphold political and administrative decisions made by their founders, even when these have proven unwise or outdated. In terms of environment, parties are influenced by a variety of contingencies, such as changing laws, sources of finance, intra-party competition and technological developments, as well as electoral results. This starting point introduces a new kind of dynamism to the static models developed by Duverger and his contemporaries because it acknowledges the often-neglected point that 'a party (like any organization) is a structure in motion which evolves over time, reacting to external changes and to the changing "environment" in which it functions' (Panebianco, 1988: 49). Based on this premise, Panebianco develops a framework for measuring the level of institutionalization achieved by a given party at a given point in time. The more institutionalized a party is, the more autonomous it is with regard to its environment, and the less likely it is to change its structure.

The conception of a political party as an open system determined by environmental conditions, rather than as a closed community living 'according to its own laws' (Duverger, 1954: 84), is well aligned with other contributions to the comparative perspective. One example is Joseph

Schleisinger's (1984: 390) characterization of parties as 'forms of organized trial and error', another is Kay Lawson and Peter Merkl's (1988: 5) description of party failure as something that occurs when parties 'do not perform the function they are expected to perform in their society' (see also Lawson, 1994). However, the most notable contribution to this 'comparative-historical' research agenda is, arguably, Richard Katz and Peter Mair's (1994) frequently cited anthology, *How Parties Organize*.

The most groundbreaking decision made by Katz and Mair (1992), during the data collection for the anthology, was to focus solely on what they called 'the official story', meaning that contributors to the project would have to rely exclusively on authorized material produced by the parties themselves. Hence, instead of approaching parties through a selection of both formal and informal data, the contributors would only consider official rules and statutes as well as 'other party reports and documents' (Katz and Mair, 1992: 7). The rationale behind this decision was that official data tends to reflect the current balance of power within party organizations, and that changes in this balance will eventually manifest in rules and regulations. Although acknowledging that the official story is not necessarily the real story, Katz and Mair thus refute Ostrogorski's (1902), Michels' (1915), Duverger's (1954) and Panebianco's (1988) warnings about not relying too heavily on authorized material as being 'fundamentally wrong in its emphasis'. The official story, they contend, provides a useful starting point for understanding the organization of political parties and offers an 'incomparable source of reasonably hard data that can be used in the analysis of party organization across both time and space' (Katz and Mair, 1992: 8).

The methodological principles spelled out in the work of Katz and Mair has had unparalleled impact on contemporary party organization literature. In fact, most studies of party organization today rely almost exclusively on 'the official story', albeit often without referring to their approach as such. One recent example is Susan Scarrow and colleagues' (2017) anthology, *Organizing Political Parties*, in which a number of high-profile authors set out to update debates about structures, resources and representative strategies in present-day parties. In this case, the editors of the volume explicitly embrace the official story approach, noting that 'this choice was made in full knowing that formal structures do not tell the complete story about actual power relations', and that 'the alternative would have been to collect expert judgements concerning these issues' (Scarrow and Webb, 2017: 13).

Such statements capture the spirit of the comparative perspective. First, they illustrate the departure from the methodological principles guiding the first two waves of literature. Participant observation, personal communication and other qualitative strategies for collecting data that were crucial to Michels and Duverger are not even considered options in more recent studies. Second, it shows how the analytical strategy has shifted from inductive reasoning and theory building to deductive reasoning and formal comparisons across time and space (see also Gauja and Kosiara-Pedersen, 2021). In that sense, the comparative perspective combines the classical perspective's interest in the orchestration of parties with the configurational perspective's focus on systematism and comparability, but completely abandons the ambition of understanding 'the inner life of the party' by almost exclusively analysing party-sanctioned material (Barrling, 2013). Fortunately, there is an emerging literature within organization studies that extends the (also limited) work of political anthropologists working with parties from a qualitative, in-depth perspective.

Fourth wave: the cultural perspective

The fourth wave of party organizations literature is perhaps less of an actual wave and more of a slow tide rolling in. Some of the earliest contributions to what I call the cultural perspective appeared in the 1990s, where political anthropologists such as Myron Aronoff (1993) and David Kertzer (1996) published ethnographic accounts of life inside political parties. Aronoff's study was actually first published in the late 1970s but was initially met with dismissive reviews that failed to appreciate the depth and freshness of his analysis of 'power and ritual' in the Israeli Labor Party. The second edition of the book was more successful, but Aronoff (1993: 3) still had to work hard to explain and justify what he rightfully called 'an unconventional approach' to the study of parties. What made Aronoff's study stand out from the majority of research on party organization was not only his focus on the symbolic aspects of party organization, such as the way in which rituals are used to promote particular understandings of the party and suppress others, but also his firm reliance on ethnographic observations. As he notes in the preface to the second edition (Aronoff, 1993: xiii), published one year after Katz and Mair launched their 'official story' approach:

> To the best of my knowledge, this is not only the first, but remains the only anthropological study of a major national political party. The use of extensive participant observation from the grass-roots branches to the most sensitive and closed inner forums of the national party institutions was without precedent, and regrettably has not (to the best of my knowledge) been emulated. The symbolic analysis of the manipulation of issues and the ritualization of politics in a modern socialist political party was innovative at the time [in 1977] and remains more unconventional that I would have anticipated or hoped it would be a decade and a half after the original publication.

In many ways, Kertzer's (1996) analysis of the Italian Communist Party's (PCI) transition to the post-communist era can be seen as the successor to Aronoff's work because it shares a focus on symbolism and builds on participant observations. Kertzer's main point is that symbols such as the hammer and sickle, verbal signifiers such as the word 'comrade' and rituals such as the singing of the 'Internationale' played a central role in the struggle between PCI's reformist majority and its traditionalist minority, and that the leadership successfully facilitated the party's process of becoming the Democratic Party of the Left by using these symbols, signifiers and rituals strategically. This approach to cultural analysis is later picked up by contemporary political anthropologists such as Florence Faucher-King (2005), in her remarkable study of party conferences across four British parties, and Emma Crewe (2015), in her equally impressive study of the UK House of commons. Both studies use anthropological methods to get below or beyond the well-polished surface layer and explore what actually keeps the party machine running. Only in doing so are they able to show that the 'official' story rarely corresponds to the real story, and that actual power relations do not always materialize in rules and regulations.

In the past few years, a handful of organization scholars have taken inspiration from this approach and helped popularize the idea the political parties can tell us something interesting about organizational culture in general. Examples include, but are not limited to, Leopold Ringel's (2019) study of the 'transparency-secrecy nexus' in the German Pirate Party (see also Reischauer and Ringel, 2023), Paresha Sinha and colleagues' (2021) account of Jeremy Corbyn's dramaturgical leadership practices in the British Labour Party (see also Smolović Jones et al, 2021), and some of my own work on Alternativet in Denmark and a local party in south-west England called Independents for Frome (for example Husted, 2020 and 2021).

However, unlike the three other perspectives, the cultural perspective lacks a consistent analytical strategy. This may have something to do with so few party researchers hitherto engaging with anthropological issues and methods, but it may also be caused by the somewhat slippery character of the concept of 'culture'. What are we actually talking about when we talk about culture, and where do we look for it? To remedy this shortcoming, I use Chapter 8 in this book to suggest an analytical strategy for the study of party cultures that build on the work of Joanne Martin (1992) in particular. Without going into detail, Martin outlines three approaches to organizational culture that seem oppositional at first sight, but which can actually be combined into what Sara Louise Muhr and colleagues (2022) call a 'multi-dimensional' framework for analysis.

When combining these three approaches, we are able to paint a comprehensive and holistic picture of organizational cultures that helps us see that some things unite all members of a party, while other things cause opposition and conflict, and that a number of additional things produce ambiguity and serve as a source of disintegration. This way of thinking about culture in political parties represents one way of moving the literature on party organization forward, since it helps us analyse phenomena that are otherwise overlooked by the other perspectives because they simply 'cannot be measured' (Eriksen, 2021: 21). However, to fully appreciate the value of the cultural perspective as well as the other three perspectives, we need to apply them and gauge the results. This is why one half of this book is dedicated to a detailed description of perspectives, while the other half is dedicated to their application. This leads us to the case at the centre of this book, namely the Danish green party called Alternativet.

Alternativet

This book is, as mentioned, partly about four theoretical perspectives on party organization and partly about a political party in Denmark that calls itself Alternativet ('The Alternative', in English). The book is structured so that one chapter outlines one of the theoretical perspectives, and then the following chapter applies it to the case of Alternativet. Chapter 2 unfolds the classical perspective, and Chapter 3 applies it to Alternativet; Chapter 4 describes the configurational perspective, and Chapter 5 applies it to Alternativet; and so on. In Chapters 3 and 5, I unfold the origin story of the party and analyse its organizational development. I will therefore not say much about that here, but some basic facts are useful to understand what kind of party Alternativet is, and why it makes sense to use it as a case for this particular book.

Alternativet was launched in late 2013 as a response to a number of perceived crises in contemporary society, such as the financial crisis, the climate crisis and what the party described as a 'crisis of trust' and a 'crisis of empathy'. It was officially founded by the former minister of culture in Denmark, Uffe Elbæk, and a union leader called Josephine Fock, but many less well-known activists worked hard to realize the project in practice. One thing that made Alternativet stand out from other parties was that it initially had no (or, at least very little) political direction. There was no political programme, no key campaign issues and no commitment to a particular ideological position. Instead, the idea was to involve members in a bottom-up process of policy making. Hence, all Alternativet initially had was a one-page manifesto, six lofty values (empathy, humility, generosity, transparency, humour, courage) and a handful of debate principles that were meant to guide the deliberative part of the policy-making process.

In early 2014, Alternativet organized a number of *political laboratories*, which are perhaps best described as themed workshops where members and non-members could debate particular policy issues (such as taxation, education or health). These laboratories served as the foundation for the policy-making process, and, a few months later, Alternativet could present its first political programme: a 64-page document bursting with radical proposals for how to make Danish society alternative. Many proposals concerned environmentalism and climate-change mitigation; others addressed problems related to mental health, education, culture, entrepreneurship and democratization more broadly.

A year later, Alternativet was elected to the Danish parliament with 4.8 per cent of the votes, which translated into nine parliamentary seats. The success story continued for a couple of years, but, in 2017, things turned sour. Internal conflicts arose, rumours of top-down management proliferated, and rival parties started to 'steal' Alternativet's thunder by branding themselves as greener or more democratic. This threw the party into a self-perpetuating downward spiral, which culminated in 2020 when surveys showed around 0.3 per cent public support for Alternativet. On top of that, more than 90 per cent of the party's members resigned their subscription in frustration, and four out of five MPs (including Elbæk) left Alternativet for a new rival party called Independent Greens, leaving just one MP, Torsten Gejl, to fight for the party's parliamentary survival. Prior to the elections in 2022, Alternativet surprisingly managed to regain some of its strength by forging alliances with a couple of minor parties and by electing a new leader, Franciska Rosenkilde, who genuinely seemed committed to restoring Alternativet's political and organizational legitimacy. At the time of writing (November 2023), the party is polling at around 3 per cent nationally and has six seats in parliament.

Throughout this book, I will describe Alternativet as a European green party, but it would perhaps be more accurate to categorize it as a *Nordic* green party. What characterizes green parties in general is that they typically originate outside parliament and emerge as a response to perceived environmental and democratic crises (van Haute, 2016). This kind of emergence has consequences for their ideological dispositions, which typically reflect a strong commitment to issues such as sustainability, ecology and veganism, and for their organizational setup. In fact, green parties are often described as the most internally democratic party family overall (Bolin et al, 2017). However, green parties are generally reluctant to be pigeonholed on a traditional left/right scale, preferring instead to identify with a third position outside 'old' politics, which is sometimes framed as non-ideological and driven purely by natural necessity (Stavrakakis, 1997). This final point is particularly true for the Nordic green parties, most of which see themselves as neither left nor right, nor centre (van Haute, 2016). All of these characteristics apply to Alternativet. The party emerged as a reaction to a number of perceived crises, it is heavily committed to green policy issues, it has (or had) an extremely democratic organizational set-up and it actively refuses to be associated with either the left (and the colour red) or the right (and the colour blue), preferring instead to be classified as the only true member of the 'green block' in Danish politics.

I have personally studied Alternativet and written extensively about its rise and fall in journal articles and book chapters (for example, Husted and Plesner, 2017; Husted, 2018; Husted, 2020; Husted and Just, 2022; Husted and Mac, 2022). Some of the following chapters draw on these publications, and this is one reason why the book centres on Alternativet. The more substantial reason is that Alternativet holds the potential to bridge the gap between political science and organization studies because of its unconventional nature both politically and organizationally. Alternativet has proved to be one of the most innovative political parties in Danish politics for decades, and it has rewritten the rules of the game in many respects. Hence, Alternativet is a curious phenomenon for people interested in electoral politics and for those interested in organizational dynamics and institutional entrepreneurship more broadly. As already mentioned, I view political parties as 'critical cases' of organizing in general (Husted et al, 2022), but I see Alternativet as a particularly interesting case of *alternative* organizing because it has so evidently challenged the dominant order and the established modes of governance in its field (see Dahlman et al, 2022).

In short, Alternativet allows us to see things that we might not otherwise be able to see in other organizations, let alone in other political parties, and the following chapters will hopefully make that clear. I am forever thankful for the unconditional level of access that I was granted by members of Alternativet from 2014 to 2017, and I am impressed by the fact that I have been invited to give talks and host seminars within the party, despite some of my more critical conclusions. In that respect, the party certainly meets its own standards of transparency and generosity. Rarely have I met such open and accommodating people. I can only hope that they too can see the value in what I have been doing for the past decade. A special thanks to those members and ex-members of Alternativet who took the time to discuss and/or read parts of the book. Here, I would like to mention Nilas Bay-Foged, Mark Desholm, and Nils Brøgger. You might not know it, but your help has been invaluable and a great source of encouragement all along.

2

The Classical Perspective

As soon as a party, were it created for the noblest object, perpetuates itself, it tends inevitably towards power, and as soon as it makes that its end, its master passion is to maintain itself against all opposition, with no scruple as to the means.

Moisei Ostrogorski (1902: 355): *Democracy and the Organization of Political Parties*

Introduction

In the previous chapter, we saw that the rise of political parties in the Western world coincided with the gradual emergence of mass democracy, represented most clearly by the expansion of male voting rights in the mid-19th century. As more people were given a voice in the formal political system, organizations were needed to mobilize and unify these voices, and to direct the ineffable 'will of the people' at the incumbent government. Although the first proper party may have been the Jacobins in post-revolution France, several countries in Europe saw the establishment of formal party organizations and party systems from the 1830s onwards. One might thus think that scholars interested in politics and government would have thrown themselves onto parties, just like researchers today take pride in studying various cutting-edge phenomena. However, most scholars of that time still dismissed parties as uninteresting or even unethical study objects based on holist ideas about society as a harmonious and unified community. Nancy Rosenblum (2008: 25) explains:

Because parties have partiality and opposition *as their aim*, they stand out among parts as the most esthetically, morally, politically unabidable. ... It is one thing to accept division and to institutionalize pluralism in a system of political representation. It is another thing to organize political conflict within or among acceptable parts by means of accusatory 'party'.

Certain influential scholars, such as Alexis de Tocqueville (1838) and James Bryce (1888), nonetheless did develop an interest in parties, but they predominantly focused on the role of parties as elements in different party systems (the US system in particular) and paid little attention to parties as organizations in their own right. The first to produce a text truly concerned with political parties is usually said to be Moisei Ostrogorski who, in 1902, authored a two-volume treatise that chronicles the rise of parties in the US and England. What made Ostrogorski's work stand out from previous studies was, according to himself, his interest in the *political forces* that drive democratic governments. Instead of extending his predecessors' focus on *political forms* (laws and institutions), he developed an interest in the practical reality of organizing popular rule, which served to direct his analytical gaze at the 'concrete individuals' who 'create and apply' these political forms in everyday life (Ostrogorski, 1902: li). This led him to conduct a longitudinal study of English and US parties and it forced him to develop new methodologies and novel research strategies for studying the orchestration of democracy as carried out by political parties. In that sense, he may be regarded as one of the first (unrecognized) organizational sociologists.

Ostrogorski's study was, however, quickly overshadowed by the work of his German colleague Robert Michels, who is responsible for the perhaps most (in)famous study of political parties hitherto conducted. Simply entitled *Political Parties*, the study reports on the concentration of power within European socialist parties and trade unions at the turn of the 20th century. Utilizing many of the same methods and strategies that Ostrogorski perfected (ethnographic observations in particular), Michels goes to great lengths to prove the 'universal validity' of what he calls 'the iron law of oligarchy' (Michels, 1915: 319). This law, in short, purports that any organization that pursues its objectives through the formal political system (such as parties) will eventually succumb to elite rule. Even the most egalitarian and democratic organizations (such as socialist parties) will, in time, transform into minor aristocracies with leaders that may have been elected democratically but remain practically irremovable. This bleak conclusion led Michels directly to the claim that democracy is a beautiful but fundamentally unachievable ideal. Towards the end of his career, he even began referring to himself as a 'scientific opponent' of popular rule (Scaff, 1981: 1281). This does not mean that we should stop trying to counter the oligarchization of modern democracy, Michels claims; it merely means that we are destined to fail.

It is difficult to overestimate the impact that Michels' study, especially, has had, not only on party research and political science but also on related disciplines such as sociology and organization studies (Tolbert and Hiatt, 2009). This is why these two studies constitute the backbone of this chapter. However, as often happens with 'classics', the reception of Ostrogorski and Michels rarely extends beyond their most colourful conclusions. Although there is much left to learn from the founders of party organization research, the two authors are often lumped together and undeservingly used as strawmen in much contemporary literature. This chapter, therefore, unfolds the two studies in greater detail, relates their contributions to other classical texts, and point outs what I believe organization scholars can learn from classical research on party organization.

Ostrogorski and the corruption of democracy

The pedigree of party organization literature is usually traced back to a Russian civil servant and politician named Moisei Yakovlevich Ostrogorski, born in 1854 in the city of Grodno, located on the western border of present-day Belarus. Having completed a law degree at the university in St Petersburg, Ostrogorski spent a number of years working as a civil servant at the Russian Ministry of Justice, where eventually he was promoted to head of the legislative department. In this first part of his life, Ostrogorski authored a number of school books on Russian history, in which he emphasized some of the emancipatory reforms undertaken by the tsarist regime during the 1860s (Barker and Howard-Johnston, 1975). However, when the authoritarianism of the regime suddenly re-intensified following the bloody assassination of Tsar Alexander II (also called 'Alexander the Liberator') in 1881, the reform movement suffered major setbacks and police brutality escalated as a consequence. Being an overt proponent of liberalization, Ostrogorski went into voluntary exile in Paris, where he enlisted in the Ecole Libre des Sciences Politiques (today known as Sciences Po) at the age of 30. Here, he was taught and supervised by the founder of the school, the liberal-elitist writer Emilie Boutmy, who significantly influenced Ostrogorski's future work and eventually shaped his attitude towards political parties (Quagliariello, 1996).

While studying at Ecole Libre, Ostrogorski crafted three papers on the development of the political party in America, the most advanced Western democracy at that time, and it was this work that gradually developed into his famous two-volume treatise *Democracy and the Organization of Political Parties*, in which one volume is dedicated to England and another to the United States (Ostrogorski, 1902). Although widely read, the book initially received a cold reception from some of the most prominent party scholars of the time, such as James Bryce and Abbott Lawrence Lowell who had both written extensively on political associations in America (for example, Lowell, 1908; Bryce, 1921). Their main criticisms were that Ostrogorski attached too much significance to the role of party organizations in controlling parliamentary affairs and that he overestimated the similarities between America and England (Pombeni, 1994). Nonetheless, his work was praised by many contemporaries for its historical approach and for being based on meticulous on-the-ground fieldwork, which allowed Ostrogorski to make novel observations about the inner-workings of political parties (Quagliariello, 1996).

Although Ostrogorski's name and credentials today appear on the first page of most academic reviews of party organization research, his actual writings have been surprisingly forgotten by the established literature on the topic. In fact, only a handful of texts seriously ponder the merits of his arguments and the consequences of these arguments for the study of political organizations and democracy more broadly. As Rodney Barker and Xenia Howard-Johnston (1975: 415) note: 'Though everybody knows about Ostrogorski, nobody reads him. There are uncut pages in the seventy-two-year-old first and only edition of his major work in university libraries, and there is remarkably little scholarly writing on him.' This was true some 50 years ago, and it remains correct to this day, which obviously raises the question: why count a figure that no one apparently reads among the founders of a densely populated academic discipline? One answer might be that any discipline worth its name needs founders, and that the search for pioneers can sometimes lose touch with reality. A more plausible explanation is that Ostrogorski did inaugurate the advanced study of party organizations, but that his main theses were – and are – so antithetical to the interests and objectives of modern political scientists that they have been conveniently overlooked, or perhaps even rejected as liberal romanticism with few implications for contemporary politics.

Those who spend some time unearthing writings about Ostrogorski will quickly encounter somewhat simplified reiterations of his most famous points: (1) The expansion of male suffrage rights across the Western world spawned an unprecedented need for organizations that could channel the will of the masses into the formal political system. Hence, mass democracy created the political parties. (2) The *raison d'être* of political parties is to win elections, and once party leaders realize that this goal is best achieved by softening the party's political ideals, the organization goes from being a *means* to becoming an *end* in itself. Hence, political parties are self-preserving by nature. (3) One consequence of this is that parties quickly become hierarchical and bureaucratic, with leaders demanding unwavering loyalty from the rank and file in return for electoral success, thereby constraining members' ability to think and act independently. Hence, the power of the party machine expands over time. (4) Another unwanted by-product is that the ideological differences between parties become gradually smaller to the point where it is sometimes impossible to distinguish one party from another. Hence, party-based democracy leads to a general loss of ideals and visions. (5) And finally, the only logical solution to this predicament is the abolition of all 'permanent' parties.

Since, however, these short reiterations are indeed simplifications, the following section is dedicated to an outline of what I consider Ostrogorski's most important arguments. This leads to a discussion of what I believe organization scholars could learn from his work, and how some of his insights on political parties might be transported to the study of other types of organization. Before embarking on this excursion into *Democracy and the Organization of Political Parties*, it should be noted that the primary focus here is the volume dedicated to England. The main reason for this is, as often highlighted in critiques of Ostrogorski, that European and US party systems differ substantially (US parties are not membership organizations in the same way that European parties often are, for example), and since the following chapter focuses on a European party – Alternativet – it makes sense to focus on the English volume here. Another reason for focusing on England is that many discussions of Ostrogorski's work centre on the historical significance accorded to the 'Birmingham plan' in the development of party organizations (Tholfsen, 1959). In what follows, we begin by considering precisely this aspect of Ostrogorski's overall argument.

Birth of the caucus

Ostrogorski's primary concern was not the organization of political parties per se, but the practical orchestration of democracy after the break-up of the 'old society', understood as the aristocratic order that existed in Britain prior to the gradual expansion of male suffrage in the mid-19th century. The old society was, according to Ostrogorski, one of clear social stratification but also of relative political harmony. In parliament, the Tories and the Whigs fought each other in a perpetual rivalry for seats and influence, but the positions were more or less predetermined. The Whigs always represented the 'attacking' side, constantly advocating liberal progress and societal reformation, while the Tories represented the defensive side of institutional preservation. Outside parliament, the middle class openly admired the privileges of the aristocracy but without the sense of antagonism seen elsewhere, while the working class almost entirely abstained from revolutionary activity. In Ostrogorski's view, this order represented the complete subordination of the individual to society, in the sense that personal liberty and independent thinking was heavily constrained by a combination of legal arrangements and stultifying social discipline. Everyone played their part in a harmonious but undemocratic society with little room for breaking out of old customs.

The first blow to the old English society was dealt in 1832 with the passing of the first reform act, which enfranchised property owners of a certain status. The second blow came in 1867, when the second reform act extended voting rights to the urban male working class through the notion of household suffrage (one vote per household), thereby doubling the total number of electors. This immediately created a new situation for the two political parties. Not only did they have to secure support from larger and more diverse constituencies, they also had to deal with a new minority clause, which introduced a system of limited voting, intended to protect minorities against the absolute power of the majority. In practice, the minority clause meant that the parties could no longer count on winning all seats in otherwise loyal constituencies because the limited voting system always left seats open for minority representatives. The parties thus needed to find a way of enlisting minority voters, to secure maximum electoral support versus their arch enemies on the other side of the parliamentary floor.

In Ostrogorski's version of events, the solution to this predicament was initially conceived in the city of Birmingham by the radical liberal politician Joseph Chamberlain, who was planning to run for office in the mayoral elections of 1873, and his chief strategist Francis Schnadhorst. Faced with a situation, in which they had to win support from middle-class and working-class voters across multiple city districts, Chamberlain and Schnadhorst devised a plan to discipline voters through a system infamously known as 'vote-as-you-are-told' (Ostrogorski, 1902: 169). The idea was to convince people to vote in a strategic fashion, with certain segments voting for certain candidates and other segments voting for other candidates, thereby ensuring that the liberals claimed the overall victory and ousted nearly all conservative candidates from city hall by 'stealing' their minority seats. To realize this plan, the liberals needed an elaborate organizational set-up, in which a network of ardent supporter would spend most of their time canvassing and registering voters. By travelling around town to instruct voters on how to vote and by constantly referring to the conservative party as 'the enemy', while sometimes even disturbing Tory meetings through violent methods, the liberals eventually succeeded: Chamberlain was pronounced mayor of Birmingham and re-elected three years later, while the Tories were reduced to relative insignificance. As Ostrogorski sarcastically remarks, 'the discipline in the electorate was perfect' (Ostrogorski, 1902: 171). Hence, when the Liberal Party surprisingly lost the national elections a year later, having been in office for almost half a century, everyone looked to Birmingham for a comeback strategy (Ostrogorski, 1902: 172, emphasis in original):

> The Liberals, who imagined that the country had given them a perpetual lease of power, could not get over it; and, as generally happens to beaten parties, they looked outside their own conduct for the cause of the electoral catastrophe and found it chiefly in the fact that they *were badly organized*. The 'Birmingham plan' claimed to supply a perfect remedy for this deficiency. The defeated candidates took a special interest in it, they accepted it with the naïve confidence of certain gamblers who swallow puffs of an 'infallible method of winning' at *rouge et noir*.

This highly organized way of electioneering, born in Birmingham and adopted nationally, in which an extra-parliamentarian organization orchestrates the campaigning strategy, was given a nickname by observers of a more conservative persuasion: *caucus*. In a US context, the notion of caucus was originally used to designate 'wire-pullers' working behind the scenes to marshal support for political causes, and it was in this somewhat derogatory sense that the word was used by British conservatives to describe the 'Birmingham plan'. Himself sceptical of this new mode of political organizing, Ostrogorski (1902: 120) likewise use the word caucus to describe 'a small committee of men who settle electoral affairs privately beforehand'. According to Ostrogorski, the success of the caucus forever changed the workings of Western democracy, as it turned electoral politics into a matter of *organization* rather than a matter of political deliberation. The key to winning elections was no longer about constructing the best policies or presenting the best arguments; it was a matter of disciplining the electorate and pitting them against opposing parties. The caucus thus represents a re-subordination of the individual to the collective. This time, however, it was not society that imposed itself on the individual but the raw power of the party machine.

The machine at work

Although Ostrogorski is often portrayed as the high priest of the 'blame-it-on-the-parties movement' (Heidar and Koole, 1999: 1) and generally characterized as a relentless critic of organized politics, he maintained that the rise of the caucus in the late 19th century served several legitimate democratic functions. For one, the caucus helped democratize electoral politics by removing some of the power vested in MPs and pushing it downwards to the local party associations. As a natural consequence, the caucus also helped make those in the lower strata of British society interested in politics in a way that they had never been before. The caucus accomplished this by composing a liturgy of meetings, dinners, demonstrations and other social gatherings 'intended to keep the voters always on the go' (Ostrogorski, 1902: 558). Through these meetings, people were enlisted as members or supporters of the party and encouraged to view the party as a place associated with social belonging. For instance, Ostrogorski recounts how the liberal caucus gave 'the people fêtes and entertainment to amuse them, and consequently to advertise the party' (Ostrogorski, 1902: 436), and how it would organize picnics with 'good-looking women' as a way of ensuring 'the presence at the meeting of several young men' (p 438).

However, these social initiatives also helped move politics away from the realm of intellectual reasoning and towards the realm of feelings and seduction. One unfortunate consequence of this was, according to Ostrogorski, that the caucus manufactured a type of group mentality that seriously diminished the space for freedom and independence within the party. The price for political participation and social belonging, both of which the caucus supplied, was the surrender of independent thinking and action on the part of its members. The rise of the caucus did, in other words, introduce a whole new level of party discipline that, in Ostrogorski's view, stifled the possibility for enlightened discussions by requiring absolute loyalty from the rank and file: 'Every attempt at asserting the freedom and independence of political thought was now repressed; for every difference of opinion was a blow struck at the unity of the party of which the Caucus had constituted itself as the permanent guardian' (Ostrogorski, 1902: 586). In that sense, Ostrogorski held the caucus directly responsible for the dwindling of individualism and freethinking within political parties and representative democracy more broadly.

The power of the caucus was exercised not only through the introduction of party discipline but also through an elaborate system of manipulation or 'wire-pulling'. This type of manipulation was most visibly displayed through the selection of candidates to run for office. Although the decision to field candidates rested with the local associations, the 'central committee' in London would frequently interfere with local affairs and 'suggest' to local organizers 'excellent candidates' deemed congruent with the predetermined objectives of the party (Ostrogorski, 1902: 507). So, the organization of the caucus constituted a 'hierarchy of wire-pullers', in which the central committee pulled the strings of county associations who then pulled the strings of district associations who then pulled the strings of town associations who then performed the selection of candidates.

This shadow structure contributed further to Ostrogorski's disillusionment with caucus-style party organization, but what bothered him most was arguably the fact that the caucus also exercised considerable influence on elected politicians and their political decisions. The caucus achieved this through its status as an intermediary between the representatives and the represented. Previously, members of parliament were in direct contact with their constituencies and had feelings of 'devotion and affection' towards their electors (Ostrogorski, 1902: 606), but with the rise of the caucus, a wedge was inserted between the politician and his constituency. The role of mediator allowed the caucus to once again 'suggest' that the MPs vote in certain ways, effectively taking over or supplementing the role of the parliamentary whip. In Ostrogorski's view, this was perhaps the biggest crime against the promise of democracy, committed by the 'professionals' in charge of the party machine.

From permanent parties to temporary organizations

The main democratic problem with caucus-style government is, according to Ostrogorski, that it severely impairs the individual's ability to think freely and act independently (what he called the 'free play of opinion'). Not only are the rank and file subjected to suffocating party discipline, which curbs the egalitarian hopes invested in mass franchise, but the fact that duly elected members of parliament are exposed to political alignment in the name of party unity constitutes a violation of the deliberative foundation of democratic politics. Ostrogorski considered the encroachment of the caucus on the individual freedom of both MPs and ordinary members an outright corruption of democracy, in the sense that it represents a return to the aristocratic order where the few control the many – this time, however, the few have not even been elected! There is thus a dilemma at the centre of Ostrogorski's analysis. One the one hand, democracy requires some kind of organization of the masses – a way of channelling the will of the people into the political system – but, on the other hand, the organizational template supplied by political parties represents a return to a pre-democratic state of affairs where individualism is eclipsed by discipline and uniformity.

This dilemma led Ostrogorski to propose a solution to the pathologies of party politics, for which he is probably best known today, namely the abolition of all 'permanent' parties. In the absence of permanent parties, the formal political system would be structured around a multiplicity of 'temporary' or single-issue organizations that would exist only for as long as their particular cause remained unresolved. In that way, Ostrogorski believed, the problems of whipping and wire-pulling would be eliminated because people would know in advance precisely what an organization stood for and how it planned to achieve that objective. As soon as its mission was completed, the organization would automatically dissolve instead of turning into a self-preserving entity whose 'master passion is to maintain itself against all opposition, with no scruples as to the means' (Ostrogorski, 1902: 355). Once structured around temporary, spontaneously created organizations, democracy would finally be able to realize its full potential of emancipating the individual from aristocratic oppression.

Hence, it is only fitting that, when Ostrogorski returned to Russia in 1906, he was elected to the Duma as a representative of the Grodno province, and, although he often collaborated with the liberal-minded Constitutional Democratic Party (also known as the Kadets), he remained an independent thinker and politician, listed in the proceedings of the First Duma as a 'non-party member' (Barker and Howard-Johnston, 1975: 420).

Ostrogorski's unrecognized contribution to organization studies

In his introduction to Ostrogorski's *Democracy and the Organization of Political Parties*, the renowned sociologist Seymour Martin Lipset (1964: xiv) claims that Ostrogorski should be seen as a pioneer not only of the sociological study of political parties but also of organizational sociology more broadly.

Yet, conventional books or articles on organization theory or organizational sociology hardly ever mention Ostrogorski's name, let alone consider his work in detail (for example, Knudsen and Tsoukas, 2005; Adler, 2009). This immediately brings us to the questions: what might organization scholars learn from digesting Ostrogorski's 1,000-plus-page monograph on the historical development of the US and English party systems, and what might his rather bleak analysis tell us about organizations more generally?

As Lipset further notes in his introduction, Ostrogorski pioneered a type of functional analysis that, implicitly at least, bears some resemblance to the work of Robert Merton and Talcott Parson, who are otherwise seen as the main originators of the functional approach to social science (Eisenstadt, 1990). Lipset never really unfolds this argument, but I would argue that Ostrogorski's historical analysis represents a functional approach to organization studies in a double sense, which might help us get beyond the crude functionalism and social reductionism that is often associated with this particular approach to sociology (what Niklas Luhmann calls 'kausalfunktionalismus'). I will refer to these two aspects of Ostrogorski's functional analysis as *problematization* and *evaluation*.

The first sense is perhaps the one most associated with functional analysis. In its original iteration, as espoused by Talcott Parsons in particular, functional analysis relies on the assumption that behavioural patterns in groups or societies can be explained with reference to the function they serve in terms of maintaining these groups or societies. For instance, one might think of certain rituals in contemporary organizations (Christmas parties, away days, team-building exercises and so on) and the role they play in terms of maintaining a particular organizational culture. The problem, of course, is how to prove the existence of a causal relationship between the behavioural pattern, its function and the group in question (see Douglas, 1987). This is one reason why 'structural-functional analysis' has been largely abandoned within the social sciences. Another reason is that it assumes a type of overly harmonious 'social consensus' that seems to suppress marginal voices and ignore the empirical complexity of real-life organizations, and its deterministic perspective furthermore leaves very little room for individual agency (Eisenstadt, 1990: 246).

The work of Ostrogorski shares the ambition of understanding how organizations emerge and how they develop certain types of organizational behaviours as a response to societal events. In that sense, he is well in line with Parsons and Merton – and half a century ahead of his time. However, instead of trying to delineate some kind of causal link between environmental factors and organizational configurations (although there are elements of this knowledge interest in his work as well), Ostrogorski seems more interested in asking: *to what problem is this particular organization and this particular behaviour an answer?* Here, focus is removed from the objective factors driving some kind of social development and placed firmly at the organization itself and its own justification for existence. As Ostrogorski explains in the preface to his book: 'I broke up my generalizations into concrete and often very matter-of-fact questions which I put to my interlocutors, *whom I treated not only as witnesses, but also as subjects of direct observation*, whether they belonged to the staff of the party organization or to other classes of the community' (Ostrogorski, 1902: lv, emphasis added). Although this may seem like hair-splitting, there is an enormous difference between focusing on cause-effect relations and focusing on problem-answer relations, as the latter is less preoccupied with general laws and more concerned with exploring the empirical complexity of a given organizational set-up. In Ostrogorski's own analysis, the caucus is the Liberal Party's (contingent and arbitrary) answer to the problems posed by the second reform act and the minority clause.

The second sense in which Ostrogorski's research strategy could be called functional has to do with the *evaluation* of the function that a particular organization was originally meant to serve. Here, Ostrogorski leaves his meticulous descriptive approach behind and ventures into normative territory, clinging firmly to his radical individualist philosophy. Although it is widely recognized that the expansion of male suffrage in 1832 and especially the establishment of household suffrage in 1867 helped pave the way for the emergence of modern democracy in Britain (see, for example, McKenzie, 1955), there is less consensus about the role that political parties played in realizing the potential for human emancipation embedded in democracy. While many observers agree that political parties often subordinate voters to bureaucratic procedures and stifle what Ostrogorski calls the 'free play of opinion', many classical thinkers claim parties to be essential to the functioning of democratic society (see Rosenblum, 2008). As Elmer Eric Schattschneider (1942: 1) has it, in one of the most overused quotes within political science: 'The political parties created democracy and modern democracy is unthinkable save in terms of the parties.' Ostrogorski certainly did not accept this view. In his mind, the political parties did not create democracy (they only reluctantly followed the winds of change) and democracy is certainly not unthinkable without them. In fact, democracy might be more accurately described as unthinkable *with* them.

But this does not really answer the question of whether parties fulfil the function they were originally meant to serve. As we have seen, Ostrogorski regarded parties as having the potential to serve some important functions in democratic society (such as educating ordinary people politically and acting as an umbilical cord between state and civil society). However, as Ostrogorski (1902: liv) notes, the study of political parties requires direct observations of 'real life' because the *realization* of democracy is often far removed from the *ideal* of democracy. What he found through these observations is that parties rarely serve any of the functions they were originally meant to serve. Instead of channelling the 'will of the people' towards the state, they discipline the electorate into voting as told; and instead of enlightening the lower strata of society about political issues, they cater to the lowest common denominator by only organizing events with easy entertainment and 'beautiful women' to attract voters. The parties' failure to deliver on both promises, and their associated tendency to discipline elected politicians, were key drivers behind Ostrogorski's proposal to abolish all permanent parties.

In terms of analytical strategy, Ostrogorski thus pioneered a type of functional analysis that oscillates between descriptive problematization and normative evaluation. In terms of methodology, he also preferred a mode of observation that went against the grain. Instead of focusing on institutions and laws (what he calls 'political forms'), he focused on the practices of 'concrete individuals' (what he calls 'political forces'); and instead of basing his inquiry solely on official material and party propaganda, he took inspiration from the burgeoning field of anthropology and ended up producing one of the first studies in organizational ethnography (Ostrogorski, 1902: li). However, this particular aspect of Ostrogorski's work was quickly overshadowed by another ethnographic study of party organization, namely Robert Michels' famous account of oligarchy in European socialist parties and trade unions.

Michels and the iron law of oligarchy

Although reviews of party organization research often begin with the mention of Ostrogorski's name and credentials, they usually skip quickly forward to a more detailed examination of the perhaps most influential party theorist of all times, the German–Italian sociologist Robert Michels. Born in 1876 in Cologne, Michels grew up in a relatively affluent household with significant international outlook, which enabled him to travel extensively during his youth and to study at some of Europe's finest schools. Initially, Michels was destined to follow his uncle's military career, leading him to spend a few years in the Prussian army. Perhaps as a reaction against his bourgeois Catholic upbringing, Michels soon quit the army and, in his mid-20s, became an avowed socialist. He later enrolled in the German Social Democratic Party (present-day SPD), the vanguard of the socialist movement at the time, where, in 1907, he ran unsuccessfully as a parliamentary candidate for the Alterfeld-Lauterbach constituency (Cook, 1971). The failure to enter parliament, and his growing disillusionment with the SPD and other socialist parties in Europe, led Michels to change career paths again, turning from a practitioner of party politics into an observer of party politics. However, owing to Otto von Bismarck's notorious anti-socialist laws, Michels was barred from working at German universities and found himself in a position where he once again had to migrate to pursue his academic interests. He soon moved to Italy (his father was of Italian descent) and accepted a position as docent at the University of Turin. It was during his time in Turin that he authored his magnum opus, *Political Parties: A Sociological Study of the Oligarchical Tendencies of Modern Democracy* (Michels, 1915), based primarily on his own personal experiences. Michels' work on party organization is known in academic circles for its remarkable main thesis, which is usually summarized in two sentences, extracted from the book's concluding chapter (Michels, 1915: 365):

> The fundamental sociological law of political parties ... may be formulated in the following terms: 'It is organization which gives birth to the dominion of the elected over the electors, of the mandataries over the mandators, of the delegates over the delegators. Who says organization, says oligarchy.'

The idea behind this powerful conclusion is that any formal organization, no matter how egalitarian in its perspective, will eventually succumb to elite rule once it embarks on the pursuit of political power. The reason for this inevitable drift towards oligarchy is that, as political organizations mature, they become dependent on the state for resources and influence. Their leaders then acquire an interest in preserving rather than overthrowing the established system, leading them to view the preservation of the organization as the party's primary objective, while simultaneously turning its revolutionary ideals into conservative ambitions.

Formal political organizations such as political parties are thus caught in a vicious circle of self-preservation, which Michels saw as absolutely detrimental to democracy. In fact, his experiences with different socialist parties even led him to denounce the very possibility of democracy as a mode of government and, towards the end of his life, turn to Mussolini-style fascism for salvation. Before we jump to conclusions, however, let's take the time to consider Michels' work in more detail.

Democracy means organization means oligarchy

Although Michels supposedly claimed to never have met 'the Polish scientist' (Quagliarello, 1996: 220), his argumentation shares many similarities with that of Ostrogorski, and in the final pages of *Political Parties*, he even references his Russian (not Polish) predecessor's proposal to substitute party organizations for 'temporary leagues', but rejects it based on the conviction that it would be impossible to suppress the self-preserving drive of traditional party organizations (Michels, 1915: 328). On other matters, the two giants of classical party research are much more in line. One particularly important similarity between Ostrogorski and Michels is their description of the events leading to the rise of political parties in the Western world.

Just like Ostrogorski, Michels argues that party organization is the natural consequence of the gradual expansion of suffrage in the latter part of the 19th century. The advent of mass democracy did indeed liberate ordinary people from the old aristocratic order, but *freedom from* (the aristocracy) only becomes *freedom to* (instigate change) when it is supported by an institutional set-up that allows the weak to challenge the strong. This is why, as Michels notes (1915: 61), 'democracy is inconceivable without organization':

> A class which unfurls in the face of society the banner of definite claims, and which aspires to the realization of a complex of ideal aims deriving from the economic functions which that class fulfils, needs an organization. Be the claims economic or be they political, organization appears the only means for the creation of a collective will.

This quote, however, also reveals a major difference between Ostrogorski and Michels. Whereas Ostrogorski based his argument on a philosophy of radical (and sometimes elitist) individualism, which led him to denounce the encroachment of the party machine on the will of duly elected members of parliament, Michels represents a position that seems ideologically closest to anarchist socialism or syndicalism (Linz, 2006). The most important consequence of this discrepancy is perhaps reflected in the level of political participation that the two authors believe is required for a system to call itself a democracy. Ostrogorski believes that democracy will be realized only if the 'free play of opinion' remains unconstrained, regardless of how this type of free play is organized, while Michels regards political leadership as undemocratic by default (Cook, 1971). This is arguably the reason why Michels is much more pessimistic about the prospect of realizing the promise of democracy than Ostrogorski, and it is certainly the reason why only Ostrogorski proposed solutions to the problems associated with formal political organization.

Michels begins his book by proposing a distinction between democracy and aristocracy, with the latter signifying the complete negation of ordinary people's right to self-determination (as seen in hereditary monarchies) and the former signifying something like the end of political representation altogether. In between these two extremes, we find several variations that can be identified in different political systems where the old aristocratic order may have been challenged but where the full potential of democracy remains far from realized. One variation is what Michels calls 'democratic aristocracy', which is a condition where the masses have been enfranchised but where their ability to participate in the process of political decision-making is denied by their own representatives. According to Michels, this condition is best captured by the notion of oligarchy, meaning government by the few, which to him is an unavoidable consequence of formal political organization. Democracy can only be realized if the masses organize in a way that allows them to voice their grievances collectively, but since organizations require leadership, and since political leadership represents a re-subordination of the masses, democracy seems to Michels an unattainable ideal. In this scenario, the people may be free *de jure* but not *de facto*; it is 'democracy with an aristocratic content' (Michels, 1915: 50).

There are several factors contributing to the process of oligarchization within political parties, some of which are technical while others are psychological. The most important *technical* factors are size and education. In Michels' view, democratic organizations should preferably be governed by a system of direct participation, meaning that ordinary members should be allowed to register their opinion on all matters of concern, effectively eliminating any kind of formal representation. However, this is obviously not an option for large-scale organizations such as the SPD, which, at the dawn of the 20th century, represented several million members across Germany. Even when split into local subunits, these consisted of thousands of people, many of whom had little time to engage in party-related issues. It is therefore no surprise that such collectives need leadership to operate both efficiently and effectively, but the introduction of hierarchical structures always signifies the beginning of oligarchization for the simple reason that representation transfers decision-making power from the many to the few. As such, organizational size is arguably the most important obstacle to the realization of what Michels perceives as democracy proper.

The other main technical factor leading to internal oligarchy is educational differences. Some members have received better training than others prior to enlisting as rank and file, and the party itself supplies training programmes for those aspiring to become leaders. For instance, Michels observes how more and more parties create 'nurseries' to accommodate the need for an increasingly professional workforce, and, in 1906, the Socialist Party even established its own 'party school' that instructs pupils in the art of party management (Michels, 1915: 68). This kind of training creates a small cohort of members, seen as capable of steering the organization into the future. This dynamic is self-perpetuating because it introduces a certain language and skillset that one must acquire to be seen as leadership material. The social stratification known from the traditional educational system and society more broadly (for example Bourdieu and Passeron, 1977) is thus mirrored by party-internal training programmes that provide certain members with more cultural capital than others. As such, the technical need for leadership (caused by the size of the organization) and the intellectual perpetuation of leadership (caused by various training programmes) ultimately serve to widen the chasm between the leaders and the led. The more developed the organization gets, the more complex its administration appears, the wider this dividing line becomes. Hence, as Michels (1915: 73) claims: 'For democracy ... the first appearance of leadership marks the beginning of the end.'

Qualities of leaders and the led

Technical factors like size and education are not alone in driving the process of oligarchization. According to Michels, psychology plays a part as well. To make this argument, Michels draws on the then emerging science of crowd psychology, represented most prominently by figures including Gabriel Tarde and Gustave Le Bon (the latter directed the translation of Michels' book into French). This intellectual legacy adds a less-than-flattering image of 'the masses' to the account of oligarchy presented by Michels. The rank and file are continuously described as a herd of passive and incompetent dupes, guided by emotions and desires rather than by rational considerations. They are portrayed, for instance, as less interested in party meetings that focus on political deliberations and more attracted to meetings that involve easy entertainment such as 'cinema-shows' or 'a popular scientific lecture illustrated by lantern-slides' (Michels, 1915: 87). Furthermore, the masses are characterized as completely lacking the will and ability for self-direction. They need guidance and desire leadership, which clearly frustrates Michels, as it disturbs his image of democracy as freedom from representation. His discontent with the members' general indolence is visible in passages such as the following (Michels, 1915: 90), of which there are numerous throughout *Political Parties*:

> Accustomed to being ruled, the rank and file need a considerable work of preparation before they can be set in motion. In default of this, and when signals which the rank and file do not understand are unexpectedly made by leaders, they pay no attention. The most striking proof of the organic weakness of the mass is furnished by the way in which, when deprived of their leaders in time of action [such as strikes], they abandon the field of battle in disorderly flight; they seem to have no power of instinctive reorganization and are useless until new captains arise capable of replacing those who have been lost.

This view of the masses as people who are 'incapable of looking after their own interests' (Michels, 1915: 111) has earned Michels a reputation as an elite theorist (someone who believes society to be governed by a small minority of powerful individuals), alongside sociologists such as Gaetano Mosca and Vilfredo Pareto, both of whom share his view of democracy as an unattainable ideal (see Burnham, 1943). Nonetheless, Michels has little sympathy for party elites. In fact, he often holds leaders directly responsible for intensifying the otherwise inevitable process of oligarchization and, consequently, for curbing the party's revolutionary ideals in an attempt to maintain their own status and position in the political system. Michels observes, for instance, how the leaders of European socialist parties hold on to their positions for remarkably long – the SPD leaders seem 'practically irremovable' – even though leadership rotation is an oft-cited principle in democratic organizations. Michels attributes this not so much to the qualities of the leaders but to the organizational set-up created to protect the leaders: tailor-made voting procedures, clandestine wire-pulling, unconstitutional veto-rights, economic privileges, access to the party press and so on. This set-up allows the leaders to 'isolate themselves' and create a 'cartel' of like-minded associates who will stop at nothing to ensure the preservation of their leaders (Michels, 1915: 126).

Psychologically, Michels characterizes party leaders as people who are: extremely strong-willed, knowledgeable enough to impress others, fanatic about their own convictions, self-sufficient and proud, and capable of appearing good-hearted and disinterested in a manner that 'recalls in the minds of the crowd the figure of Christ' (Michels, 1915: 100). These characteristics give his description of socialist party leaders an aura of megalomania, which is further confirmed when Michels discusses political leaders' recurring habit of threatening to resign when faced with internal opposition; a tactic supposedly perfected by Ferdinand Lassalle in the context of the German labour movement. In that sense, the process of oligarchy is completed by the psychological conditions of party leaders and party members (Michels, 1915: 205):

> The apathy of the masses and their need for guidance has its counterpart in the leaders [and their] natural greed for power. Thus the development of the democratic oligarchy is accelerated by the general characteristics of human nature. What was initiated by the need for organization, administration, and strategy is completed by psychological determinism.

This is what, in Michels' view, makes the drift from democracy to elite rule an 'iron law' in relation to organized politics. Avoiding the rise of an internal oligarchy within political parties is simply impossible because of the technical and psychological factors. In fact, Michels believes the process to be so irrefutable that he characterizes oligarchization as one of the most important 'sociological laws of universal validity' (Michels, 1915: 319). His case selection is meant to emphasize this point. If oligarchy can be detected in even the most democratic and egalitarian organizations in continental Europe (socialist parties and trade unions), then it logically means that it can be found anywhere – and not only in political parties. In fact, Michels maintains that elite rule will inevitably emerge in 'every kind of human organization which strives for the attainment of definite ends' (Michels,

1915: 50). As Jodi Dean (2016: 171) explains: 'even groups with aspirations to anarchism, all ultimately take on a whole slew of oligarchic characteristics. Rule by the few is unavoidable.'

Countering oligarchy

The presumably inevitable character of oligarchization led several of Michels' contemporaries to discuss the possibility of countering elite rule. One example is Mary Parker Follett's (1918) influential account of neighbourhood-based group organizations. Though Follett shares Michels' discontent with political parties and trade unions, she does not agree with his pessimistic view of democracy in general. In fact, her work is primarily dedicated to rediscovering democracy as something radically different from the dominant view of common rule, where balloting represents the only real mode of public participation. As she claims on the very first page of *The New State*, perhaps with a slight reference to Michels: 'We talk about the evils of democracy. We have not yet tried democracy' (Follett, 1918: 3). Hence, while Michels refrains from offering solutions to the ills of party-based democracy, Follett sets out to revive democracy through group organization as a particular mode of political association. Follett's point is that the diversity of the group will permeate the individual to the point where the group's participants develop a 'conscious responsibility' for society as a whole. Group organization is thus to be seen as something different from not only representative government but also direct democracy, where majority voting remains the only means of expression. In the group, individuals are allowed to exchange arguments in the absence of hierarchies while simultaneously developing a sensitivity towards each other; and that is ultimately how the individual is 'found' and democracy revived (Follett, 1918: 6).

Although it is unclear whether Michels and Follett ever exchanged views, the influence that fellow German sociologist Max Weber had on the work of Michels (and vice versa) is well documented (Scaff, 1981). Weber clearly shared Michels' analysis with respect to its descriptive conclusions: that parties will ultimately (and fairly quickly) develop a bureaucratic structure that serves to centralize power in the hands of a small elite, thereby barring the rank and file from any kind of direct participation. As Weber puts it: 'The electors only participate in the sense that both programmes and candidates are adapted to, and chosen in accordance with, the chances of winning their votes' (Weber, 1918: 150). However, Weber was more reluctant to accept Michels' normative conclusion: that the centralization of power was necessarily detrimental to democracy. In fact, Weber argued that parties are essential to mass democracy, in the sense that popular rule cannot function without mediating institutions. The inevitably bureaucratic structure of parties, however, creates what Weber calls an 'officialdom', which is a form of organized rule that relies on the authority of officials who – like political leaders – make decisions that directly affects their constituencies. This is why Weber considered legitimate political leadership, as carried out by elected representatives rather than bureaucrats, instrumental to the functioning of democracy. In his lectures 'Politik als Beruf' ('Politics as vocation'), Weber (1919) argues that politicians should continuously strike a balance between what he calls an 'ethics of responsibility' (disinterested risk assessments) and an 'ethics of ultimate ends' (unshakable moral convictions). Only when the latter eclipses the former does oligarchy, in Weber's view, constitute a democratic problem.

On the final pages of *Political Parties,* Michels himself discusses several strategies for countering oligarchy. One strategy, pioneered by the Swiss cantons, is frequent referendums. At first sight, the referendum seems like the most tangible method for eliminating elite rule: it is arguably the most defining feature of modern democracy and therefore a key ingredient in maintaining some kind of popular government. However, as Michels (1915: 309) concludes, 'the history of the referendum as a democratic experiment utilized by the socialist parties may be summed up by saying that its application has been rare, and that its results have been unfortunate'. So, the questions posed to ordinary party members has been poorly formulated and the participation rate has been correspondingly low. According to Michels, there are two reasons for the unfortunate results obtained through referendums: the 'incompetence' of ordinary members, as outlined earlier, and a general lack of time in everyday life. These, combined with the fact that plebiscites tend to eclipse the possibility for proper democratic deliberations (see also Gerbaudo, 2019), make referendums an undesirable strategy for countering oligarchy. Other possible counter-oligarchic strategies discussed by Michels include renunciation (stripping leaders of privileges), syndicalism (union-based organizing) and anarchism (anti-hierarchical organizing). Although Michels seems to favour the latter (anarchists are, for instance, portrayed as 'morally superior' to socialists), he never veers from the basic argument that oligarchy is a necessary consequence of formal political organization. Attempts at countering oligarchy are thus naïve at best and self-defeating at worst: 'who says organization, says oligarchy' (Michels, 1915: 365).

The iron law in organization studies

Since the publication of Michels' *Political Parties*, numerous organizational studies have attempted to test empirically the book's main hypothesis. While most studies have explored the limits of the iron law (Tolbert and Hiatt, 2009), others have confirmed the thesis that formal organization implies elite rule (for example Selznick, 1949; Messinger, 1955; Piven and Cloward,

1977; Mansbridge, 1980; Gulowsen, 1985; Varman and Chakrabarti, 2004; Courpasson and Clegg, 2006). One of the first comprehensive studies to seriously challenge the law-like status of Michels' thesis is Seymour Martin Lipset and colleagues' renowned analysis of power relations and decision-making in the International Typographical Union (ITU), as reported in their academic bestseller *Union Democracy* (Lipset et al, 1956). What is interesting about this text is not only that the authors challenge the supposed 'universal' validity of the iron law by illustrating how oligarchy can be countered in a real-life setting, but also that the book places itself firmly in the intersection of political science, sociology and organization studies, thereby contributing to the diffusion of the iron law across various disciplines.

What allegedly makes the ITU stand out from average US trade unions (as well as most voluntary organizations at the time), which were often structured precisely as tightly knitted oligarchies, is that the ITU was organized around a sophisticated two-party system that resembled the US political system but without any formal connections to the Republican or Democratic parties. This allowed otherwise 'secret societies' within the union to openly contest each other by presenting manifestos, preparing strategies, selecting candidates and eventually competing in the biannual leadership elections. According to the authors, oligarchy can thus be countered by a sufficiently democratic organizational structure that may be bureaucratic in its rule-based mode of operation, but which nonetheless allows ordinary members to register their preferences in duly constituted elections. This model is thus close to Michels' own discussion of referendums; a model that he perceived as inadequate based on his limited faith in the political competences of 'the masses'. What Lipset et al (1956) show through their rich account of life in the Typographical Union is that Michels was too quick to dismiss referendums as a means of instituting more democratic structures in large-scale organizations and that ordinary members are indeed capable of participating in decision-making processes if given the opportunity (particularly the highly skilled craftsmen of the ITU), and that formalized leadership does not necessarily lead to political conservatism. In that sense, the authors are thus more in line with Weber than with Michels.

This latter point is, however, made more forcefully in J Craig Jenkins' (1977) study of the transformation of political goals within the US National Council of Churches (NCC). Although Jenkins accepts the iron law's most basic tenet – that organizational growth leads to formalization, which then leads to oligarchy – he disputes the additional corollary that this development automatically serves to water down the organization's ideological position. When oligarchy emerges, the organization's overall objectives will naturally reflect the leadership's personal beliefs, but these beliefs are not necessarily conservative or self-preserving. They may just as well be *more* radical compared with the original position held by the organization, meaning that oligarchy can sometimes serve to radicalize organizational goals and possibly create conflicts between the 'radial oligarchy' and more reactionary 'lay members' (Jenkins, 1977: 580). Hence, as Mayer Zald and Roberta Ash (1966: 327) note: 'Neither greater conservatism nor organizational maintenance are iron laws' (see also Diefenbach, 2019). Similar arguments are advanced by Suzanne Staggenborg (1988) in her account of the pro-choice movement, by Mayer Zald and Patricia Denton (1963) in their study of the YMCA, and by William Gamson (1975) in his investigation of 'challenging groups'. The common denominator across such accounts is that formal organization is seen as an indispensable resource that facilitates rather than suppresses radical politics.

More recently, organization scholars have returned to the question of whether the consequences of oligarchy can be avoided in large organizations, but have abandoned the strong focus on organizational structure in favour of 'softer' areas of concern. One example of this trend is Paul Osterman's (2006) study of the Southwest Industrial Areas Foundation, which focuses on the consequences of oligarchy in terms of membership 'becalming' (losing energy and commitment), by exploring the mitigating role of organizational culture within the foundation. Osterman's point is that, if a particular type of agency is engrained in the membership, and if a culture of contestation is encouraged within the organization, it is possible to curb the negative consequences of oligarchy in terms of becalming as well as goal displacement. If ordinary members are taught to assert themselves and to constantly question authority (such as through frequent training sessions), and if this assertion is welcomed by the otherwise oligarchic leadership (through ongoing evaluations, for instance), organizations can maintain membership commitment and preserve their original goals (see also Husted, 2020). A similar point is made by Wini Breines (1980) in her analysis of the New Left's rejection of institutionalized party politics. Breines shows how the movement's culture of participation, predicated on the notion of 'prefigurative' politics, helped the New Left keep oligarchization at bay. In doing so, she challenges the dominant understanding of what it means for political movements to act strategically: instead of seeking influence through the electoral system, anti-hierarchical organizations are often better served working around the system because this allows them to maintain a strong democratic foundation that prefigures – at the organizational level – the societal changes they advocate (see also Polletta, 2002; Maeckelbergh, 2009).

As such, the many organizational studies specifically addressing the question of oligarchy have greatly contributed to the exploration, evaluation and elaboration of the iron law thesis. They have shown that the thesis is less law-like than it appears to be, and that both structural and cultural factors can help reverse the process of oligarchization, and they have emphasized that oligarchy does not necessarily lead to goal displacement and membership becalming. So, is the thesis still relevant? Or, in other words, what can organization scholars today learn from the work of Robert Michels? I believe there are, at least, a couple of things to learn from Michels' main thesis.

By strategically selecting what Bent Flyvbjerg (2006) calls 'critical cases' – those that intensify otherwise commonplace phenomena – Michels alerts us to the fact that even highly egalitarian organizations such as the SPD risk succumbing to elite rule. This awareness has sparked a number of studies of oligarchization in democratic organizations, as discussed, and has created an increased focus among practitioners on the potential dangers of formalization and institutionalization (see Breines, 1980; Polletta, 2002; Maeckelbergh, 2009). Second, the thesis directs our attention to the factors that typically drive oligarchization, most importantly technical factors such as organizational size and leadership training, but also psychological factors including self-preservation and personal decisiveness. Third, Michels' work helps us temper some of the optimism that sometimes surrounds organized attempts to prevent elite-rule, such as renunciation or decentralization, which can sometimes blind us to the fact that oligarchy may also appear in seemingly egalitarian guises (see also Courpasson and Clegg, 2006). In my view, however, the most valuable lessons offered by Michels have less to do with his thesis and more to do with his approach to the study of parties.

The classical research strategy

As mentioned earlier, Ostrogorski pioneered an approach that openly challenged those of his colleagues who based their investigations solely on authorized material, such as speeches, legal documents, financial records, organizational charts and so on, in order also to consider more informal ways of producing insights. For instance, much of the information that went into Ostrogorski's magnum opus was obtained through a 'long and minute enquiry' throughout England that often involved 'personal testimony' and 'direct observation of political life in general and of the working of party organization in particular' (Ostrogorski, 1902: lv). He further recounts how 'it has been my lot to attend ward meetings where there were not even twenty persons to elect seventy-five delegates' (p 333) to properly understand the power that the central committee exercises over local party branches. Without this type of meticulous fieldwork, Ostrogorski would arguably not have been able to produce the compelling account of the caucus machinery that we know today, for the simple reason that such incidents would have been downplayed or removed from official materials, but also because his observations provide the reader with a strong sense of presence that makes otherwise tedious ward meetings seem relevant and meaningful.

However, while Ostrogorski undoubtedly pioneered the ethnographic approach to party organization, it was Michels who first added the element of *participation* to observations (Ostrogorski was never a member of any English or US party, although he did become a politician upon his return to Russia in 1906). As a member of the German Social-Democratic Party, and as an official candidate at one point, Michels was personally immersed in the inner life of the party to a degree that arguably intensified the depth of his insights and the strictly moral character of his conclusions. Getting beyond the official story was important to Michels because, as several party scholars have recognized after him (such as Duverger, 1954 and Panebianco, 1988), the idealized picture painted in authorized documents rarely corresponds to the practical reality of party organization (for a counter-argument, see Katz and Mair, 1992). As an example, Michels highlights this discrepancy in relation to the *official* rights of ordinary members to elect and direct their leaders (Michels, 1915: 167):

> Those who defend the arbitrary acts committed by the democracy [party leaders], point out that the masses have at their disposal means whereby they can react against the violation of their rights. These means consist in the right of controlling and dismissing their leaders. Unquestionably this defense possesses a certain theoretical value. ... In practice, however, the exercise of this theoretical right is interfered with by the working of the whole series of conservative tendencies ... so that the supremacy of the autonomous and sovereign masses is rendered purely illusory.

This methodological strategy of 'immersion' (Schatz, 2009) has arguably also had an influence on organization studies as a discipline that owes its existence partly to the work of classical political sociologists such as Ostrogorski, Michels, Weber and Follett (see Chapter 1). This is evident in some of the organizational studies referenced in this chapter. For instance, Lipset and colleagues based their account of democracy within the ITU on surveys and exploratory interviews with trade union members, but they also 'familiarized themselves in every way possible with the *actual political life of the union*, attending union meetings, party caucuses, and chapel meetings' (Lipset et al, 1956: xi, emphasis added). Similarly, Jenkins (1977: 570) based his study of goal transformation within the NCC on 'intensive interviews with staff members'; Osterman (2006: 631) drew on a combination of informal interviews and observations of 'the organization in action' to develop his account of the Southwest Industrial Areas Foundation; and Breines (1980) and Maeckelbergh (2009) relied heavily on personal experiences with hands-on movement organizing to inform their arguments about the anti-oligarchic nature of prefigurative politics.

As such, one could argue that, while organization scholars have already learned a lot from classical research on party organization, there is still plenty left to ponder. One place to start would be to rediscover political parties as interesting and relevant study objects that may help us understand organizational dynamics that perhaps are more commonplace than they seem. This is why I believe it makes sense to conceive of parties as 'critical cases of organizing' (Husted et al, 2021), as argued in Chapter 1, and why we simply cannot afford to leave the study of party organization to political science, particularly given the fact that most political scientists today reject the immersive approach pioneered by Ostrogorski and Michels as unrepresentative and biased (see Scarrow et al, 2017). Hence, the resurrection of the classics is not merely an excuse to read old books and revel in a time where beautiful writing mattered more than journal rankings and impact factors, it is also an attempt to reinvigorate the study of political organizing and organizational politics by revisiting the work of those who first embarked on such research.

3

Alternativet in Classical Perspective

Introduction

The previous chapter discussed and unfolded what I call the 'classical perspective' on party organization, based on the work of Moisei Ostrogorski and Robert Michels in particular. This perspective focuses on a number of theoretical themes such as intra-party democracy, internal power relations and goal displacement, but is also defined by specific research methods and analytical strategies. In terms of methods, the classical perspective relies heavily on ethnographic approaches and personal communication, which implies a commitment to researcher participation. In terms of analytical strategies, I argue that the classical perspective is characterized by a type of functional analysis, developed by Ostrogorski, which consists of two elements: problematization (to what problem is this party organization an answer?) and evaluation (does this party organization serve the purpose it was originally meant to serve?). This particular perspective allows for analyses that are historical in nature and centre on questions related to the ability of party organizations to fulfil the role ascribed to them as 'managers of democracy' (Mair, 2003: 1). It allows researchers to explore how parties organize internally, and whether their mode of organization serves democratic ends – or whether it, in fact, constitutes what Michels (1915: 50) calls 'democracy with an aristocratic content'.

The purpose of this chapter is to apply the classical perspective to the case of Alternativet. In doing so, I focus on four distinct themes and analyse these while simultaneously chronicling the rise and fall the party, beginning with the official launch in November 2013 and ending in the present where Alternativet has been reduced to relative insignificance, although positive signs of recovery are gradually emerging. I start by exploring the democratic character of Alternativet, focusing on the invention of 'political laboratories' where members and non-members can deliberate about various policy issues in the absence of formal hierarchy and manifest party discipline. As an extension of this focus, I move on to consider the introduction of a new organizational body in 2015 called 'political forum' and discuss whether this represents a sign of oligarchization. Next, I consider the power wielded by the political forum and explore the difference between Michels' coercive conception of power and Ostrogorski's understanding of power as a strategic tool for manipulating decision-making. Finally, I explore the notion of goal displacement in relation to the overall transformation of goals and visions within Alternativet and draw inspiration from Jenkins' (1977) notion of 'radical oligarchy'. In conclusion, I follow Ostrogorski's functional approach by discussing whether Alternativet did (or does) serve the purpose it was originally meant to serve.

Alternativet: from protest to parliament

On 15 September 2011, the centre-left coalition in Danish politics managed to break ten years of right-wing dominance by winning the national elections by the smallest of margins. Only with the help of voters in Greenland and the Faroe Islands did the coalition secure enough support to form a minority government consisting of three parties: the Social Democrats, the Social Liberal Party and the Socialist People's Party. This was nonetheless an important win for the Danish left, who had witnessed a decade of severe welfare cuts and increasingly harsher immigration policies sponsored by the far-right Danish People's Party. After weeks of intense negotiations in a fancy hotel on the outskirts of Copenhagen, an elaborate coalition agreement was signed by the three parties, making Helle Thorning-Schmidt (leader of the Social Democrats) the first female prime minister in Denmark.

One of the most original characters to emerge from this agreement was Uffe Elbæk, a former communist turned socio-liberal, who had been appointed minister of culture based on his long-standing involvement in cultural life home and abroad. Elbæk was an unusual figure in Danish politics. His past was unlike those of most other politicians, including a career as founder and principal of an alternative management school called the Chaos Pilots. He also insisted on doing politics differently. For instance, during the election campaign in 2011, he opened his home to the general public and invited anyone interested to discuss his policies and help him improve his campaign strategy. He also established an association called Club Courage (*Klub Mod* in Danish), based at a gay club in Copenhagen, with the aim of highlighting and applauding people who had shown political courage by challenging the usual way of conducting politics. The common denominator in most of these initiatives was a focus on active deliberation and bottom–up decision-making.

Elbæk brought this way of thinking politics with him into the job as minister of culture. This led to many alternative working procedures meant to stir up the conventions of electoral politics. One such initiative was a recurring debate event called 'Culture on the Edge' (*Kultur på Kanten*), sponsored by the Ministry of Culture and held at a school for circus performers known as the Academy for Untamed Creativity (*Akademiet for Utæmmet Kreativitet*). Initially, the events were successful, with many people actively participating in discussions about the future of cultural politics, but pretty soon news started circulating that Elbæk's husband was employed at the academy and that Elbæk himself had been a board member at the academy. This sparked a media frenzy, in which Elbæk was accused of favouritism and nepotism. It all culminated in a parliamentary consultation where Elbæk had to explain if he had been warned by civil servants about the risk of nepotism. With his back firmly against the wall, Elbæk admitted to being warned about placing future events at the academy, thus propelling criticism to even grander proportions.

Visibly affected by the accusations, Elbæk ultimately decided to step down as minister of culture in December 2012 and went into hiatus. A few months later, however, all charges were dropped, Elbæk's name was cleared, and he resurfaced as a member of parliament. Upon returning, he quickly launched a new project called 'Under the Radar' (*Under Radaren*), which materialized in an online platform meant to draw the public's attention to all those progressive initiatives that exist outside the spotlight of mainstream media and conventional politics. Like so many of Elbæk's other initiatives, 'Under the Radar' was a glowing success for those involved, but the impact on governmental affairs remained somewhat absent. This led some of the volunteers working for Elbæk to encourage him to embark on one last political project; one that would target electoral politics more directly. At first, Elbæk was reluctant – he was approaching retirement and wanted things to slow down – but he eventually decided that if he found it easy to write some kind of founding document, he would pursue the idea of launching one last project in the name of everything alternative.

There is always an alternative!

It did not take long for Elbæk to produce the founding document of what he eventually called 'Alternativet: an international party, a movement, and a cultural voice' (Alternativet, 2013a). In that document, Elbæk starts by highlighting some of the challenges facing contemporary society, most importantly climate change and economic inequality, but also challenges that are usually overlooked in the public debate such as social marginalization and loneliness. Elbæk then proceeds to mention all those local initiatives that already work to address these problems on a daily basis and the many new forms of organization that exist as a result of these efforts. This leads him to a central question: how is it possible to 'diffuse the experiences of those local initiatives to the rest of society' and 'release the willingness to sustainable transition that exist so many places today?'. The solution for Elbæk was to unite all these initiatives in an organization focused on sustainability, everyday democracy and entrepreneurial creativity and to establish a political party 'that has the courage to imagine a radically different future' (Alternativet, 2013a: 1).

The document was well received by Elbæk's volunteers, though some initially questioned the need for a political party. Why not create an alternative *movement* instead? However, these disputes were quickly resolved, since the idea was to target electoral politics more directly, and the team set out to prepare the launch of the project. In mid-September 2013, Elbæk resigned his membership of the Social Liberal Party, and two months later he and his co-founder, Josephine Fock, summoned the press to announce the birth of a new political party and social movement called Alternativet. At the press conference, Elbæk and Fock presented their vision of Alternativet: a party that represents and promotes alternative solutions to environmental, social and economic challenges. They also presented a short manifesto and six core values meant to guide the party in relation to policies and organizational procedures: empathy, humour, courage, generosity, humility and transparency. Save for these somewhat lofty ideals, Elbæk and Fock did not present any kind of policy proposals or reform initiatives, nor did they articulate any clear ideological position. As they formulated it: 'What is the political program? What are the solutions to x-number of tangible challenges? We don't present that today. Some may be surprised that we currently don't have the grand party bible on the shelf. But that's a completely conscious decision' (Alternativet, 2013b).

In the absence of political direction, the values and the manifesto quickly became a main source of attraction for supporters. The very first line in the manifesto reads, 'There is always an alternative!' and it proceeds by characterizing Alternativet as a 'shout out' against cynicism, a 'yearning' for meaning and a 'countermeasure' to the environmental crisis. The manifesto ends by stating that Alternativet is for anyone 'who can feel that something new is starting to replace something old' (Alternativet, 2013c). These broad appeals initially mobilized a wide variety of political identities, ranging from old-school socialists to free-marketeers and from spiritualists to radical atheists. In fact, anyone attracted by the notion of sustainability and the prospect of something 'alternative' seemed capable of reading their own personal preferences into the project. As a member of Alternativet later told me during an interview session:

'In the beginning, it was completely open for everyone. Anyone could set-up a flea market in their garage and claim to represent Alternativet.

Alternativet could be anything. There was no design manual. There was just a logo that people could use for whatever they pleased. That's really how it was.'

This type of transversal mobilization generated important momentum that allowed Alternativet's name and identity to travel across political and demographic boundaries. During the first months of 2014, Alternativet began crafting a political programme. With inspiration from the open-source community and 'citizen assembly' experiments abroad, 20 public workshops called 'political laboratories' were organized. At these workshops, members and non-members discussed different topics of interest and co-produced a variety of very specific policy proposals. These proposals were then gathered by a steering committee, rewritten and turned into a 64-page document that served as Alternativet's first political programme (Alternativet, 2014a). In May 2014, the programme was accepted at a general assembly in Aarhus, after a marathon debate involving more than 150 proposed amendments submitted by members wanting to push the programme in different directions.

Throughout the rest of 2014, Alternativet continued to expand the political programme while also selecting parliamentary candidates. Much energy was spent collecting enough signatures to become eligible to run for parliament. In fact, at that time, few things seemed to matter more than the 20,260 signatures that would get the party on the ballot list. In March, 2015, more than a year's hard work paid off, when the political leadership (as the parliamentary candidates were now suddenly called) delivered 13 boxes of signatures at the Ministry of Interior Affairs. Only a few months later, the Danish prime minister called an election. Despite little preparation time, Alternativet was ready. A campaign strategy had been prepared, key campaign issues had been selected, and a host of volunteers had signed up to support the candidates.

During the campaign, I followed some of the local candidates from Copenhagen. These were all politically untried people who had little knowledge of electoral politics or how to electioneer. What struck me the most was the candidates' constant struggle to appear simultaneously *alternative* and *mainstream*. For instance, they would often come up with spectacular and unusual ideas for attracting attention, such as dressing up as superheroes or setting up an alternative dancefloor at a central square in Copenhagen, but were anxious not to come across as a 'circus party' (a nickname invented by political opponents and the tabloid press); and rightly so. In the end, none of those dressing up as superheroes or setting up dancefloors would enter parliament.

On 18 June 2015, Alternativet earned 4.8 per cent of the votes in the national elections, which translated into nine seats in parliament (of

179). This made Alternativet the sixth largest party in parliament and the third largest party in opposition, ahead of the Socialist People's Party and the Social Liberal Party (Elbæk's former party). This was a thoroughly unexpected result, not only to media pundits but also to members of Alternativet. A few had thought Alternativet would exceed the electoral threshold, but hardly anyone had expected them to earn more than a handful of seats. Although the election results were gloomy for the left – the right-wing coalition regained power – Alternativet could not have hoped for a better result. By entering parliament as a small opposition party, Alternativet would not be forced into the sort of difficult compromises that had previously broken other small parties on the left. Despite this, Alternativet had bigger dreams. 'This is only the beginning', Elbæk announced at Alternativet's election celebrations. Later that evening, he would state that the ultimate goal was to win the keys to the prime minister's office.

168,788 Danes voted for Alternativet on 18 June 2015 (out of 3,518,987 valid votes) – see Figure 3.1. Of these voters, 56 per cent were women and 57 per cent were below the age of 40. Only 1 per cent of people above 65 years of age voted for Alternativet, which served to solidify the party's reputation as a young and urban organization. In terms of income level, Alternativet had the wealthiest voter base across the three parties that are usually considered left-wing (including the Socialist People's Party and the Red-Green Alliance). Furthermore, Alternativet had the second most well-educated voter base across all nine parties, with almost 60 per cent having a university degree and almost 70 per cent having a high school diploma

Figure 3.1: The results of the national elections on 18 June 2015 in Denmark

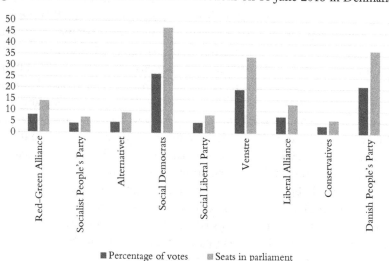

■ Percentage of votes　　▨ Seats in parliament

(Andersen, 2017). Most of Alternativet's voters previously voted for other centre-left parties, primarily the Social Liberal Party and the Socialist People's Party, although some voters did indeed venture across the political centre (Hansen and Stubager, 2017).

Problematization: an answer to everything established

We have seen that Alternativet initially saw itself as a response to various deficiencies in the established system. If we look at the party's manifesto alone, it is easy to see this counter-hegemonic self-understanding at play. In the first paragraph of what effectively amounts to a one-page document, we are told that Alternativet is 'a hope', 'a dream' and 'a yearning' for 'meaning, sense and compassionate relationships' – and that the party, therefore, should be understood as 'an answer to what is happening in the world today. All around us. With us' (Alternativet, 2013c). As mentioned, the text goes on to claim that the party is a 'shout out' against cynicism, lack of generosity and 'the ticking off which prevails in society'. It also suggests that Alternativet is a 'positive countermeasure' to the current environmental crisis, and that the party has the courage 'to look problems in the eye' (this is a somewhat direct translation of a common Danish expression), which means that openness to 'new ideas and creative solutions' is at the heart of the project. The manifesto is closed by the passage: 'Alternativet is for you. Who can tell that something has been set in motion. Who can feel that something new is starting to replace something old. Another way of looking at democracy, growth, work, responsibility and quality of life. That is Alternativet.'

We see here how the party perceives itself as the epitome of 'something new', and how this newness is positioned in an antagonistic relationship against 'something old'. It is clear from the preceding passages that the old is defined as a society characterized by distrust and selfishness, meaninglessness and incompassion, environmental depredation and resource scarcity, economic exploitation and democratic deficits, and by myopic thinking and non-creativity – but it is less clear what the new entails. In that sense, Alternativet initially saw itself as the answer to all that was wrong about the current system, which is what allowed the party to claim to represent anyone 'who can feel that something new is about to replace something old'. In a time marked by significant crises (financial, climate, refugee, representational crisis and so on) and rapid transformations (digital, environmental, political), few people would be excluded from consideration on the account that they simply could not feel things change. In other words: who does not want an alternative to the status quo? This is arguably what made Alternativet one of the most ideologically diverse parties in Denmark at the time. As the interview respondent recalled: "Alternativet could be anything."

The benefit of such a vague identity construct is that it allowed Alternativet to cater to voters who would not normally perceive themselves as left-leaning (the leader of Podemos in Spain, Pablo Iglesias (2015), frequently refers to such collective identities as 'transverval' to highlight their ability to mobilize support from across the political spectrum). This is arguably why so many different people showed up to the Alternativet's first annual meeting, which was held on the island of Bornholm in June 2014. When I first arrived at the meeting, I was greeted by enthused people chatting about political visions and the urgent need for change. Many of them did not particularly agree with each other about the political direction of Alternativet (some were former socialists or social democrats; others were liberals or even libertarians), but they all agreed that something should be done to challenge the dominant order. Several participants at the meeting had previously thought about starting their own political party – one had even thought about calling it *Alternativet* – when suddenly Alternativet offered itself as a home for the politically homeless. The discussions at that meeting reflected this diversity, with hundreds of proposed amendments to the programme and the statutes being submitted by members wanting to push the party in opposite directions. So, it quickly dawned on most participants that it would be impossible to reconcile all the voices represented by the party. There was nothing that unified, in any positive manner, the socialists and the libertarians besides their common distaste for the 'establishment'. Something had to be done to avoid ideological fragmentation or paralysis. It is in this context that the concept of political laboratories proved itself more brilliant than the founders had perhaps anticipated.

Democracy: the invention of political laboratories

It is not clear who exactly conceived the idea of political laboratories but it is mentioned in the founding paper that Elbæk wrote a few months before launching Alternativet. In this document, the party itself is described as a 'popular political laboratory' that will 'prioritize the development of serious transitional scenarios – environmental, economic, social, and cultural – so that the ambition of a sustainable society is not experienced as either a threat to the personal freedom of citizens or as a stagnant society without dynamism' (Alternativet, 2013a: 2). Initially, the idea was that the laboratory part of Alternativet should materialize in a digital platform where citizens could debate these different transitional scenarios, but the group of volunteers surrounding Elbæk and Fock quickly discovered the mobilizing power of physical workshops. So, at the press conference that officially launched Alternativet, the two founders informed the public that the party's political programme would be developed through a bottom-up process of policy making, involving non-members as well as members and even members of other political parties.

During the first months of 2014, more than 20 political laboratories were organized in various community centres across the country. While all the laboratories followed roughly the same template, they were concerned with different political issues that seemed pertinent to the founders and the organizing committee: environmental sustainability, economic sustainability, social sustainability, education, art and culture, entrepreneurship and political culture. In total, more than 700 ordinary people participated in the events, effectively shaping Alternativet's official political programme through an almost Habermasian process of deliberation. As announced at the press conference, the outcomes of the workshops were collected and edited by the organizing committee and presented to the members prior to the annual meeting at Bornholm. This, however, is where the trouble began. What became apparent during that meeting was the irreconcilable nature of the project that Elbæk and Fock had launched. Since everyone had been allowed – and encouraged – to read their own personal preferences into the party, it proved incredibly difficult to synthesize all these disparate voices into one collective statement. Following long and painstaking negotiations, as well as hundreds of plebiscites on various proposed amendments (one member later referred to the meeting as a 'thoroughly terrible day'), the meeting finally came to a resolution. Besides accepting the programme in its current form, the members agreed to continuously revise the text by organizing even more political laboratories. Regardless of whether particular issues, such as tax or education, had already been resolved at a workshop, political laboratories would be organized with the explicit purpose of contemplating whether the solutions offered in the programme were still adequate. This would allow people whose voices had initially been excluded from the programme to trust that they might one day be included (see Husted and Just, 2022).

This decision gave rise to a novel conception of political laboratories that, as it turned out, proved to be quite an invention in terms of democratic politics. Throughout the year, workshops where planned and issues were debated by people from all walks of life in a genuinely engaged manner. During my observations of these laboratories, several people told me how their faith in democracy had been restored through the many discussions they had participated in and how the simple act of exchanging views with fellow citizens produced a feeling of joy and inclusion that they had never previously experienced in relation to politics. For a moment in mid-2014, it actually seemed as if the party had managed to single-handedly reinvent and reignite the political conversation in Danish politics. Even media pundits and political opponents had to admit that Alternativet was on to something, and soon other parties followed suit by staging workshops and citizen assemblies of their own.

The democratic potential unleashed by the political laboratories during 2014 was very similar to the experience of group organization described by Follett (1918: 3–4) a century earlier as a 'new method of politics' predicated on 'the organization of non-partisan groups for the begetting, the bringing into being, of common ideas, a common purpose and a collective will'. It may be that the laboratories were organized by partisans, but the ideas discussed at the workshops were taken from all over the political spectrum – just like the participants, most of whom were not even party members. Furthermore, the laboratories were characterized by a complete absence of formal hierarchy. Parliamentary candidates and common members participated on equal terms and, in that sense, the laboratories differed entirely from regular consultation exercises in political parties where the rank and file are invited to comment on policies developed by the leadership. In the words of Follett (1918: 25): 'We find in the end that it is not a question of my idea [from a candidate, for example] being supplemented by yours [the members], but that there has evolved a composite idea.'

In terms of the ever-expanding political programme, Alternativet implicitly decided to follow what has been described as a 'strategy of addition' (Mayer and Ely, 1998) where new policy proposals are simply added to the programme without explicit prioritization and without marginalizing other proposals. This meant that Alternativet's programme quickly became one of the most comprehensive policy catalogues in contemporary Danish politics, comprising more than 60 pages packed with tangible solutions to various societal challenges. While some of these proposals articulated fairly radical ideas associated with classical left-wing thought, such as unconditional unemployment benefits and 100 per cent organic farming, others gave voice to more peculiar propositions, such as the introduction of bison in state-owned forests and the prescription of 'culture' (rather than medicine) to vulnerable people. In that sense, the programme quite neatly reflected the diversity of the membership base.

At some point, however, not too long after Alternativet earned its nine seats in parliament, the proposals developed in the laboratories ceased to enter the political programme. No one quite knows what happened, and there was clearly no official decision to stop the inflow of policies, but, as the newly elected MPs grew busy with parliamentary affairs, they gradually seemed to lose sight of the laboratories and the ideas developed there. This caused a legitimate sense of frustration among the rank and file, who slowly began to feel that the political leadership was shortcutting the official bottom-up process of policy making. The MPs, on the other hand, became annoyed with those critical voices in the membership base who, in their view, did not understand that politicians need room for manoeuvre when operating in a parliamentary setting, and that there is rarely time for consensus-based deliberations. The represented and the representatives, however, all seemed to agree that the problem could be boiled down to differences in pace. While ordinary members engaged in a type of 'slow politics' that requires both time and space to contemplate every conceivable aspect of a given policy issue, the MPs had been socialized into a high-paced working environment that requires immediate decision-making and yes/no answers to otherwise complicated questions (see also Ringel and Brichzin, 2021). Despite this common realization, the facts remained that the members wanted the MPs to commit themselves more strongly to the bottom-up process of policy making, and the MPs wanted the members to accept the simple impossibility of slowing down the pace of electoral politics.

At stake are not just differences in pace and opinion (ought the MPs to respect the official policy-making process or be free to decide for themselves in terms of policies?). There is more to it than that. At stake are different conceptions of what is required for a political party to call itself democratic with regard to the established system and, in that sense, this discrepancy mirrors the different conceptions of proper democratic participation espoused by Ostrogorski and Michels. While the former believed that democratic participation should be defined as the 'free play of opinion', and that the MPs should be left to deliberate among their peers, the latter firmly believed that 'for democracy ... the first appearance of leadership marks the beginning of the end' (Michels, 1915: 73). In that sense, Ostrogorski would have sided with the representatives, arguing that an unelected caucus should abstain from interrupting the political process as it unfolds in parliament. Members should obviously be invited to participate in political discussions and encouraged to attend party conferences, but they should not be allowed to restrain duly elected MPs' space of action. Michels, on the other hand, would clearly have sided with the represented, claiming that the shortcutting of the policy-making process signifies an attempt to centralize power in the hands of the few; and such attempts are, in his view, always detrimental to democracy. This brings us to the question of oligarchy, as discussed by Michels and others, because the alteration of Alternativet's innovative policy-making process did not end with the parliamentary entry.

Oligarchy: the introduction of political forum

In early 2015, Alternativet commissioned an internal report on the political laboratories, which was to propose a number of recommendations for how to improve the outcome of the workshops. The feeling in the board, as well as the political leadership (the MPs), was that the quality of the policy proposals developed at the laboratories was rarely high enough. Too often, the proposals were unsubstantiated, lacked coherence and were out of sync with the rest of the party's policies. This made it difficult, if not impossible, to add the proposals directly to the political programme – that was arguably one reason why proposals ceased to enter the programme. The solution proposed in the internal report was to launch a second version of the policy-making process; a version that would address the quality issue and decentralize the process even further. As one of the architects behind Alternativet's bottom-up policy-making process explained during an interview:

'I typically say that we used to have a first version, and now we have a second version of policy-making. The first version was very controlled. We were only two people who, with help from the original organizing committee, designed the process of policy-making. The process was centrally controlled and it was a small number of people calling the shots. ... So, the first version was highly structured, which meant that we could produce a lot [of policy proposals]. There was a lot of work going into it, but we were able to produce a 60-page programme in half a year. On the other hand, the process was intransparent and we failed to settle expectations in terms of what proposals that got to enter the programme ... So, we thought: Why don't we turn the process on its head? Instead of controlling the process as such, let's instead be very specific and transparent about our requirements for the outcome of the workshops.'

This solution seemed obvious when first proposed. Instead of controlling the design of the political laboratories and the issues discussed at the workshops, it intuitively made more sense to control the quality of the proposals coming out of the laboratories. After all, the problem was not the process itself but the outcome. This effectively decentralized the process even further. Whereas previously, political laboratories where scheduled and organized centrally, they were now set free: anyone could organize a laboratory at any time and discuss any kind of political issue. Even a dinner conversation or a tea party could count as a laboratory if only it was widely advertised and open to all. In return, the outcome of these deliberations had to be written into a fixed template and submitted to the steering committee for consideration (for a more detailed examination of the process, see Husted and Plesner, 2017).

However, this solution immediately raised the question: who is to decide whether an incoming proposal is good enough to enter the political programme? To this end, a new organizational body was conceived and inaugurated. It was called *political forum*, to signal a direct connection to the political laboratories, and consisted of three distinct groups of partisans: (1) the board, in charge of the party's organizational affairs; (2) the MPs, in charge on the party's political affairs; and (3) a number of local representatives. This amounted to approximately 40 people tasked with deciding which proposals to accept as policy and which to reject. So far, so good. But how were these people to make decisions – on what grounds? The answer to this, which again seemed quite obvious to most of the involved, was to make Alternativet's six core values the basis of decision-making. The problem with this decision premise was, of course, that it can be quite challenging to decide in any consensual manner whether a policy proposal concerned with healthcare or education is *empathetic, humorous, generous, transparent, courageous* and *humble*. This initially sparked some thorny debates within the party about bias and impartiality, until the forum eventually realized that yes/no decisions could rarely be made based on the values alone. The proposals almost always had to be modified in order to align with the rest of the political programme, which often meant that the forum would move beyond the role assigned to it. As one of the organizers of political forum meetings put it in an interview:

> 'The statutes clearly state that political forum has the mandate to develop policies, but they are not supposed to use their meetings to further develop and modify proposals. ... It seems like, just because they are members of the forum, they must have the final say over policies. That's not the idea behind this process. Almost all proposals are accepted on the condition that a group [consisting primarily of forum members] are mandated to re-write the policy. ... And I often say to the forum members: If you want to develop policies, then you should participate in the *laboratories*. The forum should only ratify or not ratify, but decide whether the proposals make sense in relation to the values.'

The introduction of political forum, and especially the forum's decision to frequently edit incoming proposals to match a particular political direction, is easily interpreted as a sign of oligarchization. Prior to the launch of policy-making 2.0, the annual meeting (sometimes also known as the general assembly) was the highest authority in terms of political questions. In practice, however, there was no easily discernible political authority within Alternativet, since the ambition was to allow policy proposals to move from laboratory to political programme in an unmediated fashion. If ever a genuinely democratic party existed, one that even Michels might have recognized as anti-aristocratic, this would have been it. The launch of version 2.0, however, effectively suspended this radically horizontal mode of operation by introducing a governing body at the top of the policy-making process. And in that sense, Michels' iron law of oligarchy once again seemed confirmed: even the most egalitarian associations succumb to elite rule once the quest for political power really kicks in. It might not be an iron law in any strict scientific sense (Diefenbach, 2019), but it is nonetheless a tendency that seems to resurface whenever a political organization realizes the value of self-preservation.

More interestingly, perhaps, one might contemplate how different modalities of power are being exercised in the case of political forum. Sticking to the work of Michels, it is easy to recognize what Peter Fleming and André Spicer (2014) call the 'coercive' face of power in the forum's oligarchic power to either accept or reject incoming policy proposals. Forum members have a clear right *over* ordinary members, in the sense that they can force their will onto ordinary members, which in Michels' (1915: 50) view is the defining aspect of 'democracy with an aristocratic content'. Ostrogorski would probably agree with Michels in this regard, although most likely he would have been less opposed to the introduction of political forum since all members of the forum are duly elected. Considering his view on what Rye (2014: 75) calls 'strategic' power (the ability to manipulate others into compliance), however, we might supplement our analysis with an examination of the hidden agenda-setting exercised by the forum through the recurring decisions to modify and rewrite incoming proposals. This could easily be interpreted as a type of manipulation, by which the scope of possible outcomes are limited to issues that are 'relatively innocuous' (Bachrach and Baratz, 1962: 948) to the forum. Instead of exercising coercive power by simply rejecting unwanted proposals, the forum engages in a more strategic power game where unwanted aspects are removed from the proposals in a somewhat clandestine manner, before being accepted as policy. The following description, which is based on observations as well as interviews with those involved, is an interesting example of how such power dynamics play out in practice:

Around the time of the 2015 elections, a group of ordinary members had been working for months to write up a proposal for the party's taxation policy. They had organized three political laboratories where different aspects of the proposal had been discussed by members and representatives alike. After completing the laboratories, the group got together on several occasions to draft the proposal. Finally, after weeks of hard work, they submitted the proposal to political forum, hoping it would be accepted as official policy. What ensued turned out to be a 'pretty rugged process', as one group member recalled. The proposal should have been considered by the forum within 14 days, but that did not happen. Instead, the group was met with silence. When they approached the forum again, they were told that the proposal would be considered at the next forum meeting. However, 24 hours before the forum meeting, the group was contacted by the party's secretariat who had some 'suggestions' for how to improve the text. Most importantly, they suggested shortening the text significantly, effectively turning an elaborate proposal into a short declaration of intent. The group reluctantly accepted the suggestions, knowing that the forum meeting was only 24 hours away. At the meeting, however, the forum participants ironically complained about the lack of detail in the proposal and decided that the text had to be substantiated before entering the political programme. As such, a new task force was established to rewrite the proposal. The final text turned out to bear some resemblance to the original proposal, but as one of the group members noted: 'It is a good text, but it is just not *my* text.'

Ostrogorski would probably have characterized this as a type of backstage wire-pulling, carried out by a caucus, whose real business 'amounts to manipulating the electorate in the interest of the party, with the pretention of doing this on behalf of and by the people' (Ostrogorski, 1902: 329). Once again, the characterization of political forum as a caucus-like association is arguably not fair, given that members of the forum are elected rather than appointed. However, the fact that the party's secretariat – of unelected bureaucrats – interferes with the policy-making process, 'suggesting' changes in order to prepare the ground for political forum, is pretty close to Ostrogorski's description of caucus-driven wire-pulling.

Goal displacement: coffee at the prime minister's

Alternativet's role as part of the 2015 centre-left opposition did not prevent the newly elected MPs from engaging actively in day-to-day politics and from passing bills sponsored by the right-wing government. For instance, shortly after entering parliament, Alternativet helped pass a tax-deduction bill that reduced taxation on sustainable renewal of private homes. Even though the National Energy Council estimated that the €115,000,000 solution would reduce carbon dioxide emissions by less than 0.02 per cent, Alternativet's political leadership still considered it a good deal. As the party's spokesperson on financial affairs explained in a newspaper article: 'what we are interested in is pushing all bills in a green direction' (Kristensen, 2015). Such incidents spawned a debate in the media, as well as internally, about the alterity of Alternativet. Could a bill that costs so much and does so comparatively little good for the natural environment really be considered alternative? Or, was the MPs' support for the bill more an attempt to look professional; that is, a way of appearing competent enough to make a good impression with their new colleagues in parliament?

Other decisions made by Alternativet's political leadership were met with similar scepticism from the membership base. For instance, after taking office in June 2015, the right-wing government quickly decided to shut down a commission (established by the previous centre-left government) tasked with investigating the legal basis for the wars in Iraq and Afghanistan. Since it had been a right-wing government that initially decided to join the US in declaring war on Saddam Hussein's regime, it made sense that a right-wing government would try to obstruct an investigation meant to clarify whether that decision was legal or not. However, much to the surprise of both members and observers, Alternativet supported the decision to cease funding for a legal investigation. Instead, the government and Alternativet (as the only party left of centre) decided to commission a 'historical' report on the events surrounding the wars, which many lefties saw as a pointless and toothless exploration. Alternativet's self-styled 'peace spokesperson' defended the decision by saying that he would have preferred both a legal *and* a historical report, but, since the government insisted on shutting down the former, he would now work hard to push the latter in a positive direction. Once again, the party appeared more concerned with professional pragmatism than political idealism, and that caused some of Alternativet's more left-leaning members to disengage in disbelief.

On several occasions, Alternativet tried to revive its political idealism by articulating radical proposals that seriously challenged the established order. In autumn 2017, for instance, the party managed to pass a bill that allowed citizen-driven policy proposals to be discussed in parliament. Similarly, in spring 2018, Uffe Elbæk published a paper entitled *The Next Denmark*, in which he (continuing the previous *strategy of addition*, but entirely disregarding the bottom-up process of policy making) formulated 38 ideas for how to reinvent the Danish welfare state. One of his ideas was to abolish private property rights with respect to land, on the grounds that 'nature is not our property'; another idea was to reduce the average working week to 30 hours and offer every adult one year of free education every decade (Alternativet, 2018a). Finally, in August 2018, Alternativet published a plan for how to rethink the current stock of ministries in Denmark, which among other things involved establishing a Ministry for Green Transitions that would hold all other ministries accountable in terms of carbon footprint and resource depletion. Such bills and proposals, however, could not keep voter support for Alternativet from plummeting. Having peaked at almost 8 per cent in mid-2016, support for the party was close to the 2 per cent electoral threshold at the end of 2019.

At this point, Elbæk decided to step down as political leader of Alternativet, citing retirement age as the main reason (although insiders would suggest internal disagreements between MPs as the main cause). This created a significant vacuum, as Elbæk had been the face of the party since the very beginning and no other MP seemed capable of replacing him as the incarnation of alternativity. Although the selection of party leaders is often a task exclusively undertaken by the political leadership, Alternativet's board agreed to let the members decide by voting for their favourite candidate, thereby momentarily restoring the sense of democratic participation that initially made the party so innovative. Five people entered the race for the leadership position, but only three had a real chance of winning: Rasmus Nordqvist (Elbæk's own protégé and crown prince), Theresa Scavenius (a respected university professor and environmental activist) and Josephine Fock (the co-founder of the party who, in the meantime, had resigned from parliament due to a personal conflict with Elbæk and Nordqvist).

When the votes had been counted, there was no doubt: the ordinary members clearly preferred Josephine Fock, with one of the reasons being that she was neither a complete insider, like Nordqvist, nor a total outsider, like Scavenius. She had been involved with the party from the very beginning, but had since distanced herself from the things that made support for Alternativet drop to dangerously low levels by resigning her seat in parliament. While the members recognized the value of this position, and although observers like myself had identified Fock as the favourite candidate, the MPs and the secretariat were flabbergasted. Elbæk in particular could not get over the fact that the members had elected his friend-turned-enemy as the new leader of the party. To him, she represented all that he was not. She was no longer an MP; she had a much more formal leadership style; she was known to have difficulties controlling her temper; and – perhaps worst of all – she advocated a political strategy that involved even closer collaboration with the government. Fock summarized the gist of her own strategy like this: 'One of the first things I will do as political leader is to schedule a meeting with the prime minister – invite myself for coffee and hope she says yes' (Alternativet, 2020). When representatives from Elbæk's constituency a few months later demanded, in no uncertain terms, that he publicly declared his support for Fock, he immediately decided to leave Alternativet. Shortly after, all but one of the remaining MPs follows suit, leaving the party in what can only be described as a fatal condition.

Alternativet's short but eventful history provides an interesting window to understanding how processes of goal displacement unfold in practice. In general terms, the gradual transformation of Alternativet's political objectives is easily described as an example of the ideological dilution that often follows oligarchization (Messinger, 1955). When the party was first launched, it advocated a sweeping reconfiguration of Danish society. For instance, in the preamble to the first version of the political programme, it is stated that 'the time for half-measures is over', and that 'small adjustments and symptom treatments no longer suffice' (Alternativet, 2014a: 5):

> Instead, what we need is new forms of collaboration, new decision-making processes, and a new approach to the redistribution of earth's resources, where economic growth and material consumption is no

longer the only measure of success. In other words, Alternativet wants to redefine the established understanding of welfare and value.

Such passages ring hollow when compared with some of the first bills sponsored in parliament, such as the sustainable tax-deduction bill that appears very much to be a 'half-measure' and a 'small adjustment', as well as the decision to cease funding for the Iraq Commission, which sits uneasily with 'transparency' as a core value. In fact, this was the official approach advocated by the political leadership when they first entered parliament. Here, the idea presumably was to push all bills in a slightly progressive direction instead of maintaining a strong and idealistic stance; a vision that Elbæk himself described as 'visionary pragmatic' to emphasize that the MPs were not going to 'sit in the corner' and do nothing (Alternativet, 2015a). This strategy was extended during the following years and thoroughly solidified by the new leader, Josephine Fock's, analogy of inviting herself for coffee at the prime minister's office. In other words, pragmatic collaboration was generally prioritized at the expense of idealist resistance, with *reform* replacing *revolution* as the primary political objective.

That said, there have indeed been moments of re-radicalization. One example is Elbæk's aforementioned 38 ideas for the 'Next Denmark', in which he articulates proposals that may have been discussed at political laboratories but never turned into official policy. One such proposal centres on the notion of universal basic income (UBI), understood as an unconditional and periodic cash payment to all citizens in a given community. Basic income initiatives have historically been met with resistance from both left and right, but have recently gained traction in the public debate (Petersen et al, 2022). The same kind of resistance could initially be identified within Alternativet, where many believe that UBI would be too radical and too expensive and give rise to welfare free-riding. Elbæk's decision to include the proposal in his paper could thus be interpreted as a sign of what Jenkins (1977) calls 'radical oligarchy', understood as instances where an organizational elite espouses ideas that are *more* radical than those promoted by 'lay members'. Hence, although the overall development of Alternativet seems to mirror the process of oligarchization, described by Michels and others, moments of renewed idealism in terms of political content and democratic participation are indeed detectable.

Evaluation: conquering oneself to death

At the time of writing (autumn 2023), Alternativet has managed to stop the bleeding and begin a process of gradual recovery. For a while, however, the party was heading straight for political extinction. After Fock took over as leader, opinion polls dropped to even lower levels, reaching a point below 0.5 per cent in 2020. At the same time, more than 90 per cent of the party's members decided to leave the organization from 2017 to 2020 (see Chapter 7). In fact, at that point, very few people – including myself – seriously believed that Alternativet could survive the national elections in 2022. In early 2021, however, Fock decided to step down after fewer than ten months at the helm, and another leadership referendum was announced. This time, a member of the Copenhagen City Council, Franciska Rosenkilde, won the election and promised to turn things around. Against all odds, through hard work and dedication, she succeeded in bringing Alternativet back to life. A few months before the 2022 elections, Alternativet successfully forged a number of alliances with minor green parties such as Momentum and the Vegan Party – thereby reducing the risk of 'wasting' green votes on parties that would never make it across the electoral threshold – and relaunched some of the democratic procedures that worked so well during the party's early years. At the elections, Alternativet won 3.3 per cent of the vote and increased its parliamentary seats from one to six.

To adequately summarize Alternativet's contribution to Danish politics and to round off this classical analysis of party organization, we need to revisit the second aspect of Ostrogorski's functional analysis: *evaluation*. As such, we need to ask: did (or does) Alternativet serve the purpose that it was originally meant to serve? I believe there are two answers to this and they are, unsurprisingly perhaps, *yes* and *no*. Let's unfold these answers one at a time, beginning with the second. First, Alternativet was primarily established to reinvigorate the democratic dimension of Danish politics by serving as a home for all those who longed for an alternative to the status quo and by reinventing the otherwise oligarchic processes of policy making that dominate contemporary politics. In fact, in many ways, Alternativet was conceived as the institutionalization of deliberative democracy, where focus is on edifying dialogue, public participation and consensus-based decision-making (for a detailed examination of Alternativet's deliberative potential, see Husted and Mac, 2021). For a number of years, and certainly prior to the 2015 parliamentary entry, the party clearly served this purpose, hosting political laboratories and inventing debate principles that effectively abolished mudslinging and unproductive conflicts. However, the invention of political forum – and the 'fast politics' associated with parliamentary life – drove a wedge into this super-democratic set-up and moved the party dangerously close to the type of oligarchy described my Michels. Today, there are few laboratories and very little membership participation left in Alternativet. As such, it seems fair to conclude that the party no longer delivers on its promise to reinvigorate Danish democracy by representing all those 'who can feel that something new is starting to replace something old', although it probably did inspire other parties to momentarily consider how their internal processes could be democratized.

In terms of the first, positive, answer to our evaluative question, Alternativet was also established as a response to the ongoing climate and biodiversity crises. In the party's first political programme, the notion of sustainability was by far the most dominant signifier, giving meaning to Alternativet's position in relation to environmental issues and in relation to economic and social policy. Similarly, in the founding document written by Elbæk prior to the launch of Alternativet, the party is described as prioritizing 'the development of serious transitional scenarios – environmental, economic, social, and cultural' – all of which would serve as stepping stones for the realization of a sustainable future (Alternativet, 2013a: 2). Alternativet's position as Denmark's number one green party was further confirmed in 2019 when Elbæk refused to back any of the two candidates for the Prime Minister's Office (the centre-left parties usually back the Social Democrat's leading candidate). Instead, Elbæk decided to announce his own candidacy for the office of prime minister, citing the fact that Alternativet was a *green* party, not a *red* party.

Although the elections in 2019 proved nearly fatal for Alternativet, reducing their total number of seats from nine to five, the party's impact on the election was clearly visible. A few months before the elections, a public poll revealed climate change to be the most important issue for Danish voters, which significantly tainted the electoral race and forced all parties to up their game in relation to environmental policies. Suddenly, almost all parties in parliament were willing to accept reduction levels of CO_2 emissions that would have been absolutely unthinkable just one year earlier. Much of this was attributed to Alternativet and its success in terms of making green politics mainstream in Denmark. In the end, the 2019 election was characterized as a 'climate election' and saw the Social Democrats regain power after four years in the opposition. Shortly after being voted into office, a clear majority in the Danish parliament backed a climate law that committed the government to reduce CO_2 emissions by no less than 70 per cent by 2030, thereby restoring Denmark's position as a global leader in terms of green transitions. In that sense, one could argue that Alternativet has had an immense impact on Danish politics and that the party clearly served its (sustainability-related) purpose, but that it somehow conquered itself to death. Given that most other parties are now championing a green stance, and that Alternativet's core agenda has (ironically) become mainstream, it has proven difficult for the party to maintain distinctiveness and uphold its identity as a truly alternative home for the politically homeless.

4

The Configurational Perspective

For present-day parties are distinguished far less by the nature of their programme or the class of their members than by the nature of their organization. A party is a community with a particular structure. Modern parties are characterized primarily by their anatomy.

Maurice Duverger (1954: xv): *Political Parties*

Introduction

In Chapter 2, we saw how Moisei Ostrogorski and Robert Michels pioneered a type of party research that privileges the empirical reality of party *organizations* at the expense of macro-level phenomena such as party *systems* and constitutional frameworks. Instead of focusing on what Ostrogorski (1902: li) calls the political 'forms' of representative democracy, as figures such as James Bryce and Alexis de Tocqueville had previously done, they developed a concern for the political 'forces' that govern everyday life in parties and parliaments. This approach would come to dominate the literature for decades, with countless studies attempting to either verify or reject the conclusions reached by these founders of party organization research (see Lipset et al, 1956). What primarily characterizes this body of research is that it blends sociological descriptions with moral judgements, provides tangible solutions to the problems observed, and focuses on the ability of political parties to deliver on the democratic hopes invested in them in terms of liberating the individual from aristocratic rule.

Halfway through the 20th century, a new but clearly related approach to party organization research emerged. Instead of focusing squarely on political forces, it shifted focus back to forms, but maintained an interest in parties as organizations in their own right. This resulted in a perspective that emphasizes the importance of achieving a much more systematic understanding of the structural anatomy of parties, based on the conviction that it is *the nature of their organization* that distinguishes political parties from one another. The approach that I have chosen to call the 'configurational perspective' is overwhelmingly informed by the work of French jurist and political scientist Maurice Duverger. Although he might be best known for formulating high-profile hypotheses about the correlation between electoral systems and the number of parties operating in those systems, it is his work on party organization that will concern us here. In an attempt to update and systematize the findings reported by classical authors such as Ostrogorski and Michels, Duverger produced a general but 'preliminary' theory of political parties that centres on three related themes: organizational structures, membership modalities and leadership dynamics. Combining insights on these three themes, Duverger launched a way of thinking about parties that is configurational through and through; that is, he provided a theoretical tool-kit for analysing how political parties consist of multiple organizational elements that, when combined, converge into distinct party models. Two of the configurations most commonly associated with the work of Duverger are the 'mass' party and its logical counterpart, the 'cadre' party. Both configurations may, however, be seen as relics of a distant past where parties played a much more central role in the mobilization of the masses.

Since the publication of Duverger's (1954) theory of party organization, a wide range of scholars have followed his lead by developing and modifying different party configurations (Krouwel, 2006). One of the most famous configurations to emerge from this body of literature is the 'catch-all' party, which Otto Kirchheimer (1966) famously framed as a transformation of the traditional mass party along the lines of centralization and de-ideologicalization. Another configuration that could be said to advance this transformation even further is the 'cartel' party, conceived by Richard Katz and Peter Mair (1995) as a political formation that establishes symbiotic ties with the state apparatus. This chapter considers each of these configurations in turn, alongside other prevalent party models such as the authoritarian 'business firm' party (Hopkin and Paolucci, 1999), the egalitarian 'movement' party (Kitschelt, 2006) and the techno-utopian 'digital' party (Gerbaudo, 2019). All of these will help to develop an understanding of how the configurational perspective works, and what research strategies and methodological choices it relies on, and they will provide useful thinking tools that can assist in analysing Alternativet as a mixture of several configurations (see Chapter 5). The realization that existing parties rarely correspond to one single party model also illuminates the fact that configurations are ideal types, meaning that they isolate and emphasize certain tendencies that may be found in many parties. The task for the empirically informed party researcher is then to explore how different configurations allow us to perceive the structural anatomy of party organizations more clearly, and how this new understanding provides us with novel insights that bring us closer to comprehending the inner life of parties.

Duverger's general theory of parties

In the pantheon of party scholars, only one author properly measures up to Michels and Ostrogorski in terms of intellectual influence and that is Maurice Duverger. Born in 1917 in the provincial city of Angoulême, on the southern bank of the Charente, Duverger went to school in nearby Bordeaux where he later enrolled 'unenthusiastically' in the Law Faculty (Hoffmann-Martinot, 2005: 304). Although he personally would have preferred to become a 'famous writer ... like François Mauriac', Duverger (1977: 68) excelled in his legal studies, winning several prizes for outstanding scholarship. In 1940, Duverger earned his PhD within the field of public law and quickly assumed a professorship at the University of Bordeaux. In this early part of his life, Duverger was a controversial figure in the French public debate, owing largely to his questionable accounts of anti-Semitic legislation, which led observers to make comparisons between him and Martin Heidegger (Hoffmann-Martinot, 2005). In the latter part of his life, Duverger played an important role in establishing political science as an independent discipline at French universities as well as internationally. His political sympathies shifted considerably after the Second World War, with Duverger openly associating with leftist forces such as the French Socialist Party and the newspapers *Libération* and *Le Monde* (Elgie, 2011). In 1989, he even accepted to represent the Italian Communist Party in the elections for the European Parliament. He remained an MEP for five years, but disengaged from politics as well as academia towards the end of the 1990s.

Most political scientists will undoubtedly have heard of Duverger's Law, a widely tested hypothesis developed by Duverger in the 1950s and 1960s, which holds forth the idea that proportional representation in parliamentarian elections gives rise to multi-party systems, whereas plurality voting (such as 'first past the post') affords Americanized two-party systems (see Duverger, 1954: Book 2). Political scientists might also have come across Duverger's (1980) notion of 'semi-presidentialism', which signifies a constitutional set-up where the president's power is matched or at least constrained by those of the prime minister and the parliament. However, none of these famed contributions to the literature on party *systems* is of immediate relevance for our purposes. Instead, and in line with the rest of the book, I want to consider Duverger's (1954) work on party *organization*, as outlined in the first part of his bestselling monograph *Political Parties: Their Organization and Activity in the Modern State*. What makes this an important contribution to party organization research is Duverger's attempt to draw up 'a preliminary general theory of political parties' (Duverger, 1954: xiii) by focusing predominantly on the administrative structure of parties (their 'anatomy'). Combined with his taste for ostensive classifications and systematism, Duverger's work on party organizations represents a radical break from the colourful and moralizing descriptions of life inside parties, as produced by classical authors like Michels and Ostrogorski. In many ways, this more systematic and formalized approach to research represents both the immense strength and weakness of Duverger's theory of party organization.

I begin this section by detailing the core elements of Duverger's comprehensive theory, following his lead by focusing on party *structure*, *membership* and *leadership*. I then proceed to consider how his work on parties relates to organization studies – particularly to the structuralist or formalist part of the literature – highlighting what I believe organization scholars might learn from engaging with Duverger's writings. In the end, I use Duverger as a stepping stone for introducing the work of other party scholars who have adopted and developed the configurational perspective on party organization.

The basic anatomy of parties

Classifications require distinctions. Developing ostensive categories and sorting the empirical world accordingly necessarily entails a process by which something is demarcated from something else, often in a rather simplified fashion, which serves to reduce complexity but heighten analytical utility. In the established literature on party organization, this trend is nowhere as visible as in Duverger's work on party structures. As Robert Elgie (2011) notes, the first part of *Political Parties* is replete with analytical distinctions between various categories associated with party organization, although Duverger (1954: xxx) readily admits that these represent 'general tendencies rather than clearly differentiated types' (see Figure 4.1 for an overview of Duverger's distinctions). Nonetheless, the aim of Duverger's investigation clearly lies in 'defining these basic distinctions with maximum precision' (p 3) in an attempt to develop a general theory of parties that allows us to see how 'present-day parties are distinguished far less by the nature of their programme or the class of their members than by the nature of their organization' (p xv).

The first distinction that Duverger asks his reader to contemplate concerns the origins of parties, since 'the whole life of the party ... bears the mark of its origin' (Duverger, 1954: xxxv). Here, he seems to draw extensively but implicitly on the work of Ostrogorski (see Chapter 2), when asserting that it makes sense to consider whether parties originate inside or outside the parliamentarian system. The first type of party – originating 'from within' – begins as informal parliamentarian groups or as electoral committees, united around particular views or geographical belongings. Examples include the Conservative Party and the Liberal Party in Britain, both of which grew out of loosely affiliated parliamentarian groups – the Tories and the Whigs – and splinter parties such as the US Republican Party, which was born in 1854 as a consequence of an internal disagreement on the issue of slavery in the now-extinct American Whig Party (see Gienapp, 1987). The second type of party – originating 'from without' – is created by extra-parliamentarian forces. Examples of such forces traditionally include religious communities (such as Catholic parties), trade unions (labour parties), intellectual societies (elite or 'radical' parties), social movements (such as green parties) and corporate interests (libertarian parties, for instance). Although most parties represent a mixture of the two types, Duverger nonetheless maintains that certain characteristics can be ascribed to each type. Surprisingly perhaps, he claims extra-parliamentarian parties to be more centralized and ideologically consistent than parliamentarian parties.

Duverger's second distinction is closely related to the first. It concerns the difference between parties that consist of rank and file, who pay their monthly membership fees and attend meetings to exercise their influence, and parties that consist of an elaborate network of support groups, lobbying for influence. The former are labelled 'direct' parties, since they rely directly on the will of their members, and the latter are 'indirect' parties, since the link between the represented and the representatives is mediated by external groups. In many ways, indirect parties thus correspond to what have more recently been called 'memberless' parties (Mazzoleni and Voerman, 2017), in the sense that the parties themselves have no official members. All those who appear to be members are, in fact, members of affiliated organizations such as trade unions and worker cooperatives (in the case of certain socialist parties) or religious communities and capitalist associations (in the case of certain Catholic parties). However, many indirect parties tend to assume structures that are more direct over time, and to free themselves of the constraints imposed by the support groups. In that sense, 'direct parties are the rule, indirect parties the exception' (Duverger, 1954: 13).

Duverger's third distinction – or rather, cluster of distinctions – sets the scene for the rest of his book, as well as for much of the established literature on party organization. Having discussed, first, the origins of parties and the *horizontal* composition of parties, Duverger turns to 'basic elements', understood as the building blocks that constitute the foundation of a party's *vertical* structure; that is, the administrative form of the organization. While once again recognizing that each party has its own unique structure, and that no party will ever be based exclusively on one kind of basic element, Duverger highlights four types that are prevalent in modern parties: caucuses, branches, cells and militias.

The caucus, understood as a closed elite committee at the centre of the organization (see also Chapter 2), constitutes the basic element of conservative parties and US parties. Caucuses are generally composed of influential and accomplished notabilities, often selected through a process of 'tacit co-optation' (Duverger, 1954: 18), who govern the party by giving orders and pulling wires. The caucus is limited, meaning that it does not seek to expand, and it is therefore not readily open to new members. In that sense, it represents an administrative structure that sits uneasily with popular demands for intra-party democratization, which may be why it is less prevalent today than in the era preceding the invention of universal suffrage.

The branch, understood as a decentralized subdivision of ordinary members, constitutes the negative image of the caucus and is the basic element of socialist parties and Catholic parties. Unlike the caucus, the branch is 'wide open' in terms of recruitment (Duverger, 1954: 23), rendering it an instrument for appealing to the masses. Branches meet regularly – also outside election season – and their role in socializing members into the party culture and educating them politically is therefore significant. Branch-based organizing remains the most dominant way of structuring mass parties, with both left- and right-wing formations adopting the configuration (Janda and King, 1985), making it an 'interesting example of contagious organization' (Duverger, 1954: 25).

The cell, understood as a clandestine group that operates within a particular workplace or neighbourhood, constitutes the backbone of old-school communist parties. Like branches, they tend to represent a certain geographical area, but cells are usually much smaller in terms of membership (around 15 or 20 people in Duverger's estimate) and have a stronger hold on their members. The shared experiences of life at work or in the local community help to build a strong sense of party solidarity and discipline that cannot be matched by the other organizational configurations. The tight link between party and workplace, facilitated by the cell, also renders collective actions such as strikes and the dissemination of propaganda highly effective. In that sense, a cell-based party is best understood as an 'instrument of agitation' rather than an organization 'intended for the winning of votes, for grouping of representatives, and for maintaining contact between them and their electors' (Duverger, 1954: 35). This tendency, however, is even more pronounced in the case of the fourth and final element.

The militia, understood as a highly disciplined private army, is characteristic of fascist parties. Members of militias resemble soldiers in every way: they are incredibly obedient, well trained, often uniformed, often armed and ready to engage in violence if necessary. They have sworn allegiance to the leader – rather than the party – whose actions they justify with reference to his presumed divinity. Militias exist at different levels. For instance, in the case of Adolf Hitler's dreaded Storm Troops, the lowest level was called a squad. It consisted of four to twelve men. The second level was made up of sections of three to six squads. The third level was a company, consisting of four sections. The fifth level was a battalion, consisting of two companies, and so on. Mussolini's Fascii followed the same organizational template. Like the cell, the central purpose of the militia is not to win votes or to connect representatives with their constituencies, but to inspire discipline in the electorate. Cells achieve this through propaganda and agitation; militias achieve it by violence. In essence, as Duverger rightly notes, the militia is not an instrument for organizing democracy but for overthrowing it.

Duverger's fourth distinction concerns the strength of the link between a party's basic elements and the degree of formalization within the party organization. If close ties connect the basic elements (perhaps through regional divisions), and if the administrative structure of the party is sufficiently formalized (for example through detailed regulations and accurate organigrams), it is characterized by Duverger as an example of 'strong articulation'. If, on the other hand, the basic elements remain loosely connected, and if the administrative structure of the party is only vaguely defined or cast in darkness, it is characterized by Duverger as an example of 'weak articulation'. Parties based on cells and militias tend to be more strongly articulated than parties based on branches and caucuses. This shows why the notion of strong articulation should not be confused with intra-party democracy: a party can easily exhibit a high degree of formalization without being democratic in any meaningful way. However, as Duverger asserts in a conclusion that anticipates discussions about the 'tyranny of structurelessness' (see Freeman, 1972): 'It is, of course, true that weak articulation is not democratic' (Duverger, 1954: 44). Duverger's point is that weak articulation often curbs the ability of ordinary members to exercise their influence, and tends to create favourable conditions for oligarchy. As we saw in Chapter 3, and as will become evident in Chapter 5, this point can help us understand the dynamics that may have led to Alternativet's downfall.

Duverger further distinguishes between 'vertical' and 'horizontal' links. Vertical links connect elements that are in a hierarchical relationship with one another (such as branches and sections), whereas horizontal links connects elements on the same level (different branches). The notion of articulation concerns both links, in the sense that a party may have strong vertical links but weak horizontal links. According to Duverger, this is often the case in communist parties, whereas the opposite may be the case in movement parties (which we shall consider later). The final distinction to consider here concerns the difference between centralization and decentralization, which clearly bears some resemblance to the distinction between vertical and horizontal links. However, whereas the latter distinction signifies the direction of *collaboration*, the former represents the concentration of decision-making *power*. The more power each of the basic elements wield, the more decentralized the party is, and vice versa.

An interesting observation that emerges from Duverger's final distinction is that parties, which claim to be decentralized, may sometimes be highly centralized. This is why, according to Duverger (1954: 56), we cannot 'allow ourselves to be misled by the constitution but must analyze its application in practice before coming to a conclusion'. This assertion is worth keeping in mind, not only because it tells us something about the methodological ethos that undergirds the configurational perspective, but also because it alerts us to dynamics that we will consider in the application of the configurational perspective to the case of Alternativet.

Duverger differentiates between four types of decentralization – local, ideological, social and federal – and two types of centralization – autocratic and democratic. Centralized parties are characterized by strong national management, where a small elite unite – caucus – single-handedly decides issues of relevance to the organization. In decentralized parties, on the other hand, the basic elements enjoy significant autonomy from decisions made by the national or regional leadership. First, *local* decentralization corresponds to the intuitive understanding of the concept: 'the local leaders of the party come from the bottom; they enjoy wide powers; the centre has little control over them; the fundamental decisions are taken by them' (Duverger, 1954: 53). Second, *ideological* decentralization has to do with the 'free play of opinion', as Ostrogorski calls it; that is, the absence of enforced party discipline, which often provides favourable conditions for wings or factions to arise within the organization. Third, *social* decentralization concerns the autonomy granted to various demographic segments within the organization. In Duverger's time, class or occupation was arguably the most relevant identity marker in this regard, but today we may encounter modes of decentralization that follow racialized, gendered or sexuality-focused patterns. Finally, *federated* decentralization, which signifies a process where the party is split into autonomous divisions that mimic geographical or ethnic demarcations, is perhaps the most radical way of delegating power.

Membership modalities

What does it mean to be party member? Although very few people today are members of a political party (van Biezen et al, 2012), most probably have an intuitive idea of what it entails, such as paying fees, receiving newsletters and perhaps attending conferences. However, as Duverger convincingly shows, the notion of party membership is equivocal and varies substantially from party to party. For instance, the literature often distinguishes generically between registered party 'members' and casual 'supporters' who follow the organization without being listed as rank and file, but this distinction is often difficult to maintain in practice. Sometimes supporters are allowed to vote on issues that are usually reserved for members (this trend is prevalent in digital parties), and sometimes parties operate entirely in the absence of formal memberships (the case in memberless parties). Considering this equivocality,

Figure 4.1: Duverger's six distinctions of party configurations

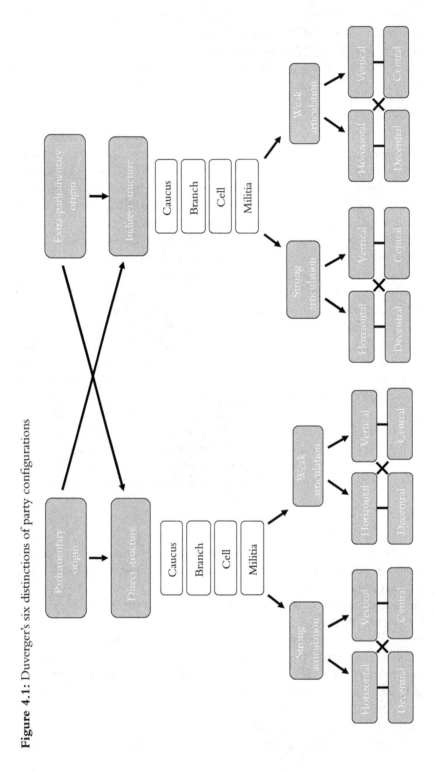

Duverger decides to approach the topic of membership from another angle. Instead of outlining various formal requirements for what it truly means to be a party member, he defines different membership modalities according to the level of participation (Duverger, 1954: 90, emphasis added):

> Within parties in which no formal membership exists three concentric circles of participation can be distinguished. The widest comprises the *electors* who vote for the candidates put forward by the parties at local and national elections. ... The second circle is made up of *supporters* ...: the supporter is an elector, but more than an elector: he acknowledges that he favours the party; he defends it and sometimes he supports it financially; he even joins bodies ancillary to the party. ... Finally the third, the inmost circle, is composed of *militants*; they consider themselves to be members of the party ...; they see to its organization and its operation; they direct its propaganda and its general activities. ... In parties that have *members*, these constitute a fourth circle, intermediate between the last two: wider than the circle of militants, narrower than the circle of supporters: membership involves a greater degree of participation than the sympathies of the supporter, but less than militancy.

Let's consider each of the circles in turn. The widest circle, consisting of *electors*, is by far the easiest to define: an elector is a person who votes for a party in duly constituted elections. Today, in European democracies, this circle is typically somewhere between 25 and 35 times bigger than the circle of registered members (in Duverger's time, the difference was much smaller). Electors rarely enjoy any privileges within a party and, if they do, they will probably not take advantage of these privileges in any meaningful way. This leads us to Duverger's definition of the second widest circle, the *supporters*, who are understood as electors that openly commit to a particular party by declaring their support in public or by assisting the party financially. Hence, in Duverger's (1954: 102) words, 'an elector who says how he has voted is no longer an elector'. As such, what separates electors from supporters is the willingness to commit to a particular party through various means of informal participation. This type of commitment, in which a person 'confesses his political preferences', serves a couple of important functions that substantiate the difference between electors and supporters (Duverger, 1954: 101). First, the public declaration of support – attending rallies, putting stickers on cars, joining online groups and so on – helps create a sense of community that may be fundamental to people's personal identity and social relationships. Second, it often installs a particular mode of being in people that implicitly compels them to act in accordance with the principles of the party they claim to support.

There might be several reasons why supporters may not want to formalize their commitment to a particular party by becoming registered members: financial (subscription fees), work commitments (conflicts of interest) and a simple lack of time. As Duverger maintains, however, less tangible reasons for avoiding enrolment also exist. For instance, people may experience a certain resistance to the prospect of being 'regimented'; that is, an unwillingness to be subjected to the homogenizing force of party rules and discipline.

Those that do become party *members*, however, clearly enjoy more rights and privileges than those who remain electors or supporters. Nonetheless, in contemporary Europe, fewer than 5 per cent of the population are registered rank and file (van Biezen et al, 2012). Surprisingly, perhaps, Duverger does not discuss the characteristics of 'normal' party membership in detail. Instead, he defines it negatively by claiming that members are more active and committed than supporters, but less involved than those he calls *militants.* These are members who, without necessarily occupying formal positions, constitute a caucus within the party. Militants are not always leaders (and leaders are not always militants), but they nonetheless exercise a significant influence on the organization and its members. They do so by voicing opinions at meetings, by circulating slogans, by manufacturing propaganda, by recruiting members, by raising funds and by enforcing party culture. As such, without militants, it simply would not be possible for voluntary organizations such as political parties to carry out their activities. This leads us seamlessly to the question of party leadership.

How to rule the party

Duverger starts from the assertion that formalized modes of leadership in all political parties, with the possible exception of fascist parties, have one thing in common: they are 'democratic in appearance and oligarchic in reality' (Duverger, 1954: 133). Given that parties typically portray themselves as indispensable to the proper functioning of democracy, they must naturally 'take the greatest care to provide themselves with leadership that is democratic in appearance' (Duverger, 1954: 134), even though the empirical reality of party organization often pushes in the opposite direction. According to Duverger, a range of factors influence the extent to which a party adopts an oligarchic structure: the composition of members, the party's internal culture, ideological commitments, the size and age of the organization, as well as factors related to inter-party competition. Duverger thereby adds nuance to the technical and psychological causes for oligarchy, established by Michels (see Chapter 2), although he clearly recognizes that the account provided by his predecessor 'continues to hold true' (Duverger, 1954: 134).

The assumption that oligarchy is inherent to all party organizations leads Duverger to an interesting distinction between 'open' and 'disguised' autocracy, with the latter being the rule and the former the exception. In open autocracies, the party does little to conceal the fact that vast powers are invested in a single person. This set-up is typically seen in fascist parties and, to a certain extent, in business firm parties and memberless parties, where oligarchy is justified with reference to the perceived divinity of the leader. New party leaders and parliamentarian candidates are here appointed or 'co-opted' by the incumbent rather than elected by the members. In disguised autocracies, on the other hand, oligarchy is concealed through elaborate voting procedures and opaque decision-making processes. In the previous chapter, we saw how such processes unfolded in relation to Alternativet's open-source approach to policy making. Members were promised direct influence on the content of the political programme, but when policy drafts developed by ordinary members were submitted, the leadership would often redraft them in a manner than could be described as oligarchic.

Another way of disguising autocracy is through processes of 'indirect representation', which refers to the practice of having delegates vote on behalf of ordinary members. We recognize this phenomenon from US politics where each party sends delegates to the Electoral College to vote for their preferred presidential candidate. Although these delegates almost always follow the popular vote (the outcome of the presidential elections in their home state), there have indeed been instances where delegates have defied the will of the people. Delegates who betray their pledge to vote for a particular candidate are known as 'faithless electors'. Similarly, prior to the presidential elections, each party will typically host a national convention where delegates elect the party's presidential candidate. These delegates are selected either by popular vote or by caucus appointment but, in either case, delegates may decide to remain unpledged; that is, they can reserve the right to choose the candidate they personally prefer without declaring their opinion in advance. This naturally opens the door for undemocratic forces to influence the preferences of delegates.

While delegates may be most widely used in an US context, they are also frequently deployed in European parties. Even in highly egalitarian parties such as Alternativet, delegates are used to render decision-making processes smoother. Here, we may again recall the example of open-source policy making explored in the previous chapter. Although all members (and non-members) are allowed to participate in the drafting of policy proposals, the drafts are always ratified – and sometimes redrafted – by members of the political forum (the MPs, the board and local representatives). The members of the forum are, in that sense, delegates who act more or less faithfully in terms of adequately representing the interests of ordinary party members. This example also illustrates what Duverger (1954: 138) calls a 'pyramid election'; an elaborate system where members of local branches select candidates to represent the branch at regional level, and where new candidates are selected to represent the section at national level. As Duverger (1954: 140) sarcastically remarks, such methods are an 'admirable way of banishing democracy while pretending to apply it'.

A final means of disguising autocracy to consider here is the distinction between 'titular' and 'real' leaders. While titular leaders are elected by popular vote, real leaders are appointed autocratically: 'The former enjoy power in theory, the latter exercise it in reality or else share it with them' (Duverger, 1954: 146). Paolo Gerbaudo (2019) observes this phenomenon in digital parties. According to Gerbaudo, what titular leaders such as Beppe Grillo (Movimento 5 Stelle), Pablo Iglesias (Podemos), Rick Falkvinge (Swedish Pirate Party), Jeremy Corbyn (Momentum) and Jean-Luc Mélenchon (France Insoumise) have in common is that they personify the party to the extent that their name becomes almost synonymous with the organization. This means that they serve as an object of identification for a multiplicity of political identities, effectively rendering him (for it is somehow always a man) a 'hyperleader', in the sense that he has to represent a wide chain of political demands. To do so, titular leaders of digital parties often employ a charismatic leadership style that allows them to assume the role of talismans who embody the 'authentic' spirit of the party, rather than day-to-day managers who make tough decisions. Hence, the management of the organization is almost entirely left to 'hidden demiurges' like Gianroberto Casaleggio in the case of Movimento 5 Stelle or Iñigo Errejón in the case of Podemos who operate(d) well out of public sight (Gerbaudo, 2019: 160).

Having outlined the most important parts of Duverger's work on party organization, we can now take a step back and observe how each part of his theory is tied together by a common reference to the basic elements of political parties. For instance, parties that rely on caucuses (referred to here as cadre parties) will automatically generate a very small but very active membership base, consisting almost entirely of militants. By contrast, parties that are based on branches (mass parties) are predisposed to fostering a large but somewhat passive pool of members, where only a small fraction can be considered militant minded. Similarly, although most parties are said to exhibit some degree of oligarchy, the means for legitimizing elite rule varies, with militia-based parties openly embracing the divine rule of their leader and cell-based parties disguising it through various 'electoral tricks' (Duverger, 1954: 146). Towards the end of this chapter, I will discuss the merits of this approach to organizational analysis. Beforehand, I will review what might be called Duverger's legacy: the more recent body of literature that follows his lead by exploring parties through a configurational lens.

Duverger's legacy

Duverger clearly supplies a nuanced framework for analysis that makes it possible to distinguish party organizations along at least seven lines, but he also conceived of two ideal-typical configurations that would come to dominate party research for decades: the cadre party and the mass party. For all intents and purposes, the two configurations constitute each other's opposites (Krouwel, 2006). With the word 'cadre' (according to the Merriam-Webster dictionary, 2023) referring to a core group of 'trained personnel able to assume control' of a particular enterprise, the cadre party represents a configuration that is exclusively organized around a small elite of notabilities and experts (also known as a caucus). As such, it quite accurately corresponds to what Max Weber (1922) calls the 'party of notables'. The cadre party has no members, in the sense of subscription-paying supporters who enjoy rights and privileges within the organization, and it therefore has no interest in things that concern other party configurations, such as membership participation, socialization and political education. Accordingly, the party's finances are not supplied by ordinary members who pay their monthly dues but derived primarily from resourceful stakeholders 'who can bring the sinews of war' (Duverger, 1954: 64). In terms of recruitments, cadre parties rarely select representatives from their own ranks, and they certainly do not elect them democratically.

Unlike the cadre party, the mass party is a membership organization through and through. It is an organization that measures its strength in sheer numbers. As such, it seeks to mobilize otherwise marginalized segments of society and goes to great lengths to socialize 'the masses' into a particular party culture, thereby cultivating a strong sense of identification and commitment in ordinary members. In mass parties, members are organized in branches and educated politically through a 'dense network of ancillary organizations' such as trade unions and sports clubs (Krouwel, 2006: 254). Sigmund Neumann (1956) famously describes mass parties as 'parties of social integration' to emphasize how these formations typically venture beyond 'individual representation' by fostering a feeling of belonging within the membership base. In other words, mass parties provide parliamentarian representation for specific interests and they provide a home away from home for people longing for some kind of community. To accomplish this socialization, mass parties are typically committed to a relatively distinct ideology that is espoused through party propaganda, which is what sets this configuration apart from more recent party models that operate with more vague political profiles. According to Duverger (1954), however, the most important factor that distinguishes mass parties from cadre parties is their source of finance. Whereas cadre parties rely on donations from wealthy financiers, mass parties are dependent on members who pay their dues. This is also what potentially makes mass parties more democratic, in the sense that they have an obligation to serve members rightfully, although some of the most well-known studies of oligarchization centre on European mass parties such as the German Social Democratic Party (see, for example, Michels, 1915).

In the following sections, I will describe some of the most well-known party configurations that have emerged from the literature on party organization. Most of these reflect basic distinctions made by Duverger in his systematic work on party structures and, in that sense, the entire configurational perspective can be viewed as a product of Duverger's intellectual legacy. In order to provide a comprehensible overview, I will focus on three contemporary 'party clusters', identified by André Krouwel (2006): the catch-all party, the cartel party and the business firm party. Then, to prepare the ground for the following chapter, I will add two further configurations that can assist in applying the configurational perspective to Alternativet: the movement party and the digital party.

The catch-all party

One of the most famous and contested configurations to emerge from the post-Duvergerian literature on party organization is the catch-all party, originally developed by the German political scientist Otto Kirchheimer (1966), to explain the emergence of a new breed of political parties that seemed to reject the ideological dogmatism of traditional mass or cadre parties. At its most fundamental level, the thesis holds that catch-all parties resemble mass parties (or 'mass integration' parties), in the sense that enrolling ordinary members in local branches is a key ambition. Catch-all parties might be a degree more centralized than mass parties and focus more on electoral efficiency, but they generally mimic the organizational structure of mass parties. Unlike mass parties, however, catch-all parties are characterized by a much vaguer ideological stance. Watering down the party's political ideals allows it to cater for the 'median voter' (Downs, 1957), thereby positioning itself as capable of catching 'all categories of voters' – or, at least, 'more voters in all those categories whose interests do not adamantly conflict' – and 'to that extent its potential clientele is almost limitless' (Kirchheimer, 1966: 186). Although he never provided any hard and fast definition of the catch-all party (Krouwel, 2003), Kirchheimer did indeed outline several characteristics that are common to this configuration (Kirchheimer, 1966: 190):

a) Drastic reduction of the party's ideological baggage. ... b) Further strengthening of top leadership groups, whose actions and omissions are now judged from the viewpoint of their contribution to the efficiency of the entire social system rather than identification with the goals of their particular organisation. c) Downgrading of the role of the individual party member, a role considered a historical relic which may obscure the newly built-up catch-all party image. d) Deemphasis of the class-gardée, specific social-class or denominational clientele, in favour of recruiting voters among the population at large. e) Securing access to a variety of interest groups for financial and electoral reasons.

A few of these characteristics stand out as particularly interesting. First, because of the weak ideological stance, catch-all parties de-emphasize the *classe gardée* and focus instead on the recruitment of members from all segments of society. This development corresponds to the general waning of class-consciousness and the emergence of 'liquid loyalties' in the electorate throughout the latter part of the 20th century (Ignazi, 2017: 201), and in that sense the catch-all party may be described as a product of its time. Second, catch-all parties downgrade the role of the individual subscription-paying member and focus instead on the relationship with interest groups for financial and electoral reasons. This point resonates with Duverger's notion of 'indirect' parties that rely on a network of support organizations instead of ordinary members, although catch-all parties clearly are membership organizations. In that sense, one could say that the catch-all party represents an unexpected and untold break from the dominance of 'direct' parties in modern society – or, that they at least signal the emergence of a hybrid format where members are enrolled in a widespread fashion but are significantly deprived of influence. This down-prioritization of ordinary members furthermore anticipates the rise of the cartel party (Katz and Mair, 1995).

Notably, the catch-all party thesis also contains assumptions about the relationship between a party and its institutional environment (Wolinetz, 1991). Although the catch-all party may be described as a product of its time, Kirchheimer believed the causal link between organization and environment to run in both directions. The success enjoyed by catch-all parties since the middle of the last century has, according to Kirchheimer, created an isomorphic pressure that implicitly forces other parties to adopt similar structures. The isomorphism of the catch-all configuration has created an immensely competitive environment where several parties today fight for the same votes with indistinguishable ideological content.

In Kirchheimer's view, these organizational developments have caused significant changes to Western European party systems; most importantly to the way in which parties campaign and the democratic link between citizen and government. In terms of the former, contemporary parties are increasingly concerned with what Jennifer Smith (2009) calls 'persuasion campaigning': instead of seeking to mobilize known supporters (for example based on class affiliations or socioeconomic demographics), parties today appeal to the undecided voters at the centre of the political spectrum. This also means that many party systems have become more homogeneous and less fragmented as a consequence of catch-all partism (see Wolinetz, 1991, for a counter-argument). In terms of the latter, contemporary parties are less concerned with mass integration compared with those in previous eras. Whereas an important task for mass parties was to socialize members into a particular culture and educate them politically, catch-all parties focus more on the simple aggregation of voters (see Wolkenstein, 2021). A consequence of this is a weakened focus on decentralization and intra-party participation, which ultimately deteriorates the democratic link between represented and representatives.

The cartel party

The cartel party thesis begins with a paradox. On the one hand, the emergence of catch-all partism in the mid-20th century reflects a tendency for political parties to gradually distance themselves from civil society and focus on perfecting their electioneering strategy by centralizing decision-making power. This development has significantly contributed to the dominant view of political parties today, which sees them as illegitimate and undemocratic representatives of common interests (Ignazi, 2017). On the other hand, parties today are stronger than ever. Financially, at least, political parties have never been more robust. In fact, most European parties receive more than two thirds of their income from state subsidies alone (Falguera et al, 2014). On top of this, a range of countries are currently going through a process of 'constitutionalizing' political parties, thereby acknowledging them legally as 'desirable and procedurally necessary for the effective functioning of democracy' (van Biezen, 2012: 187).

Richard Katz and Peter Mair's (1995) explanation for this paradoxical situation is that we should stop measuring the strength of parties in terms of their link with civil society, since this is no longer a key criterion for success. If we instead focus on the relationship between political parties and the state, the situation suddenly makes sense. During the last 50 years, parties have sought to expand their voter base by watering down their ideological position and they have sought to compensate for falling membership rates by turning to the state for resources (after all, it is the parties themselves that decide what spoils they receive from the state). This has created a situation where parties have begun to form symbiotic ties with the state apparatus, which has meant increased public funding for parties, partisan use of civil servants, and patronage appointments in the state bureaucracy. In short, parties have established a cartel with the state, to weather the consequences of waning public support. As such, the party becomes less of a popular movement and more of a career route for politicians and functionaries (Katz and Mair, 2009). See also Figure 4.2.

Figure 4.2: The development from mass party to cartel party

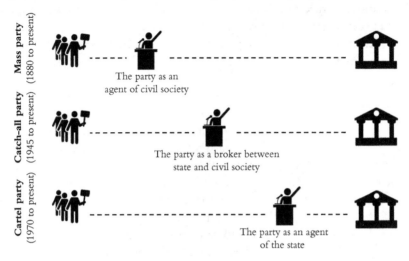

A few features characterize cartel parties. The obvious ones are 'the interpenetration of party and state' and a clandestine 'pattern of inter-party collusion' (Katz and Mair, 1995: 17), with the latter referring to the tendency for larger parties to settle political affairs behind closed doors and perform a type of 'symbolic competition' in public (Katz and Mair, 1996: 530). At an organizational level, the cartel party is more centralized and professionalized than the mass party and the catch-all party. The party leadership constitutes a fully fledged oligarchy that will use all means at its disposal to advance the (short-term) interests of the organization and, in that sense, the emergence of the cartel party appears to constitute a critical proof of concept for Michels' (1915) iron law. Furthermore, campaigns organized by cartel parties are typically capital-intense and developed by professional advisers and media specialists. This leaves little room for membership participation, with registered members usually relegated to the status of passive supporters. Although members may in principle enjoy considerable rights within the organization, these are rarely exercised in practice. Moreover, when given the odd chance to make their voices heard, members tend to participate in the decision-making process as individuals rather than as groups or through delegates. Katz and Mair (1995: 21) refer to this as an 'atomistic' conception of party membership to emphasize how rank and file rarely coordinate their efforts collectively, thus allowing the party leadership to reign supreme.

Curiously, however, cartel parties tend to allow local branches considerable autonomy to engage in regional affairs, just as the local branches tend to abstain from challenging the central leadership in terms of national affairs. Samuel Eldersveld (1964) characterizes this type of horizontal autonomy (understood in Duverger's terms as the freedom to cooperate with units at similar levels in the party bureaucracy) as a 'stratarchy' to underscore the stratified nature of this party configuration. This concept is important for the forthcoming analysis, in which I intend to show how much of Alternativet's initial success was predicated on a stratified decoupling between the 'movement' and the 'party'.

The business firm party

An important feature of both the catch-all and cartel party, as well as similar configurations such as the 'electoral-professional' party (Panebianco, 1988), is the widespread professionalization of the organization. Whereas earlier party configurations (most importantly the mass party) recruited staff and candidates among their members who were trained and educated politically inside the organization, these more recent configurations prefer to recruit external professionals who are evaluated based on technical skills alone. To serve as an adviser in one of these parties, one does not necessarily have to agree with the political priorities that the organization is promoting, nor does one have to fully understand the party's ideological backdrop. What matters is that core messages are communicated effectively via well-selected media outlets and that tangible results are achieved by the smooth operation of the party machine. In practice, however, very few parties completely abandon their ideological stance to maximize votes, just as very few politicians focus exclusively on short-range goals. Nonetheless, with the emergence of yet another breed of parties during the 1990s, processes of de-ideologicalization and professionalization drastically intensified. These are formations that effectively lack a historically situated identity and operate in the absence of discernable ideological commitments, since they are established for the sole purpose of attaining political power for private motives (status, money, privileges and so on); these are formations than have come to be known as 'business firm' parties (Hopkin and Paolucci, 1999).

The business firm party is usually characterized as a lean organization that can operate effectively because its bureaucratic structure is reduced to an absolute minimum and because power is centralized in an autocratic fashion. Tasks that would normally be handled by party bureaucrats such as campaign management and public outreach are outsourced to private enterprises with no formal ties to the organization. Although business firm parties may enrol ordinary members, these are totally disconnected from the party leadership and enjoy very few privileges in terms of participation and deliberation. In fact, they tend to be regarded merely as a 'reservoir of votes and a ready-made electoral machine' instead of an active political movement (Paolucci, 1996, quoted in Mazzoleni and Voerman, 2017: 784). The ideological dispositions of such configurations are, as mentioned, very difficult to identify. In lieu of political ideals, the business firm party tends to pursue tangible goals such as tax breaks or state subsidies without necessarily legitimizing these objectives ideologically. Policy proposals are, furthermore, based on extensive 'market research' and 'wrapped in attractive package' before being 'aggressively put into the market' (Krouwel, 2006: 261).

According to Krouwel (2006: 260), there are two types of business firm parties: 'one is based on an already existing commercial company, whose structures are used for a political project, while the other type is a new and separate organization specifically constructed for a political endeavor'. Such parties are still relatively rare in a European context, but there are noteworthy examples such as Ano, founded by the former prime minister and second-richest person in the Czech Republic (Kopeček, 2016), and to some degree also the Norwegian Progress Party (Jupskås, 2016). However, as Hopkin and Paolucci (1999) observe, Silvio Berlusconi's now-defunct Forza Italia probably constituted the clearest expression of this configuration. In a time of political turmoil, Berlusconi thought it necessary to secure his own monopolistic position in the commercial television industry by establishing an 'organizational weapon' (Selznick, 1952) that would serve his private interest in the public realm (Hopkin and Paolucci, 1999: 320–321):

> In Forza Italia the distinctions between analogy and reality are blurred: the 'political entrepreneur' in question is in fact a businessman, and the organisation of the party is largely conditioned by the prior existence of a business firm. … Hence, originally FI was little more than a personal instrument, created for this specific private purpose: to win the elections in order to prevent a hostile left from jeopardizing Berlusconi's economic empire.

The business firm party accentuates dynamics that have gradually emerged during the past century such as de-ideologicalization and professionalization. However, it also softens dynamics that have been extensively criticized by party scholars such as the widespread cartelization that we examined earlier. Instead of forging close ties with the state apparatus, to absorb public resources, the business firm party turns to interest groups and corporations for financial reasons. Although people concerned about the 'interpenetration of party and state' (Katz and Mair, 1995) might celebrate this move, it clearly does not render the business firm party a democratic organization. Fortunately, other party configurations have emerged during the past few decades that seem to deliver on the promise of democratization.

The movement party

The movement party is, in many ways, the business firm party's conceptual counterpart. The business firm party is fiercely centralized; the movement party is decentralized. While the business firm party focuses almost exclusively on vote maximization, the movement party prioritizes membership participation and deliberation. On the other hand, the two configurations also share certain characteristics. For instance, both may be described as vehicles for 'political entrepreneurs' (Sheingate, 2003) who seek to alter the rules and norms of conventional party politics. However, unlike many of the configurations reviewed here, the movement party has a less developed conceptual pedigree, and it may therefore be known by other names such as the 'grassroots' party (McCulloch, 1983), the 'hybrid' party (Chironi and Fittipaldi, 2017) or the 'alternative' party (Husted, 2021).

According to Herbert Kitschelt (2006: 280), 'movement parties are coalitions of political activists who emanate from social movements and try to apply the organizational and strategic practices of social movements in the arena of party competition'. Understood as such, the Spanish party Podemos is a good example of a movement party, as it was initially established for the express purpose of providing the 15M movement with parliamentary representation (Fominaya, 2020). However, in his oft-cited characterization of the movement party, Kitschelt ventures beyond this basic definition by adding features that seem to sit uneasily with contemporary movement parties such as Podemos. First, he suggests that movement parties 'make little investment in a formal organizational party structure', which means that they have 'no formal definition of membership' and that they lack salaried staff and communicative infrastructure (Kitschelt, 2006: 280). This characteristic arguably says more about Kitschelt and his time than about movement parties today. Podemos, for instance, may allow both members and non-members to participate in political deliberations, but it has a well-articulated organizational structure as well as a professional media strategy that includes various channels for membership participation. In fact, the party has compiled a 60-page document that spells out precisely how it gives life to values such as participation, transparency and democratic control (della Porta et al, 2017).

Second, Kitschelt (2006: 280) maintains that movement parties 'invest little in the process of solving problems of social choice', meaning that they 'lack an institutionalized system for aggregating interests through designated organs and officers with authority to formulate binding decisions and commitments on behalf of the party'. Observing contemporary movement parties such as Podemos or Movimento 5 Stelle, however, this characteristic appears equally outdated. Owing largely to the advent of new digital technologies, movement parties have developed elaborate infrastructures that allow precisely for the aggregation of interests. In fact, one might contend that contemporary movement parties are superior to traditional party bureaucracies in this regard, although the digitalization of party organizations clearly involves many problems as well (Husted, 2019). Finally, Kitschelt (2006: 281) claims that movement parties 'attempt a dual track of combining activities within the arenas of formal democratic competition with extra-institutional mobilization'. Unlike the first two characteristics, this point gets to the heart of movement parties. As Donnatella della Porta and colleagues (2017: 7) put it in their book on 'anti-austerity' movement parties:

> [W]e can speak of movement parties when relations with social movements are particularly close. Social movements are usually defined as networks of groups and individuals, endowed with some collective identification, that pursue goals of social transformation mainly through unconventional forms of participation. ... Political parties are instead ... free associations built with the aim of achieving institutional power. ... Movement parties emerge as a sort of hybrid between the two, when organizational and environmental linkages are very close: to different degrees, they have overlapping membership, co-organize various forms of collective action, fund each other, address similar concerns. As organizations, they participate in protest campaigns, but also act in electoral arenas.

This conceptualization of the movement party as a hybrid between social movement and political party provides us with a more fruitful perspective for understanding this configuration (see Chironi and Fittipaldi, 2017). For instance, della Porta and colleagues (2017: 79) argue that Podemos is characterized by a 'nebulous border between the inside and the outside of the party'. There was until recently no registration fee, and it only requires a few clicks on a web page to become an official member of the party. As the authors note, 'this is similar to the kind of belonging established by the Indignados Movement' (15M) that initially gave birth to Podemos (della Porta et al, 2017: 79). In terms of organizational structure, Podemos is characterized by a mixture of vertical and horizontal lines of command and cooperation. The basic unit of the party is the 'circle', which may be defined as discussion group where participants debate certain issues and conjure solutions in the absence of formal hierarchies. The circles are based on participatory ideals, they have no leaders or spokespersons, and decisions are always made unanimously (Pavía et al, 2016). The party's vertical structures are represented by the Citizen Council, which is the executive body of Podemos (della Porta et al, 2017: 80). This mixture of horizontality and verticality is emblematic of movement parties: they are based on subunits that adopts processes and procedures from social movements, but these always exist alongside executive organs that allow the parties to compete in elections (see Anria, 2019).

The digital party

As we have seen, there are several overlaps between the movement party and the digital party, just as many of the empirical cases used to exemplify both configurations recur. (See Table 4.1 for an overview of the configurations.) For instance, Podemos is usually treated as a critical case of a movement party, but it is also seen as a digital first-mover (Rodríguez-Teruel et al, 2016). Similarly, Movimento 5 Stelle has been credited with disrupting Italian politics, but the literature often explains the party's success with reference to digital technology (for example Bickerton and Accetti, 2018). That said, there are indeed examples of parties that are easier to characterize as digital parties than movement parties, in the sense that the emphasis on the positive aspects of digitalization are more pronounced within these formations (see della Porta, 2021). The perhaps most frequently cited example is the International Pirate Party, which was founded in Sweden in 2006, with the extremely particularized ambition of 'legalizing file sharing and protecting freedom on the internet' (Almqvist, 2016: 98). Since then, the party's objectives have clearly widened, as the notion of pirate politics has spread across the globe. However, the fact that the party was established with an explicit focus on internet freedom speaks volumes about the techno-optimism that pervades the organization (Miegel and Olsson, 2008).

Paolo Gerbaudo is often considered coiner of the term 'digital parties' (although accounts of 'cyber parties' have existed for some time; see Margetts, 2001). In his celebrated book on the topic, Gerbaudo (2019) defines digital parties as political organizations that rely on digital technology for internal processes related to coordination, deliberation and participation. Hence, while most parties today struggle to adapt to a digital reality that affords novel opportunities for outreach and intra-party democratization, a small group of parties such as the International Pirate Party have taken these trends to the extreme. Obviously, this has consequences for the organization of these parties (see Gerbaudo, 2021a). It means that the boundaries of the organizations become much more permeable than they were previously, and that decision-making processes are more inclusive than they used to be. However, it also means that power relations are sometimes opaquer, and that the relative transparency of formal rules and regulations is sacrificed at the altar of structurelessness and spontaneity. In that sense, digital parties cannot readily be considered more democratic than traditional party configurations, although this is a key element in the digital parties' self-narrative. In fact, the opposite seems closer to the truth. As Gerbaudo (2021d: 740) concludes, based on an in-depth analysis of online activities in Podemos and Movimento 5 Stelle:

> [I]n both M5S and Podemos there is a clear discrepancy between the lofty promise and the prosaic reality of digital democracy. It is therefore

doubtful whether these parties are more democratic than traditional political parties. While participatory platforms were presented as a way to disintermediate party politics and directly involve ordinary member in political decisions, their practice has been strongly plebiscitary and top-down. The participation of members has been severely limited in qualitative terms, often amounting to little more than a 'reactive democracy' in which users are called to rubber-stamp decisions already taken at the top and crowdsource policy ideas, but with no binding mandate.

Although this observation contrasts starkly with the techno-optimist hype surrounding many discussions of digital technology and democracy, it confirms the findings of researchers working in similar settings. For instance, Michael Margolis and David Resnick (2000) claim that the disruptive potential of online media is 'normalized' by the practical reality of party organizations and other political actors. That conclusion was later corroborated by Karina Pedersen and Jo Saglie (2005) who found little evidence of ordinary party members being impacted by the increased use of information and communication technology in two Scandinavian countries, although digitalization did make work processes smoother for top- and mid-level party elites. More recently, Ursula Plesner and I followed the open-source process of policy making in Alternativet and found that its digital platform afforded a disengaging and 'affirmative' type of participation for party members (Husted and Plesner, 2017). The overall picture painted by such accounts is that online democracy is a very difficult thing to achieve, particularly in political parties where the centralization of power constitutes a seemingly inescapable iron law (Michels, 1915).

According to Marco Deseriis (2020), it makes sense to distinguish between two 'variants' of the digital party: the *platform* party and the *networked* party. The latter corresponds quite accurately to our definition of the movement party, in the sense that it is a decentralized configuration focused on active participation and deliberation, while the former represents a less democratic and more leader-oriented model. In many ways, the platform party mirrors the FAANG corporations (Facebook, Amazon, Apple, Netflix and Google) by harvesting massive amounts of data about followers, operating with a free membership model and relying heavily on the free labour of its members (see Gerbaudo, 2019: 70). This configuration is problematic in democratic terms because the platformization of organizations generally tends to 'create significantly more value for platform owners than for platform users' (Deseriis, 2020: 899). However, the networked party represents a more positive example of how digital technology can be employed in the service of democratic ends. As Deseriis (2020: 913) notes: 'By combining social movement practices with deliberative and collaborative software, networked

Table 4.1: Overview of seven party configurations

Configuration	Characteristics	Examples	Key contributions
Cadre party	• Parliamentarian origin • Indirect structure • Based on caucus • Weak articulation • Centralized and vertical • No/few members	Former conservative parties and US parties (e.g. Republican Party, US)	• Ostrogorski, 1902 • Duverger, 1954 • Neumann, 1956
Mass party	• (Extra)parliamentarian origin • Direct structure • Based on branches • Strong articulation • Decentralized and horizontal • Many members	Former socialist parties and Christian parties (e.g. Social Democratic Party, Germany)	• Michels, 1915 • Duverger, 1954 • Neumann, 1956
Catch-all party	• (Extra)parliamentarian origin • Direct structure • Based on branches • Strong articulation • Centralized and horizontal • Many members	Large centrist parties in multi-party systems (e.g. Labour Party, UK)	• Kirchheimer, 1966 • Wolinetz, 1991 • Krouwel, 2003
Cartel party	• (Extra)parliamentarian origin • Direct structure • Based on branches • Strong articulation • Centralized and horizontal • Several members	Large centrist parties in countries with strong state support (e.g. Social Democrats, Denmark)	• Katz and Mair, 1995 • Detterbeck, 2005 • Katz and Mair, 2009
Business firm party	• Extra-parliamentarian origin • Indirect structure • Based on caucus • Weak articulation • Centralized and vertical • Few/no members	Libertarian and/or authoritarian parties (e.g. Ano, Czechia)	• Hopkin and Paolucci, 1999 • Kopeček, 2016 • Mazzoleni and Voerman, 2017
Movement party	• Extra-parliamentarian origin • Direct structure • Based on branches • Weak articulation • Decentralized and horizontal • Several members	Alternative parties on both sides of the political spectrum (e.g. Podemos, Spain)	• Kitschelt, 2006 • Della Porta et al, 2017 • Anria, 2019
Digital party	• Extra-parliamentarian origin • Direct structure • Based on branches • Weak articulation • (De)centralized and horizontal • Several members	Alternative parties on both sides of the political spectrum (International Pirate Party)	• Margetts, 2001 • Gerbaudo, 2019 • Deseriis, 2020

parties advance a model of [the] digital party that leverages the decentralized affordances of the Internet to make the party line (and the relative division of labor) emerge from the network itself.' That said, both variants of the digital party face similar difficulties, most importantly related to what Deseriis calls 'scalable deliberation': how can local discussions on political issues be channelled into decision-making processes that go beyond simple plebiscites? Until such questions have been resolved in practical terms, the digital party will most likely continue the current trajectory of 'seriously under-delivering on its lofty promise' of online democracy (Gerbaudo, 2019: 127).

Configurational contributions to organization studies

Configurations, typologies, ideal types, systems and syntheses: these are by no means concepts that are new to organization studies. In fact, the literature sometimes seems replete with hypothetical models and metaphysical matrixes that somehow report to represent reality more or less faithfully. To get the picture, one only needs to think of Henry Mintzberg's (1979) hugely influential work on structural configurations. In fact, there are several evident overlaps between Duverger's and Mintzberg's approaches to organizational analysis. For instance, they both focus on the basic elements of an organization and highlight the importance of understanding whether its structural configuration relies on vertical/centralized or horizontal/ decentralized modes of collaboration and decision-making. Moreover, they both consider the causal relationship between organization and environment to be a two-way process, in which the former may push back upon the latter, but emphasize the relative importance of situational variables.

It is worth noting, however, that Duverger authored his most important work at least a decade before the rise of 'structuralism' within organization studies (*Political Parties* was originally published in French in 1951). Notable contributions to this body of research include Tom Burns and George Stalker's (1961) work on the relationship between dynamic/stable environments and organic/mechanistic structures, Alfred Chandler's (1962) account of the relationship between corporate strategy and organizational structure, Joan Woodward's (1965) study of the relationship between production technology and administrative structure, Paul Lawrence and Jay Lorsch's (1967) inquiry into the relationship between subunit integration and the level of structural formality and Peter Blau and Richard Shoenherr's (1971) writings on the structural consequences of membership growth. What characterizes these works is precisely their interest in organizational structures and the relationship between structural configurations and various situational variables such as technology, size, strategy and environmental (in)stability. Just as Ostrogorski may be viewed as an unrecognized pioneer within the field of organizational sociology, Duverger may thus be seen as an early contributor to what is sometimes called the 'contingency theory of organization' (Donaldson, 2001).

What sets Duverger's theory of party organization apart from other early attempts to grapple with the determinants of structural configurations is the level of nuance he brings to the discussion at a point in time where rather simple distinctions were commonly used to determine the 'fit' between organization and situation. Although Duverger likewise employs simple distinctions, his account of party configurations is characterized by relative nuance. One source of this nuance is his large number of distinctions, summarized in Figure 4.1, which consider a multitude of situational variables such as origin, funding, power distribution, mode of collaboration, membership participation and formality levels. However, an arguably more crucial source of nuance is to be found in Duverger's ability to escape those deterministic traps that often serve to simplify studies of organizational structures. Woodward (1965) is frequently accused of technological determinism, but other hallmark contributions to the structuralist literature is characterized by the same type of mono-causal thinking. For instance, Chandler's (1962) work has achieved widespread fame and drawn equal criticism because of the slogan 'structure follows strategy', just as Burns and Stalker's (1961) claim that dynamic environments force organizations to adopt organic rather than mechanistic structures has been said to rely on a type of determinism that neglects the 'scope of choice' that actors have in terms of deciding the appropriate design of an organization (Schreyögg, 1980). Duverger escapes such determinism by repeatedly showing how certain parties can defy expectations and adopt configurations that appear unfit for their present situation.

More recent work on party configurations follows the same pattern. Instead of outlining precisely what ostensive criteria that decides whether a party should be classified as a catch-all party, a cartel party or perhaps a business firm party, most contributors to the configurational perspective prefer an approach to organizational analysis where certain tendencies are sketched and illustrated, but where the inclination to conclusively group and categorize actual parties according to some essentialist standard is kept at bay. Ironically, the literature on party configurations has been heavily criticized for its refusal to provide clear guidance on how to box up the empirical world into predefined categories. For instance, Krouwel (2006: 250) laments the fact that 'most of the proposed models of party do not include clear empirical indicators that would allow us to determine which parties actually fall into each of the categories or when they have transformed into a different type'. In my view, the beauty of the configurational perspective is that it only provides ideal types, and that it therefore recognizes that no party falls squarely into one category. Like all organizations, parties have idiosyncrasies that make them stand out, and a scope of choice that allows them to resist environmental pressures. This awareness is precisely what makes the configurational perspective a valuable source of inspiration for organization scholars.

For formal organization

Another way of thinking about the contribution of configurational party research is to view it as an antidote to what Paul du Gay and Signe Vikkelsø (2016) call a 'metaphysical' or 'anti-empirical' stance. According to these authors, contemporary research within organization studies is dominated by a staunch preoccupation with *processes* rather than substances, with *change* rather than stability and with *informality* rather than formality. Moreover, it is less concerned with the empirical reality of formal organizations and more interested in developing 'an elaborate theoretical simulacra' that effectively dissolves the idea that organizations exist as ontological substances (du Gay and Vikkelsø, 2016: 17). Instead of viewing organizations as purposefully established enterprises where individuals collaborate and work towards a common goal, the 'metaphysicists' of organization studies tend to view organizations as 'myths' (Weick, 1969) or 'fictions' (Jensen and Meckling, 1976) that conceal the fact that only spontaneous interactions and ephemeral processes supposedly exist.

According to du Gay and Vikkelsø (2016), there are several problems associated with the anti-empirical stance in organization studies. One is that it draws organization scholars away from issues that are relevant to practitioners and therefore prevents them from advising inhabitants of real-life organizations. Another is that it serves to deconstruct organization studies as a distinct scientific discipline that focuses on a common study object: the *formal organization* (see also Lopdrup-Hjorth, 2015). If organization scholars no longer agree on the empirical existence of organizations, and if they thus abandon the study of formal organizations in favour of more general speculations about social organizing, then it seems fair to worry that the discipline will eventually dissolve and (re)merge with those well-established disciplines that it once grew out of, such as sociology and political science.

To revive the notion of formal organization as a common denominator for organization scholars, and to rescue organization studies from irrelevance, du Gay and Vikkelsø propose, among other things, to reconsider the importance of authority and authorization. Drawing on classical scholars such as Mary Parker Follett and Chester Barnard, they advance the claim that authority is integral to any 'system of effective coordination' because it helps establish (the limits to) the sanctioned rights that members enjoy when acting on behalf of the organization (du Gay and Vikkelsø, 2016: 150). Yet, in much contemporary research, questions of organized authority have been pushed to the margins and are frequently considered out of tune with the flexible nature of present-day enterprises. Instead of authority, many organization scholars today prefer to explore softer themes such as creativity, culture and communication. Without clear lines of authority, however, power dynamics easily become opaque and unjustified (for example Freeman, 1972), which is why the reluctance to adequately consider questions of authority within contemporary organization studies is highly problematic.

Notably, however, du Gay and Vikkelsø do not specify precisely how organization scholars should rehabilitate the notion of authority. For instance, how do we identify (the limits to) authority within organizations? And how do we represent the empirical reality of organizations in a way that accounts for authority without alienating practitioners by means of elaborate theoretical simulacra? One suggestion, occasionally alluded to by Vikkelsø (2016: 5), is to recover the discipline's long-lost interest in organizational charts because they inform us 'in a tangible and yet detailed manner' how an organization is geared towards coordination and how it relies on particular lines of command.

My contention is that the work of Duverger and other contributors to the configurational perspective could serve as a welcome source of inspiration for the revival of formal organization as a core study object for organization scholars. Not only would it supply a much-needed boost of empirical insight and nuance, it would likewise help organization scholars escape the type of determinism that sometimes sticks to studies of organizational configurations – where the structure of an organization is said to be determined almost exclusively by its size, technology, strategy or environment. Taking inspiration from this body of literature, organization scholars would be able to pose questions such as: what are the basic elements of this organization, and how do these elements influence horizontal/vertical modes of collaboration; and: how articulated is the structure of the organization, and what consequences does this have for the level of decentralization achieved in practice? Such questions could then be accompanied by organizational charts that specify lines of command, as most contemporary diagrams tend to do (Vikkelsø, 2016), and indicate collaborative dynamics within the organization and the overall level of formality. In the following chapter, I will attempt to construct an organizational chart of Alternativet that follows this way of thinking about party configurations.

5

Alternativet in
Configurational Perspective

Introduction

The previous chapter discussed and unfolded the 'configurational perspective' on party organization, based primarily on the work of Maurice Duverger. This perspective focuses predominantly on the organizational structure of political parties, understood as the lines of command and cooperation that constitute the anatomical backbone of these associations. This focus entails a commitment to empirically informed considerations about organizational origins, basic elements, structural set-ups, levels of (in)formality, degrees of horizontalism, types of decentralization, membership modalities and leadership dynamics. Combined, these themes allow the observer to make qualified assessments about the resemblance between ideal-typical party models and actually existing party organizations. Methodologically, the configurational perspective relies on similar approaches that characterizes the classical perspective: ethnographic observations, personal communication and document analysis. The configurational perspective differs from the classical perspective, however, by adding another level of systematism and quantification. It supports this addition primarily with statistical data on membership fluctuations and voter demographics, but also with visual aids such as organizational charts. Based on such data, this perspective gives observers a view into the administrative machinery of party organizations and allows them to describe important developments at the core of political parties in systematic ways. In that sense, the configurational perspective creates the theoretical foundation for the next chapter and the 'comparative perspective'.

The purpose of this chapter is to apply the configurational perspective to the case of Alternativet. In doing so, I will focus on a number of distinct themes that all originate in the work of Duverger – most notably, in the first part of his book *Political Parties* from 1954. I begin by exploring the organizational origins of the party, focusing in particular on the role of the presumed founding father, Uffe Elbæk. Here, my ambition is to show that creation myths within political parties – as in most other organizations – often paint an overly romantic and one-sided picture of the events leading up to the formation of the project, and that it requires the observer to venture beyond the official story to produce a more nuanced origin description. Next, I focus on the structural anatomy of Alternativet, which pushes me to investigate how unity is achieved within the party and how different parts of the organization interact. I then move on to consider the different membership modalities that currently exist within Alternativet and how different kinds of leadership are exercised within the organization. Finally, I summarize these findings and discuss them in relation to some of the party models outlined in the previous chapter, most notably the mass party and the movement party.

The origin(s) of Alternativet

Alternativet's creation myth appears at the official party website under the subheading 'Our history', in the section on 'Organization'. The main gist of the story is that the party was created as a legal entity in 2013, a few months prior to the press conference that informed the public about its existence, but that the idea behind Alternativet had been brewing in the mind of Uffe Elbæk for years. It all supposedly started when Elbæk was running for office in Denmark in 2011 as a candidate for the Social Liberal Party. Here, Elbæk launched several initiatives that encouraged public participation in policy making and celebrated people who had the courage to defy conventional norms and expectations. As a testament to this narrative, the Alternativet website includes a link to an unpublished paper that Elbæk wrote in the aftermath of the elections, in which he secured the position as minister of culture. The text is called 'Election campaign on the edge'. It is a spin-off on the title of one of Elbæk's bestselling books, *Management on the Edge* (in Danish, the notion of being 'on the edge' means to push the boundaries of something), and covers almost 80 pages of personal reflections on politics and life in general. In this text, a distinct moment of creation is outlined: a moment in 2010 when a well-known politician from the Social Liberal Party called Marianne Jelved asked Uffe Elbæk about his plans for the future, while secretly implying that they should include him running for office. As Elbæk (2012: 10) notes:

> Most projects are born as a product of a particular 'prehistory', an event or triggering factor. In this case, it was Marianne Jelved who posed the exact right question at the exact right time. ... Her question made me stay in Copenhagen and committed me to the task of mobilizing public

support for a change of government. But the idea behind the elections campaign ... was, in the first instance, developed by Rasmus and me.

The Rasmus mentioned in the quote is Elbæk's 'crown prince', Rasmus Nordqvist, who would end up as Chair of Alternativet's board and later MP, until he left the party alongside Elbæk in the wake of the 2020 election and the disastrous leadership contest (see Chapter 2). What is particularly interesting about this account is the way in which responsibility for a project that Elbæk, on multiple occasions, recognizes as a team effort is attributed almost exclusively to himself. This, coupled with the fact that Alternativet views itself as a direct extension of Elbæk's election campaign for the Social Liberal Party, is probably the reason why he figures so prominently in the party's creation myth. This somewhat myopic founding-father narrative is solidified by the considerable weight given to yet another document authored by Elbæk in mid-2013, in which he outlines the fundamental idea behind Alternativet. On the party's website, this is entitled 'Basic concept' and is described as 'the very first considerations' about Alternativet. Once again, full credit is awarded to Elbæk, who was 'repeatedly motivated by volunteers' to write down his own thoughts on 'a new entrepreneurial party'. The description of the document goes on to say that 'when reading the basic concept today, it is remarkable how many of the original thoughts still constitute the spinal cord of the party in terms of concept and values' (Alternativet, 2023a). As such, the official story of Alternativet is deeply intertwined with the founding father's personal story and his 'edgy' approach to politics. The many volunteers surrounding Elbæk naturally also figure in the creational myth, but they play a subordinate role, and very few of them are identified by name.

The myth of the founding father begins to crack, however, once other voices are considered. For instance, if one talks to people involved with some of the projects that Elbæk formally headed prior to the launch of Alternativet, such as 'Under the Radar' or 'Club Courage' (see Chapter 3), one quickly realizes that several volunteers played a much more central part in the formation of Alternativet than typically suggested by mainstream media as well as the party itself. One very central player is Nilas Bay-Foged, a social entrepreneur who currently occupies a position as board member in Alternativet, but who has previously inhabited most conceivable positions within the organization (head of the secretariat, PA to the leader, member of the political forum, parliamentary candidate and so on). In the formative months before the launch in late 2013, Bay-Foged worked closely with Elbæk and Nordqvist as well as eight to ten extremely dedicated volunteers, several of whom worked upwards of 80 hours a week. Recalling those hectic days, Bay-Foged describes himself as a 'steward' who oversaw everything and ensured progression, while focusing primarily on the 'content part' of the project.

Interestingly, according to Bay-Foged, the 'Basic concept' document is not the product of Elbæk's imagination alone. It is the product of the merged visions of Elbæk and Bay-Foged. He explains in an interview that I conducted with him in 2021:

'The funny thing is that, before Uffe wrote his conceptual paper, I had already written one. … I had written things like: *if* we are to make a party, what might it look like? As a political scientist, I'm very excited about all things political. Imagine being an entrepreneur at Christiansborg. Anyhow, I sent this paper to Uffe, and he's just having a laugh because the thoughts in my paper are almost identical to those in his. His was a bit longer than mine, but they were very similar. Then we made seven new versions of the paper. So, the official one is actually draft number seven.'

The document that Bay-Foged authored is dated 7 June 2012. In other words, a full year before the completion of the official version, which is today at the heart of the creation myth (and the creative process leading up to Bay-Foged's document arguably goes even further back). This helps us appreciate how long the thought of launching an alternative political party had been brewing in the minds of those surrounding Elbæk, but it also brings nuance to the idea that Alternativet is Elbæk's personal invention. In Bay-Foged's first draft, he outlines the dream of a 'cross-national' party and social movement, centred on the notions of diversity and difference. The organization's values should be sustainability, pluralism, innovation, creativity, freedom, solidarity, nearness and tactility. Politically, it should be focused on a number of core issues, such as the interdependence of humans and nature as well as the importance of culture, art and democratic processes. While the official version of the basic concept ended up being much longer and more elaborate than the version composed by Bay-Foged, many of the themes are identical. In that sense, one could argue that, during this crucial time before the launch of Alternativet, Bay-Foged constituted what Gerbaudo (2019) calls a 'hidden demiurge' who plays a key role in the development of the party without ever being formally recognized. Such figures are, as we shall see, important to many different party configurations, but perhaps especially to digital parties.

The story of Alternativet's origins is even muddier. On the party's website, the first six months of its existence are described as an edifying process of creative deliberation, where more than 700 people from all walks of life took part in developing Alternativet's official political programme as well as its organizational characteristics. This description is further solidified in the opening lines of the political programme (Alternativet, 2014a: 2), where it is stated that:

> The political document you are about to read is the result of a very special political and democratic experiment, fueled by the conviction that more people know more. Last November [2013], when we first launched Alternativet, we posed a challenge to each other: to formulate a political program through what might be called an open-source process, meaning that we invited anyone with time and interest to co-author Alternativet's political program. ... More than 700 people accepted the invitation and have thus contributed tangible proposals, critical questions, and curious thinking.

Such passages have served to bolster Alternativet's democratic legitimacy immensely because they describe something akin to direct democracy. Nowhere else in today's highly professionalized political landscape do ordinary people have the opportunity to directly influence, let alone 'co-author', an official political programme. This makes the process seem truly alternative, which is one reason why Alternativet cherishes its creation myth so dearly. However, as detailed in Chapter 3, the process was perhaps less directly democratic (and more deliberatively democratic) than often assumed, since the outcomes of the political laboratories were edited and even rewritten by a small but industrious steering committee tasked with reconciling the many different – and often contradictory – proposals that came out of those first workshops in early 2014. As the architect behind the whole bottom-up process of policy making explained in an interview, it "was centrally controlled and it was a small number of people calling the shots ... which meant that we could produce a lot. ... We were able to produce a 60-page document in half a year."

Such 'competing narratives' about the past (Lubinski, 2018) allow us to see that the official origin story is only one account of several. It also helps us realize that official materials often paint an overly idyllic and sometimes simplified picture of what happened in the early period of a party's life. The truth is typically more complex and less linear. This realization is at the heart of the configurational perspective, and at the centre of Duverger's writings in particular, but it has gradually given way to less critical examinations of official material, as we shall see in the following chapter. For now, however, we turn to the analysis of Alternativet's organizational structure and its practical manifestations.

The anatomy of Alternativet

The political pillar

As an organization, Alternativet can be divided into two relatively distinct pillars: political and administrative. The function of the political pillar is to ensure that visions and ideas are developed in a democratic fashion and that they are somehow translated into tangible policy proposals that can be presented in parliament. As we saw in Chapter 3, the basic organizational element in this pillar is the *political laboratory*, which can be defined as a thematic workshop open to the public. At these workshops, members and non-members discuss various political issues, such as tax or education, with the ambition of reaching (some level of) consensus on several proposals. For instance, the participants in one of these laboratories may agree that we need to rethink the Danish tax system along progressive lines, which might entail awarding tax breaks to artists and low-income earners. To formalize this proposal, the participants will have to describe it in a designated template and submit it to the online platform called *Dialogue* where other party members can comment (but not edit). After three weeks, the proposal moves on to the *political forum*, which should be understood as the highest authority in terms of political decision-making. The forum consists of the party leader, two members of the board, two members of each regional section, two members of Alternativet's youth party and a maximum of 15 MPs (41 people in total). This group convenes at least five times a year and is formally tasked with deciding whether a laboratory proposal should be accepted as official policy, discarded or perhaps rewritten in some way. Once a proposal has been accepted as official policy, the *political leadership* (the party leader and the MPs) is informed and instructed to comply. This is, in principle, how the political pillar of Alternativet works.

Given the fact that the party, for some time, only had one MP in the national parliament, the political leadership recently decided to appoint other members – mostly city councillors – to act as spokespersons for certain policy areas. For instance, one member of the Copenhagen city council has acted as finance and economy spokesperson, while a member of the city council in Skanderborg (a provincial town in Jutland) has acted as child and family spokesperson. Having extra-parliamentarian members as spokespersons clearly serves to democratize the decision-making processes, but it also creates certain obstacles. For instance, while these members are allowed to participate in inter-party negotiations, they are not allowed to vote on issues in parliament, nor do they have access to confidential material from the state apparatus. Moreover, it is not clear exactly how spokespersons are selected and by whom, but spokespersons are *appointed* rather than *elected*, which is a procedure that follows the modus operandi of more traditional party organizations.

In addition to the formalized elements, the party's political pillar likewise consists of two informal kinds of organs, both of which contribute to the development of policy proposals, albeit in a more subtle and indirect manner. The first is what the party itself calls 'democratic talk', a concept which the party describes as: 'an independent activity focused on conversations and dialogue, and not on creating a specific product. ... The format is completely free: it can be a dinner, a conversation salon, or a walk' (Alternativet, 2018b: 5). As such, there are certain overlaps with the political laboratories, in the sense that these too can take the shape of dinners or salons. However, while laboratories are expected to produce an outcome (a policy proposal), democratic talks are not. The other informal organ that belongs to the political pillar is what the party calls 'background groups'. These are groups of members who volunteer to specialize in a certain topic. If, for example, an MP would like to develop a new policy on higher education, she might feel the need to establish a background group that can help her qualify the outcome of a political laboratory. Hence, these groups constitute an additional way of influencing policy making.

The administrative pillar

The administrative pillar is structured in a similar way to the political pillar, with proposals moving up the hierarchy and decisions moving down, but with a considerable degree of autonomy for both 'higher' and 'lower' parts of the organization. The basic element in the administrative pillar is the *local branch*. As a membership organization with a certain size, Alternativet divides its members into branches across the country. There are currently more than 90 local branches in total, but, with fewer than 3,000 registered members, some branches are almost completely inactive. A recent report commissioned by the party leadership found that many small branches had become inactive since the 2019 elections as a consequence of too little membership engagement and too many 'boring organizational tasks' (Alternativet, 2020: 11). The most active is arguably the Copenhagen branch, which is where five of the party's 12 local and nation representatives are registered, including the current leader. In general, branches with members represented in city councils are the most active, which testifies to the importance of parliamentary representation in terms of membership engagement. All branches operate under one of the party's ten *regional sections*. The primary task for regional sections is to field candidates for national elections (candidates for local and regional elections are selected by members of the branches).

The party's *secretariat*, consisting of somewhere between 10 and 15 employees, also belongs to the administrative pillar. Most are assistants and secretaries. Some are political advisers, and others oversee the party's campaign and communication strategies. It is, however, fair to say that the secretariat is conditioned by limited resources. With the 2019 elections and the resignation of four MPs, the party's funding plummeted, leaving the secretariat in a difficult situation where external funding was needed to keep things afloat. The organizational function of the secretariat is to support the political and administrative leadership, as well as to help the regional sections organize key events, although this latter function is clearly secondary. Prior to the 2019 election, the party had two secretariats: one based in parliament – serving the MPs – and one based in a community house in downtown Copenhagen – serving the rest of the organization. The limited resources that followed the disastrous election result, however, forced the party to pool resources and merge the two secretariats. Today, the joint secretariat is located at Christiansborg.

The executive organs in the administrative pillar are the *board* and the *administrative leadership* (abbreviated as DOL for daily organizational leadership). The division of labour between these two entities is that the board makes strategic, long-term decisions on behalf of the organization, while the administrative leadership deals with day-to-day matters. The board consists of a chair, one member of each regional section, one member of Alternativet's youth party and six ordinary members (18 people in total). Each member of the board has one vote, and nine people must be present for the board to be capable of making binding decisions. The DOL consists of the chair, vice chair and three additional board members. Its primary function is to maintain close ties with the secretariat and the political leadership between board meetings.

The administrative pillar, complex as it is, likewise consists of two councils: a *dialogue council* and a *by-laws council*. The former is meant to intervene in internal conflicts and help opposing parties reach an agreement through edifying dialogue. However, most people in Alternativet (including members of the council) agree that the dialogue council does not work as intended. In fact, very few conflicts are resolved through council intervention. Interestingly, a report stipulated that one reason why the dialogue council is not really 'flying' is that members of Alternativet are 'way too conflict-averse', leading the authors of the report to suggest that the council plays a more proactive role in the future (Alternativet, 2020: 12). The other council seems to work better. The organizational function of the by-laws council is to assist other organs in interpreting and applying the party's official statues.

At this point, there is only one organ left that needs introduction, and that is the *national congress*. Held once every year, the congress represents the highest authority in Alternativet. This is where accounts and budgets are approved, where current issues are debated, and where candidates for administrative positions are formally selected. The congress is open to all members, although the meetings often have a maximum capacity of around 500 people, and are typically placed somewhere geographically neutral (so, not in Copenhagen). Extraordinary congress meetings may be called occasionally if, for instance, a new leader needs to be elected, which always causes a lot of hassle for the organization and its members. Each winter, a 'half-year' meeting is also arranged (the national congress is usually held in the summer half-year). No official decisions are made at these events, but they are often used to debate important issues in plenum and to launch visions for the future.

Organizational structure

Figure 5.1 is an attempt at visualizing the structural anatomy of Alternativet. Looking at the 'organigram', one might get the idea that Alternativet is characterized by strong articulation; that is, a highly formalized mode of operation. This may have something to do with the structural anatomy of Alternativet being heavily inspired by Elbæk's former party, the Social Liberal Party, which is one of the oldest and most articulated parties in the Danish parliament (other articulated parties also served as sources of inspiration). If one peeks below the surface, however, it quickly becomes apparent that not all formalities translate equally well into practice. For instance, as we saw in Chapter 3, the official process of policy making is often cut short by leading actors who rewrite incoming proposals or even advance their own proposals at the expense of the bottom-up ethos that otherwise permeates the organization. Furthermore, some of the units included in the organigram play a much less prominent role than we might assume from reading official party statutes or browsing the website. Examples of such units include the dialogue council, which has been more or less inactive since its inception, and the digital Dialogue platform, which is often bypassed or unintentionally neglected by leaders in particular. In that sense, one might conclude that Alternativet is actually characterized by weak articulation.

There may be several reasons why a party that describes itself as well articulated practises a much less formalized mode of operation. One reason, typically highlighted by people within Alternativet, is that the organization has been constructed on an ad hoc basis and that units or procedures have been added whenever needed ('we build the plane while flying' is a phrase commonly used by members). For instance, as we saw in Chapter 3, the political forum was created as a way of ensuring a certain level of output control in the policy-making process. The forum was not mentioned in the first statutes nor in other official documents; it was simply created in early 2015 to meet a specific need. Another reason, also emphasized by party members, is that the regulations are too complicated and opaque. For example, few people seem to know exactly how to engage the dialogue council, just like many get lost when trying to understand the official process of policy making. The final reason why Alternativet thrives on informality is, simply, that it suits those in power. It is a well-known fact that the lack of formality often benefits the strong since these people can navigate the shadow structures of the organization much more efficiently than people with fewer resources. This was the main conclusion reached by Jo Freeman (1972) in her article on the 'tyranny of structurelessness'. Freeman famously

Figure 5.1: A visualization of Alternativet's organization (in 2022)

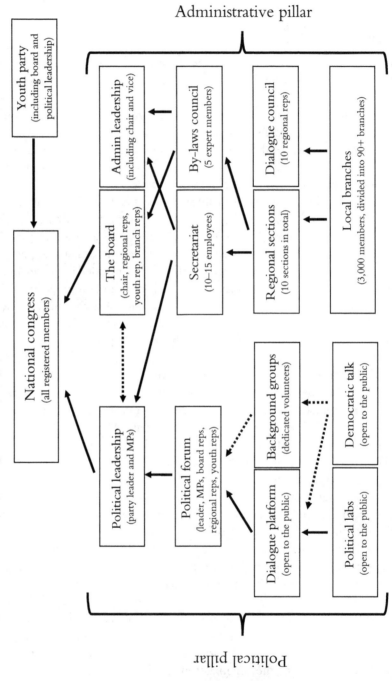

used the phrase to describe power relations within the women's liberation movement, but it could equally be used to describe life within Alternativet.

Branches and caucuses

As mentioned, branches constitute the basic elements in Alternativet's organization. There are currently more than 90 branches in the party, meaning that each regional section oversees approximately nine to ten branches, although a good deal of these have become inactive since the 2019 election and the resignation of four MPs. The more active branches, such as Copenhagen and Aarhus, as well as certain rural branches with high levels of citizen engagement, such as Samsø and Bornholm, organize regular meetings and coordinate events on their own initiative. For instance, during election campaigns, the active branches will typically organize happenings and help candidates prepare for debates, interviews and conversations with voters. Outside election season, the active branches will host events – debates, lectures, exhibitions and so on – and coordinate local activities meant to attract new members.

All branches are, in principle, treated equally. However, certain branches naturally wield more power than others. Few members object to the Copenhagen branch, being the largest and geographically closest to Christiansborg, having a more prominent voice within the organization, but, sometimes, the uneven distribution of influence across branches becomes too pronounced. This was the case during the 2017 local elections. Here, the party's leading candidate for mayor of Copenhagen was accused of violating the democratic ethos of Alternativet by forging extremely close ties with the political leadership in general and the founder, Uffe Elbæk, in particular. At certain points during the election campaign, it almost seemed that the political leadership used the Copenhagen branch as an outlet for its own ideas and visions, thereby breaking with the arm's-length principle that is meant to ensure local autonomy for branches.

Such instances have led members to speculate that certain caucuses exist within the otherwise branch-based organization; that is, a 'small nucleus of militants' who are capable of exercising disproportional influence based on their social standing within the organization (Duverger, 1954: 114). In many ways, the people running the Copenhagen branch during the 2017 local elections constituted such a nucleus, thereby creating a 'spontaneous oligarchy' among ordinary members (Duverger, 1954: 114).

Another type of internal caucus emerged in the immediate aftermath of the party's 2015 parliamentary entry, centred on the political secretariat at Christiansborg. To professionalize the organization and prepare it for attacks by political opponents and other outspoken critics, the head of the secretariat took measures to recruit a handful of talented media advisers and political assistants, well-trained in handling both internal and external opposition. Four of these professionals (all young males) drew a circle around Uffe Elbæk to protect him from critique and bad press. This small nucleus, which quickly acquired the nickname Uffe's Boy Band, wielded an unprecedented level of influence on the party's overall strategy and provoked regular accusations of top-down management. Some members even voiced fears about being regimented by the boy band if they somehow betrayed the official party line, something that seemed completely at odds with the open and inclusive spirit that initially characterized the organization. In that sense, the case of Alternativet testifies to the fact that internal caucuses do emerge in highly egalitarian, branch-based enterprises, and that they may consist of political representatives as well as professional bureaucrats.

Collaboration and power

Alternativet has always perceived itself as a collaborative project. In fact, in the party's official manifesto, collaboration is described as the very essence of the organization: 'Alternativet *is* collaboration,' it says (Alternativet, 2013c, emphasis added). As such, most members of the party are typically keen on collaborating with fellow partisans and people outside the organization. This becomes particularly clear during political laboratories where members and non-members discuss various policy issues. Here, the slogan is 'more people know more', which is an ethos faithfully enacted at the laboratories through exercises and procedures that serve to stimulate synergy and creative thinking.

For that reason, it may seem paradoxical that the level of horizontal collaboration between different units within the organization is rather low. Because of the pillar-based anatomy of Alternativet, collaborative ties are usually forged along vertical lines, meaning that the internal coordination of activities usually takes place between subordinate and superior units. Representatives from local branches coordinate activities with representatives from regional sections, and representatives from regional sections coordinate activities with the administrative leadership (for example through their membership of the board) or the political leadership (perhaps through their membership of political forum). In that sense, there is very little formal collaboration between units that exist at the same level in the organizational hierarchy. This is one reason why so many branches became inactive in the wake of the 2019 elections: they simply did not have the human resources to sustain their efforts in difficult times. As stated in the aforementioned report (Alternativet, 2020), many branches even felt abandoned by the core of the organization. To remedy this, Alternativet has recently started to experiment with frequent Zoom meetings between representatives from different branches and sections. These are meant to foster horizontal collaboration and make the branches more dependent on each other, thereby relieving the administrative and political leadership of some of the toil that comes with being an organization that mainly collaborates vertically.

From the perspective of the branches, however, there are certain upsides to being 'abandoned' by the core of the organization. One is that considerable autonomy is given to the party's basic elements. Alternativet's local branches are largely free to act as they please, as long as their actions can somehow be justified with reference to the official values and the manifesto. This set-up is very much akin to what Samuel Eldersveld (1964: 10) terms 'stratarchy', understood as a 'hierarchical pattern of stratified devolution of responsibility for the settlement of conflict'. According to Ramashray Roy (1967), there are multiple reasons why a stratarchy might emerge within a political party. One is that the notion of local autonomy somehow complies with the overall ideological position of the party; another is that differences of opinion may be recognized through a stratified devolution of responsibilities. Both factors have arguably contributed to the gradual emergence of a stratarchy within Alternativet. The most significant reason, however, is arguably the 'sparsity of activists' and the 'limited rewards available to activists' who engage in a small party (Roy, 1967: 897). The sheer lack of people who are willing and capable of overseeing the branches and the sections has simply caused a situation where local autonomy is not just tolerated but encouraged.

This leads us straight to the question of power. As mentioned in Chapter 3, the notions of vertical and horizontal links should not be confused with the concepts of centralization and decentralization since not all centralized organizations collaborate along vertical lines and not all decentralized organizations collaborate along horizontal lines. In fact, the latter quite accurately corresponds to the current condition in Alternativet: while collaboration primarily follows the hierarchical structure of the organization, decision-making power is in many ways decentralized. Recalling Duverger's four modes of decentralization – local, ideological, social and federated – there is no doubt that Alternativet's organizational configuration facilitates a type of *local* decentralization. Local leaders are selected from among ordinary members, they enjoy quite a bit of freedom and they are allowed to make decisions on fundamental issues. There is also a certain degree of *social* decentralization within Alternativet. One example of this might be the existence of a strong LGBT+ community that convenes on several occasions, most predominantly in connection with WorldPride week, thereby giving the party a prominent voice in debates on sexuality and gender issues.

More interestingly, perhaps, Alternativet can likewise be said to exhibit a type of *ideological* decentralization that allows for the emergence of factions or wings within the party. With this, we move from the administrative pillar to the political pillar in the sense that the level of ideological decentralization is perhaps most visibly felt in the political laboratories. When one visits the laboratories, it quickly becomes clear that there is very little ideological disciplining going on: participants are free to voice their own idiosyncratic opinions and to propose suggestions that run counter to the official party line. All opinions are acknowledged, and none is excluded, marginalized or ridiculed. Furthermore, although laboratories always centre on a particular issue – such as education, health or taxation – participants are often allowed to discuss issues that may seem utterly unrelated. To facilitate this type of unrestricted dialogue, many laboratories have 'dives' (*slyngelstuer* in Danish) where people less interested in the official topic can gather and debate freely. This allows people of all hues to feel included and provides them with a sense of being represented even though they might not conform to Alternativet's ideological position.

As I have argued elsewhere (Husted and Plesner, 2017), this is one reason why Alternativet handled the process of entering parliament so well. All political formations that begin life as an inclusive protest movement and transform into a political party will inevitably face what I call the 'problem of particularization', meaning that the scope of political representation will decrease as a consequence of the parliamentary entry (see Husted and Hansen, 2017). To avoid ideological collapse, such formations will have to find ways of maintaining a broad appeal while simultaneously advancing specific policy proposals. Alternativet's solution to the problem of particularization was to organize a multiplicity of political laboratories where members who might feel marginalized by the specificity of the political programme could continue to find representation and feel included. As such, the type of ideological decentralization found within Alternativet helped the party sustain its universal claim to represent all those 'who can feel that something new is starting to replace something old', as the manifesto boldly proclaims. The case of Alternativet is, unlike so many other examples, a case of positive ideological fragmentation or decentralization (see Chapter 9).

Leaders, members, participants

There can be no doubt that Alternativet is a 'direct' party, understood as a formation that relies *directly* on its members in terms of financial and political support. Members pay subscription fees and contribute to the advancement of the political project through various modes of participation. Inspired by other Danish left-wing parties such as the Red-Green Alliance, Alternativet allows members to 'tailorize the subscription fee' (Alternativet, 2023b). You can choose to pay anywhere from €2.50 each month to €80 each month. However, while certain restrictions apply in parties like the Red-Green Alliance (the subscription fee must match one's income level, for example), there is nothing stopping Alternativet members from paying an extremely low monthly fee.

Despite the direct nature of the party, Alternativet has occasionally benefitted from collaborations with external actors such as financiers and NGOs. One example is the Danish-Canadian philanthropist and co-founder of SimCorp, Ross Jackson, who, on more than one occasion, has supported the party with hundreds of thousands of euros. It is generally recognized that Jackson did not receive any immediate favours as a result of his generous donations, but it should be noted that his eldest son occupied several positions of trust within the organization, until he was expelled in 2017 for 'neglecting his extended responsibilities as a political candidate and representative' (Østergaard, 2017). Another example of indirect support is the relationships between Alternativet and NGOs like ActionAid Denmark and Amnesty International. While no financial relationship has ever existed between these organizations, they have often relied on each other for political influence and expertise. For instance, on several occasions, employees from ActionAid Denmark have participated in Alternativet events such as political laboratories (on tax policy and related areas, for example) to provide the ensuing discussions with a foundation based on expert statements.

Internationally, Alternativet has built close ties with the British think tank and pressure group Compass, which is usually seen as aligned politically with the Labour Party. The chair of Compass, Neil Lawson, has, on several occasions, participated in events organized by Alternativet, and, in 2014, he even co-authored a paper called *The Bridge: How the politics of the future will link the vertical to the horizontal* with Uffe Elbæk. In the text, the authors predict a near future where political parties will act as 'open tribes' that forge bridges between old – vertical – institutions and new – horizontal – movements (Elbæk and Lawson, 2014). Such examples illustrate that most direct parties today likewise rely on a network of support organizations to succeed organizationally as well as politically, rendering the direct/indirect distinction blurrier that it perhaps appears.

Modes of participation

Despite occasional collaborations between Alternativet and other organizations, the party remains one of the most direct parties in the Danish political system. Few parties – and certainly none of those represented in parliament – enjoy less financial assistance from networks of support organizations. While most parties on the right are funded by strong corporate interests, many on the left benefit from close collaborations with labour unions and think tanks. In fact, the idea of privileging ordinary members has been foundational to Alternativet's political project since the launch in 2013. Uffe Elbæk stated that it would have been easy for him to mobilize famous friends and strategic alliances within the political system and the cultural establishment, but he preferred to mobilize ordinary people with little parliamentary experience to prefigure the vision of a more democratic society. This commitment to direct and deliberative democracy is also at the heart of the policy-making process, which seeks to leverage the 'wisdom of the crowd' in the pursuit of better decisions and more legitimate decision-making.

This makes Alternativet an excellent example of a new breed of party organizations that Paolo Gerbaudo (2019) describes as relying on a 'participationist' discourse instead of more classical ideologies such as socialism or liberalism. According to Gerbaudo (2019: 81), such parties commit to participation as 'the normative criteria of a good politics, making legitimate only those processes that actively engage ordinary citizens while being suspicious of top-down interventions'. In other words, while parties traditionally seek to justify decisions and policies with reference to politically charged signifiers like 'freedom' or 'solidarity', participationist parties use citizen involvement as the most important standard for assessing the legitimacy of decisions. As stated in the first version of the party programme, Alternativet (2014a: 8) wants:

> it to be attractive and possible to get involved in politics, regardless of whether you are an academic or a craftsman, or whether you can contribute 8 minutes or 8 hours a day. We believe it is evident that being an active citizen matters and that we all, by being engaged, can help create better solutions for our society.

This profound commitment to participation is one reason why it seems relevant to use Duverger's (1954: 90) four 'concentric circles of participation' as a heuristic for distinguishing different modes of engagement within Alternativet. First, in terms of *electors*, the party has enjoyed varying levels of support throughout its lifetime. At the highest level in 2016, opinion polls reached almost 8 per cent, making Alternativet one of the biggest parties in the centre-left opposition. At the electoral nadir in 2021, however, polls fluctuated between 0.2 and 0.7 per cent.

If we stick to the official election results, Alternativet has participated in three national elections: in 2015 when it first entered parliament with 4.8 per cent of the votes; 2019 when it was reduced to 3 per cent; and 2022 when it recovered from near-death following the 2020 crises and earned 3.3 per cent of the votes. At the local elections, the party did significantly better in 2017 than in 2021. In Copenhagen, for instance, Alternativet secured 10.5 per cent of the votes, while the leading candidate, Niko Grünfeld, became the fourth most successful candidate across all parties in the capital. Furthermore, at the tiny island of Fanø, the party received 7.6 per cent of the votes, while the leading candidate, Sofie Valbjørn, managed to negotiate her way into the mayor's office. At the local elections in 2021, however, the party lost many city council seats across the country. In Copenhagen alone, Alternativet lost 7.6 percentage points and three seats at City Hall.

Second, in terms of *supporters* (electors who openly declare their support for the party), it can be difficult to assess the width of the circle, since people in Denmark usually express sympathy with certain parties to friends and family instead of putting signs in their garden and slapping stickers on their cars, as often seen elsewhere. With the rise of social media platforms such as Facebook and Twitter (X), however, this assessment has become a bit easier to make. Surprisingly, perhaps, at the top of its success, Alternativet was one of the strongest parties in Denmark on these platforms. A report from 2015 concluded that Alternativet outdid all other parties in terms of growth in *likes* (on Facebook) and *followers* (on Twitter). While most parties grew by 5–7 per cent in the weeks leading up to the national elections, Alternativet grew by 15 per cent (Krogsholm, 2015). Another report from 2017 showed Alternativet to be the sixth largest party on Twitter with approximately 20,000 followers, the third largest party on Facebook with almost 90,000 likes, and by far *the* largest party on the creativity-affording Instagram, with 17,000 followers (Kristensen, 2017). By late 2023, the impressive growth in SoMe support has stagnated. On Facebook, the party has even lost support, while the two other platforms have seen only modest growth rates.

Third, in terms of registered *members*, Alternativet has experienced a development, which is perhaps best described as an inverted U-curve. The party's popularity peaked in 2017, when more than 11,000 people were registered as rank and file, making Alternativet one of the biggest membership parties in the Danish parliament, only surpassed by much larger parties voter-wise such as the Social Democrats and Venstre. Following several unfortunate events in the wake of the 2017 local elections, many members resigned their subscription. Things became even worse in 2020 when internal conflicts flared up around the infamous election of Josephine Fock as leader while Uffe Elbæk left the party alongside three MPs. During only five years, Alternativet lost more than 90 per cent of its membership base, hitting an all-time low in 2022 with only 1,470 registered members. Since then, the numbers have once again increased. As of spring 2023, Alternativet currently has 2,235 members, according to its own numbers (see Chapter 7).

Finally, in terms of *militants*, it is extremely difficult to make any qualified assessments of historical developments or the current state of affairs. However, due to the ongoing membership decline, there can be no doubt the level of militancy within the organization is lower than four or five years ago. That said, the question of militancy naturally also depends on one's definition of what it means to be an extremely dedicated member. Duverger (1954: 110) is not exactly clear on this matter, as he simply defines a militant as 'an active member'. One could clearly argue that the number of people who voice their opinion, recruit members, talk to voters and organize events has decreased in parallel to the party's overall decline. However, as emphasized by several current members of Alternativet, one could equally argue that those who have not resigned their membership because of poor election results are the true militants. These are the people who are committed beyond the prospect of parliamentary influence and career opportunities. Indeed, it takes a true militant to stick around despite opinion polls that struggle to reach 1 per cent.

Modes of leadership

As in most organizations, there are different kinds of leaders in Alternativet: people with political responsibilities, people with administrative responsibilities, and people who exercise influence despite not occupying any formal leadership position. There is no need to revisit the distinction between political leaders and administrative leaders, as outlined earlier in this chapter. It seems sufficient to recall that the political leadership is constituted by the party leader and the national MPs as well as a number of appointed spokespersons, and that the administrative leadership is constituted by the head of the secretariat as well as five members of the board. In that sense, almost all formal leaders are elected one way or another. While the administrative leadership is elected by registered members at the national congress, the political leadership is elected by voters at national elections. Only the spokespersons are appointed through a process that few people really seem to understand. This opacity of these appointments has obviously been met with concern from certain parts of the party, but not enough to significantly alter the process.

This leads us to the question of informal leaders that operate in the shadows without a clear organizational mandate. In most political parties, there are whips whose job it is to ensure that the legislature follows the official party line. In certain party systems, such as the British, this has become a formal role occupied by selected MPs, but in other systems, including the Danish, the role of parliamentary whip is much less formalized. While there have indeed been instances where MPs have been disciplined for disrespecting the party line – one parliamentary candidate was, for example, reprimanded for suggesting that Hamas was a liberation movement rather than a terrorist organization – this happens less frequently than in other parties. However, the administrative pillar of the organization has occasionally shown a stronger tendency towards whipping. As we have seen, Alternativet is an organization that in many ways encourages dissensus and free-thinking, but sometimes this collides with the party's ambitions of gaining parliamentary influence. This tension became particularly pronounced in the first years after the 2015 elections. Here, the previously mentioned 'boy band' exercised a disproportional level of influence on the political strategy, disciplined members who were too vocal and sought to regulate external observers who scrutinized the party organization in unwanted ways (me included).

The existence of such whips or influencers within Alternativet's organization brings to mind Duverger's (1954: 146) distinction between 'titular' and 'real' leaders: the former is elected, but the latter is appointed. In many respects, Elbæk could be characterized as a titular leader who has been elected to represent the party but exercises surprisingly little influence over its political direction. As the charismatic figurehead of the party, he spent much of his time talking to the press and participating in events that would somehow cast the party in a positive light, instead of managing the party's internal affairs and drawing-up political strategies. These tasks were often delegated to key figures within the administrative pillar of Alternativet. For instance, although Elbæk officially authored the policy document called *The Next Denmark* (see Chapter 3 and Alternativet, 2018a), it remains a poorly kept secret that the former head of secretariat Leila Stockmarr played a crucial role in crafting the piece and conceiving many of its core ideas. Not only did the many casual references to figures such as Hartmut Rosa and Zygmunt Bauman give the highly educated Stockmarr away as ghost author, the fact that so many of the proposals deviated from the party's official line also testified to her personal influence. Other key people within the secretariat have played similar roles. The 'boy band' may be one example, and figures such as Nilas Bay-Foged, mentioned earlier, could also be described as the real leaders who influence the political direction.

In other respects, however, Elbæk certainly acted as a 'real' leader in the Duvergerian sense. This was especially true during the first years of Alternativet's life. Then, he quite actively impacted the political direction and guarded it by regulating members who deviated too much. During the initial campaign to enter parliament in 2015, for instance, several untried candidates worked hard to position themselves and attract media attention by airing policy proposals that were truly unconventional. While one candidate proposed to ban all food products that contained artificial additives (so, 80 per cent of all Danish food products), others suggested that all public transportation – including train and air travel – should be free of charge. In both cases, Elbæk had to correct the candidates and assure voters that Alternativet would stick to its political programme and not pursue proposals like these.

Configuring Alternativet

Having analysed Alternativet according to the main distinctions, proposed by Duverger in his book *Political Parties*, the time has come to consider if and how the party's organizational anatomy corresponds to some of the many party configurations that emerged from the post-Duvergerian literature, while bearing in mind that party configurations are ideal types that cannot be identified one to one in the empirical world.

Judging from Table 4.1, the configuration that fits Alternativet best seems to be the *movement* party, understood as a highly decentralized formation that caters to a wide range of voters and emphasizes participation and deliberation as fundamental values. Alternativet has ties to several social movements (including the climate movement and human rights initiatives) and it meets most of the characteristics usually associated with movement parties. In terms of origin, the party was founded mostly by extra-parliamentarian forces. In fact, Elbæk was the only person involved in the launch who had significant parliamentary experience. Furthermore, the party is clearly direct, in the sense that it primarily relies on members for financial and political support. In terms of basic elements, Alternativet is based on numerous branches, which is also what allows for the type of local decentralization that is characteristic of the party's organizational set-up. Finally, the structural articulation within Alternativet is relatively weak, meaning that many of the organizational processes are characterized by an unusually high level of informality.

The only parameter where Alternativet seriously deviates from the standard configuration of movement parties is collaboration. Contrary to what might be expected, perhaps, collaborative ties are predominantly vertical within the party. This means that local branches usually look upwards for cooperative interfaces rather than sideways. Instead of collaborating at a branch-to-branch level, branches often approach the regional sections and even the national headquarters for assistance and advice. In that particular sense, the party resembles a mass party more than a movement party. This may have a lot to do with the fact that Alternativet's organizational anatomy was initially modelled on the Social Liberal Party, which is certainly a mass or catch-all party.

From movement to mass

When trying to describe the configuration of a political party, it is worth keeping in mind that we are dealing with a moving target. Like all other organizations, parties change over time, although a certain level of inertia seems inherent to most formations (Husted et al, 2021). In the case of Alternativet, however, transformations could be said to have unfolded surprisingly fast. Not only has the party seen three leaders come and go in one single year, it has also altered many of its core processes within a relatively short time frame. One example of this might be the changing nature of the policy-making process, which went from being a genuinely open system, in which both members and non-members could participate, to a more centralized process driven primarily by the political leadership. In that sense, one could argue that Alternativet has undergone a journey from being a movement party to becoming a more regular mass party.

Another factor than indicates the party's transformation from movement to mass party is the scope of representation. Whereas traditional mass parties such as the old socialist parties and Christian parties are characterized as having a relatively well-articulated ideological position, movement parties are typically described as transversal, meaning that they seek to mobilize support from across the political spectrum by constructing more inclusive frontiers between the people and the elite or, as in the case of Alternativet, between the old political culture and the new political culture. Since the party's parliamentary entry in 2015, however, Alternativet's political project has gone through a 'process of particularization' (Husted and Hansen, 2017), in which the scope of representation has been cut short because of numerous difficult and sometimes unpopular decisions. For instance, the decision to support a tax-deduction bill for sustainable renewal of private homes, initially advanced by the former right-wing government, served to position Alternativet as a *centre*-left party rather than a radical-left party (see Chapter 3). Furthermore, the party's occasionally myopic focus on the green transition agenda has led observers to characterize it as a single-issue party, incapable of resolving problems not related to this particular concern.

There are clearly several important reasons for this overall change, but some may be related to what Santiago Anria (2019) calls 'constant causes'; that is, dynamic factors that shape a party's organizational set-up on a day-to-day basis. One of these factors is Alternativet's ambition of always having a tangible impact on parliamentary processes and forging productive collaborations with other parties instead of simply criticizing the power that be. This is arguably what led the party to support the tax-deduction bill in 2015 and what motivated it to strike additional compromises with right-wing forces. Typically, such constant causes will be countered by 'historical causes', understood as principled decisions made during the party's formative years. In the case of the Bolivian MAS, analysed by Anria, historical causes clearly helped preserve the organization's movement-like character despite institutional pressures to conform. For Alternativet, however, given its informal modus operandi as well as its relative short life, it seems fair to speculate that the constant causes simply outweighed the historical causes. In other words, the overwhelming experience of entering parliament as a party of under two years and having to achieve parliamentary impact from the get-go arguably contributed to overturning some of the fundamental decisions made during Alternativet's initial formation. Chapter 7 will consider a number of institutional factors that may have contributed further to Alternativet's organizational transformation and compare these with movement parties that have matured in different societal settings.

6

The Comparative Perspective

> But a party (like any other organization) is a structure in motion
> which evolves over time, reacting to external changes and the
> changing 'environments' in which it functions. One might suggest
> that the most important factors explaining its physiognomy and
> functioning are its organizational history (its past) and its relations
> with changing external environments.
>
> Angelo Panebianco (1988: 49): *Political Parties*

Introduction

Chapter 4 outlined the basic tenets of the configurational perspective,
which may be seen as a precursor to, or even a subdivision of, a much more
dominant perspective known today as the comparative perspective. Here,
we saw how Maurice Duverger (1954) blazed the trail for much subsequent
research by suggesting that parties are best distinguished in terms of their
structural anatomy rather than their ideological dispositions. Conservative
and socialist mass parties, he claimed, have much more in common than
ideologically similar parties with different organizational configurations. For
several years, the post-Duvergerian literature seemed to follow this relatively
novel way of thinking about parties. Some scholars refined and developed
the generic models suggested by Duverger (for example Kirchheimer, 1966)
or added 'behavioral' dimensions (such as Eldersveld, 1964), while others
extended his innovative focus to the relationship between parties and party
systems (for example Sartori, 1976).

In the 1980s, however, studies of party organization gradually began to
move in a new direction. Building on insights from both the classical and
the configurational perspective, a new breed of party researchers developed
a more specific empirical orientation. Whereas scholars like Robert Michels
and Maurice Duverger relied heavily on personal experiences and described
general tendencies based largely on anecdotal evidence, this new class of

researchers seemed less interested in theory *building* and more interested in theory *testing* (Gauja and Kosiara-Pedersen, 2021b). To this end, scholars such as Kenneth Janda (1980) launched large-scale projects that aimed to establish databases of comparable information about parties across the world, with the purpose of either verifying or falsifying grand theories proposed by their predecessors. This newfound interest gave rise to a rolling wave of comparative party studies. Although these studies varied thematically, they all subscribed to the same underlying premise: that environmental factors determine, or at least strongly encourage, a particular organizational set-up (Harmel and Janda, 1982; Lawson and Merkl, 1988). Hence, Duverger's otherwise widely accepted proposition that parties constitute closed communities, living according to their own laws, was therefore implicitly rejected as empirically counter-factual (see Janda and King, 1985).

From Duverger to Panebianco

This era of party studies was not, however, entirely devoid of theorizing. For instance, Joseph Schlesinger (1984) stitched together a theory of party organization based largely on Anthony Downs' (1957) rational-choice conception of democracy, and Samuel Eldersveld (1982) developed a framework for understanding the role played by parties in US society. However, arguably the greatest theoretical contribution to the emerging comparative perspective is of Italian descent. In 1988, a professor of comparative politics at Bologna University, Angelo Panebianco, took it upon himself to build a comparative-historical theory of political parties. His idea was to reclaim Duverger's point about party *organization* being the most important aspect of party politics, but to adjust the theory in a way that allows it to inform the new wave of comparative studies. Panebianco's most basic argument is that the structural configuration of parties is determined by a variety of factors, some of which have to do with the organization's own history while others are related to the external environment. In that way, he managed to build a bridge between the classical and configurational scholars – who emphasized the former – and the new wave of comparative researchers – who emphasized the latter. This is perhaps why Panebianco's theory has had such lasting effects on contemporary party literature, and it is the reason why I have dedicated a good part of this chapter to unfolding its most important elements.

Despite Panebianco's attempt to build an account of party organization that grants equal attention to internal and external factors, the focus on environmental factors was accentuated a few years later by a highly influential text edited by Richard Katz and Peter Mair. The two assembled a team of esteemed party researchers who were asked to gather current and historical data about party organizations in their home countries. This eventually resulted in a cutting-edge volume that provided insights into key developments since the 1960s with respect to party membership, staff, resources, expenditures and representative structures in 12 Western democracies (Katz and Mair, 1994). What made this contribution so influential was not only the idea of assembling a series of country-specific analyses, but also the methodological decisions made in the formative stages of the project. Katz and Mair (1992: 7) decided that the team of country experts should focus only on 'the official story'; that is, contributors to the project should collect authorized material submitted by the parties themselves and disregard 'unofficial' data such as interviews, observations or personal experiences. In that way, Katz and Mair not only broke with long-standing theoretical assumptions about the relationship between organization and environment, they also refuted Ostrogorski's (1902), Michels' (1915), Duverger's (1954) and Panebianco's (1988) repeated warnings about not relying too heavily on sanctioned material as being 'fundamentally wrong in its emphasis'. The point, for them, was to collect 'reasonably hard data' that could be used for comparative purposes and then only subsequently add the 'real story' (Katz and Mair, 1992: 8).

Most of the party organization research conducted today is comparative. A quick browse through field-specific journals such as *Party Politics* and designated book series on political parties reveals as much. Instead of submerging themselves in single or a few case studies, contemporary party researchers work with large-n samples and conduct cross-contextual analyses. Instead of building theories in an inductive manner, present-day party scholars typically test theories deductively. Instead of utilizing qualitative data sources such as interviews and observations, party researchers today rely predominantly on 'hard' and 'official' data. And instead of imbuing their analyses with moral judgements and normative standards, they prefer to describe their cases neutrally and without value-based prescriptions. As such, there can be no doubt that the comparative perspective, and its commitment to sober empirical observations, remains *the* most dominant approach to the study of party organization. In what follows, I will begin by unfolding Panebianco's comparative-historical theory, focusing on his conception of power as well as his account of internal and external 'contingency factors'. I then move on to a discussion of Katz and Mair's research project, concentrating on the methodological dispositions. Finally, I will consider some of the most popular themes in comparative party studies: membership, staff, income, expenditures, participation and representation. In conclusion, I will highlight what I believe organization scholars can learn from the comparative perspective on parties.

Panebianco's comparative-historical theory

Every 40 years or so, history seems to repeat itself within the field of party organization research. In 1915, the English version of Michels' *Political Parties* was first published, purporting to delineate the true nature of organized political activity. In 1954, the English version of Duverger's *Political Parties* appeared, with its systematic effort to illustrate how parties are best analysed based on their structural anatomy. And in 1988, yet another book called *Political Parties* came out, this time authored by Italian political scientist Angelo Panebianco. A certain degree of path-dependency thus seems to characterize the history of party organization research, in the sense that all three books bear the same title and because they all argue in favour of privileging the *organizational* study of parties and focus on the structural characteristics of these political formations. However, whereas Michels focused on the internal power dynamics of party organizations, such as the tendency towards oligarchy, Duverger began to consider the impact that party *systems* may have on party organizations. Panebianco's contribution is, crudely put, to take this development to its logical conclusion by showing how party organizations are determined, not only by their own decisions but by a variety of contextual factors such as organizational size, technological developments and environmental relations.

Panebianco (1988: xi) clearly recognizes this scholarly pedigree when asserting that, since Duverger, party researchers have generally prioritized 'the study of electoral dynamics, of the functioning of state institutions as influenced by parties, and of the relations between parties and social classes' – in other words, the study of 'political processes' – at the expense of genuinely *organizational* perspectives. As such, Panebianco's aim is to re-emphasize the importance of investigating organizational dynamics and to develop an analytical framework that can aid party researchers in this endeavour. As he famously notes: 'whatever else parties are and to whatever else solicitations they respond, they are above all organizations and ... organizational analysis must therefore come before any other perspective' (Panebianco, 1988: xi). To this end, Panebianco develops a 'comparative-historical' theory of party organization. The theory is historical because it seeks to take the party's past into account, and it is comparative because it likewise considers a number of contextual factors that allow researchers to compare party organizations in cross-country analyses.

Panebianco's strategy is to utilize insights and concepts from what he calls the 'sociology of organizations' and apply them to 'the case of parties' (Panebianco, 1988: xvi). More specifically, he draws consistently on theoretical resources from contingency theory – a branch of organization theory that considers organization a product of environmental relations – but adds his own party-centric points to provide a full picture. In the following sections, I will go through what I believe to be the most central aspects of Panebianco's theory, based on the premise that many of the arguments advanced in *Political Parties: Organization and Power* have had profound implications for subsequent party research.

Power and organizational stability

Panebianco begins by establishing a clear connection to Michels' seminal work on the iron law of oligarchy (see Chapter 2). He does so by positioning power as perhaps the most central theme in the study of party organization and by framing the issue of power according to the idea that parties are governed by elites or, as Panebianco calls them, 'dominant coalitions'. Unlike Michels, however, Panebianco subscribes to an understanding of power that is more nuanced than the Weberian definition employed by his predecessor. Instead of viewing power as something resembling coercion, he draws on Michel Crozier's (1964) classical conceptualization of power as the *management of uncertainty*. This allows him to decentre power by showing that even the 'lowliest activist' controls certain zones of uncertainty (Panebianco, 1988: 33) – one being the (dis)continuation of their own membership subscription – and it provides a foundation for the study of organized power as a moving target. According to this view, power relations are not static. They change all the time, and one important element in the study of parties as organizations is to examine how such changes unfold. As Danny Rye (2014: 16) explains, Panebianco sees power as a 'changing and evolving resource, where different elements and combinations of the power of leaders and members may be in play at any particular time'. In that sense, he also breaks with Michels' top-down view of power by contending that leaders must subject themselves to the will of members to sustain their position within the party's dominant coalition.

Any organization must navigate several uncertainties, some of which are more decisive than others. For instance, in Crozier's (1964) study of a monopolistic cigarette manufacturer, the maintenance engineers had a surprisingly firm grip on the organization because they controlled the company's only vital source of uncertainty: the production system. What made the engineers powerful was their ability to make others dependent on their discretionary actions – if they failed, everyone failed. This ultimately reversed the formal chain of command, forcing managers and directors to ask the engineers for advice on how to run the organization. Hence, those who control zones of uncertainty have an asset that they can 'spend' in 'unequal exchange relations' between leaders and members (Panebianco, 1988: 22). Some of these uncertainties result from internal factors, such as the production system, while others are imposed on the organization by external forces, such as the market. This also applies to political parties. Panebianco lists six primary sources of uncertainty that parties must navigate: competency, communication, formal rules, financing, recruitment and environmental factors (see Table 6.1).

The zone of uncertainty that Panebianco refers to as 'competency' has to do with the expertise of individual party members and staff. If an MP is

Table 6.1: Panebianco's six zones of uncertainty and those who control them

Zone of uncertainty	Source of power	Power wielders
Competency	Professional expertise and personal experience	Experts, analysts, advisers, members with seniority
Communication	Access to information and communication channels	Communication officers, PR consultants, advisers
Formal rules	Direct influence on (the interpretation of) rules	Formal leaders, council members, advisers
Financing	Relations with donors and impact on fundraising strategy	Fundraisers, liaison officers, large-scale donors
Recruitment	Influence on promotion and demotion, on- and off-boarding	Formal leaders, HR professionals, advisers
Environment	Insights on external factors and their future development	Experts, analysts, advisers, members with seniority

an expert in striking deals with opposing parties, she invariably controls an important source of uncertainty, because without cross-party collaboration, there can be little political impact, particularly in pluralist party systems. The second zone of uncertainty relates to 'communication'. Parties are, like other organizations, communicative systems that operate on the basis of spoken and written exchanges. This means that those who are capable of manipulating, delaying, and/or distorting official information administer a great source of uncertainty. For instance, the press officer in charge of the monthly newsletter wields considerable power, because effective communication is the key to connecting members' personal desires with the organization's overall purpose (see Barnard, 1938). Third, 'formal rules' are an equally important zone of uncertainty, since those who mould the 'playing field' effectively decide 'the terrain upon which confrontations, negotiations, and power games will take place' (Panebianco, 1988: 35). This also applies to those who are officially responsible for interpreting the rules, such as Alternativet's by-laws council, as we saw in the previous chapter.

The fourth zone of uncertainty is financing. With the rise of the 'cartel party' (Katz and Mair, 1995) and the diminished role played by membership fees in the financing of parties, this particular zone has arguably become less uncertain. In most Western countries, the state now constitutes the primary source of party funding, which has made fundraising a somewhat less central concern for party organizations (van Biezen, 2008). Nonetheless, those who oversee relations with important donors undoubtedly still control a great resource, as donations are key to growing the organization and launching expensive initiatives such as election campaigns (the donors themselves are obviously also powerful in this regard). In connection to that, 'recruitment' constitutes the fifth zone of uncertainty. Recruitment has two central dimensions. One has to do with on- and off-boarding: those who hire and fire can be seen as charged with maintaining the very border of the organization, and that task certainly represents an important element in any enterprise. The other recruitment dimension concerns internal promotion and demotion: those who are able to assign positions and responsibilities internally surely manage a great deal of uncertainty within a party since the relocation of personnel is closely connected to the constitution of the 'dominant coalition', as we shall see. In the previous chapter, we saw how this played out in Alternativet with the sudden concentration of power in relation to the formation of Elbæk's 'boy band'.

The greatest zone of uncertainty in political parties is clearly represented by environmental factors; perhaps the most important being changing laws, inter-party competition, technological developments and electoral results. Few of these factors can be controlled by party members or staff, but changes in the external environment necessarily require interpretations, and these are often conducted by powerful actors within the organization. For instance, those who are in a position to provide analyses of changing attitudes in the electorate hold the key to defining the party's next official strategy. Similarly, those who can advise the leadership about new technological inventions are in a crucial position to alter the ways of working within party organizations. The latter obviously applies more to 'digital parties' (Gerbaudo, 2019) than to other configurations, but information and communication technology is clearly central to all contemporary organizations – and particularly to those that rely heavily on public support (Plesner and Husted, 2019). However, some 'environmental' zones are not just concerned with interpretation and can be more or less directly controlled. For instance, those in charge of forging and maintaining alliances with partner organizations, such as other parties, NGOs, think tanks, social movements or even state agencies, occupy powerful positions since these effectively manage the very foundation of the party's political clout.

Having outlined these six zones of uncertainty, we can now return to Panebianco's decision to view parties as governed by dominant *coalitions* rather than by oligarchic *elites*. The main reason for this shift is to emphasize that modern parties are rarely controlled by small and homogeneous entities at the very top of the organization, but by amorphous networks of heterogeneous actors across units and organizational boundaries; the composition of these networks is a product of ongoing struggles and negotiations; and the constitution of dominant coalitions changes accordingly from one situation to the next. In that sense, Panebianco goes to great lengths to nuance the one-sided picture of oligarchy that Michels' presents as an irrefutable iron law, focusing on power and leadership as something that can be exercised by different actors at different levels in the organization.

This is why Panebianco describes the dominant coalition as a 'potentially precarious construct' (Panebianco, 1988: 38).

Contingencies in party organization

As noted in this chapter's epigraph, Panebianco sees two main factors as decisive when it comes to the organizational structure, or physiognomy, of a political party: its history and its environment (the notion of environment here should be understood in the broadest sense as representing a party's organizational context). While the latter is arguably more important than the former, the past nonetheless weighs heavily on the present, with outdated decisions sometimes being upheld simply because of inertia and path-dependency (see also Anria, 2019). The organizational set-up that a party follows in its formative stage is referred to by Panebianco as the 'genetic model'. While many dimensions of the genetic model could be highlighted, Panebianco points to three that are particularly important: (1) the relationship between core and periphery, (2) the possible existence of a financial sponsor, and (3) the level of charismatic leadership.

In terms of the first dimension, Panebianco (1988: 50) distinguishes between parties where the core determines developments in the periphery of the organization (the national party establishes local branches) and parties that emerge on the basis of 'spontaneous germination' (local branches join forces by establishing a national party). The former is called 'territorial penetration', the latter 'territorial diffusion' (see also Eliassen and Svaasand, 1975). In terms of the second dimension, Panebianco distinguishes between parties where the leadership derives its legitimacy from being associated with an external sponsor (such as trade unions) and parties where an external sponsor uses the party as its parliamentary arm (business firms, for instance). Parties that rely on an external sponsor for legitimacy are 'externally legitimated', while parties that do not are 'internally legitimated'. Finally, the third dimension concerns the existence or absence of a charismatic leader. While all popular parties will contain elements of charismatic leadership, some are almost exclusively tied to the divine leader's charisma. Such parties are often short-lived and rarely outlast the leader's reign.

Although important, we will not spend too much time on these factors here as, to some extent, they overlap with Duverger's reflections on party configurations (see Chapter 4) and they rarely constitute a primary focus point for comparative studies of party organization. Instead, we will turn to the other major factor governing the organizational structure of parties: contextual conditions.

Panebianco's focus on contextual factors represents a clear break with early theories of party organization such as those introduced in Chapters 2 and 4. For instance, whereas Michels saw oligarchy as an unavoidable tendency that unfolds across contexts and despite institutional differences (Diefenbach, 2019), Duverger (1954: 84–85) conceptualizes a political party as a 'closed community', shielded off from external forces and living 'according to its own laws'. To inform his work on the relationship between parties and their environment, Panebianco turns to one of the most popular organization theories of his day, namely *contingency theory*. The basic premise of contingency theory is that a host of situational factors, or contingencies, some of which are more important than others, determine the appropriate structure of an organization (Donaldson, 2001). Three factors are, according to Panebianco, typically highlighted as crucial for any contemporary organization: the size of the organization, recent technological developments and environmental relations. While he discusses the former and the latter in great detail, he leaves the second curiously untouched.

Panebianco begins by emphasizing the importance usually attributed to organizational size when it comes to determining the administrative structure of a party. The core argument here is that large parties usually exhibit a more hierarchical structure than small parties and, as we saw in Chapter 2, a number of psychological and technical causes are typically said to drive this tendency towards oligarchy. Panebianco, however, rejects these explanations as prejudiced and one-sided. For instance, organizational growth is often said to correlate negatively with the level of membership participation, in the sense that small parties usually engage more actively in participatory processes. Panebianco refutes this assumption, citing a lack of evidence, and points to the fact that small parties may easily structure their organization in a hierarchical and non-participatory manner. Although recent literature confirms this conclusion, stressing that the 'causal order may be unclear here' (Schumacher and Giger, 2017: 177), there seems to be some degree of positive correlation between size and oligarchy (for example, Scarrow 2002; Weldon, 2006). Nonetheless, for Panebianco, external forces related to the environment matter more.

To account for the decisive role played by environmental conditions in terms of deciding the most appropriate structure for a political party, Panebianco (1988: 204) highlights three 'dimensions of unpredictability' (environmental uncertainties that parties must navigate): complexity/ simplicity, stability/instability and liberality/hostility. In terms of the first, he draws on contingency theorists such as Charles Perrow and Henry Mintzberg in asserting that the level of environmental complexity has a direct bearing on the administrative structure of any organization. High levels of environmental complexity push the organization towards increased internal specialization and stimulate the recruitment of 'boundary personnel'; that is, people who are responsible for managing particular parts of the environment (White, 1974). Here, environmental complexity is usually associated with the degree of task analysability, with the aerospace industry (or 'rocket science') frequently highlighted as an example of an extremely complex business environment (for example, Perrow, 1967). While political parties do not operate in 'industries' or 'markets' as such, they are nonetheless engaged in a fierce competition for support. Panebianco therefore translates the classical distinction between complexity and simplicity into a question of task (un) analysability in relation to what he calls the 'electoral arena' – populated by voters – and the 'parliamentary arena' – populated by politicians.

When it comes to environmental stability, Panebianco draws on the work of contingency theorists par excellence, Paul Lawrence and Jay Lorsch (1967), in suggesting that dynamic and unpredictable environmental conditions usually breed decentralized decision-making structures, while stable and predictable conditions typically foster centralization. As we saw in the previous chapter, decentralization in political parties can take several forms, with *local* – relative autonomy for regional branches – and *ideological* – relative autonomy for factions within the party – being most prevalent. High levels of decentralization often lead to internal differentiation, which in parties as well as in most other organizations is a frequent source of conflict since it effectively destabilizes the power of the dominant coalition. Panebianco's (1988: 206) working hypothesis is thus that parties operating in dynamic environments are prone to conflicts, since the existence of a higher 'number of political solutions proposed' invariably challenges the leadership's internal legitimacy.

Finally, in terms of environmental hostility, Panebianco highlights the party's external legitimacy as an important factor for determining its administrative structure. A considerable part of this legitimacy is predicated on whether or not a party operates in a hostile or liberal environment. Although a particular environment may be hostile to some parties, it may be liberal to others. Similarly, while a particular party may find the electoral arena quite welcoming and hospitable, the parliamentary arena might be hostile and unaccommodating. That is the case, for instance, for many right-wing parties in Northern Europe. While the electorate generally supports their existence, the other parties frequently bar them from parliamentary influence (Widfeldt, 2018). Again, drawing on classical contributions to contingency theory, Panebianco purports that organizations operating in hostile environments tend to exhibit a higher level of internal cohesion, while those operating in liberal environments tend to be more fragmented. This points to an interesting observation: while instability and complexity often lead to decentralization and heterogeneity, hostility typically encourages cohesion and homogeneity. Panebianco's explanation for this apparent discrepancy is that instability and complexity represent a threat to the organizational *order*, while hostility represents a threat to the very survival of the organization: 'This fundamental difference explains their different effects' (Panebianco, 1988: 206). (See Figure 6.1.)

Figure 6.1: Environmental contingencies and their consequences for party organizations

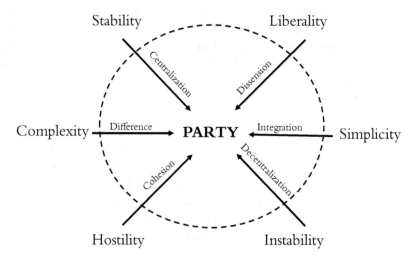

In the next chapter, we will analyse these three aspects of the environment in relation to Alternativet and the two additional cases, the Spanish party Podemos and the Icelandic Pirate Party. Throughout his work, however, Panebianco is at pains to stress that no mono-causal relationship exists between environment and party. Although parties are heavily conditioned by their external environment, they are sometimes able to dominate their surroundings and instigate field-level changes. The ability to do so depends on the level of 'institutionalization' achieved by a particular party at a particular time. This leads us to the final aspect of his comparative-historical theory.

Party institutionalization

A party can be more or less vulnerable to changes in its immediate environment. While some parties may suffer the consequences of sudden instability in the electoral arena (perhaps because their administrative structure is overly bureaucratic and centralized), others might weather the storm and even dominate their surroundings. According to Panebianco, the main predictor in this regard is the level of institutionalization achieved by the party at a given time. To substantiate this argument, Panebianco draws on another classical branch of organization theory – institutional theory (not to be confused with neo-institutional theory). In particular, he takes inspiration from Phillip Selznick's work on administrative leadership in large organizations. Here, an institution is defined as an organization that has progressed from being an 'expendable tool' to becoming an end in itself; something that has an intrinsic value 'beyond the technical requirements of the task at hand' (Selznick, 1957: 17). This means that institutionalization is a process (Selznick, 1957: 16–17):

> It is something that happens to an organization over time, reflecting the organization's own history, the people who have been in it, the groups it embodies and the vested interests they have created, and the way it has adapted to its environment. … The degree of institutionalization depends on how much leeway there is for personal and group interaction. The more precise an organization's goals, and the more specialized and technical its operations, the less opportunity will there be for social forces to affect its development.

In other words, institutionalization is a process in an organization's justification for existence. Does it merely exist as a tool for realizing certain goals, or does its very existence represent a 'source of personal satisfaction' for those involved (Selznick, 1957: 17)? Translating these insights into a framework for the study of political parties, Panebianco suggests that there are two ways of measuring the level of institutionalization attained by a particular party: (1) its autonomy vis-à-vis the external environment, and (2) the level of 'systemness', the 'interdependence of its different internal sectors' (Panebianco, 1988: 55). In terms of the former, a party is said to be institutionalized if it is relatively independent of other organizations for its survival. Some parties may rely heavily on external donors such as trade unions or other interest groups (externally legitimated parties), while others may have acquired positions of power in the political field that allows them to operate autonomously without risking their own survival (this applies to cartel parties in particular, but also more generally to mass parties with large membership bases). In terms of 'systemness', a party is deemed an institution if it displays a considerable degree of internal structural coherence. In other words, the more integrated the subsections, the more institutionalized the party, since internal integration generally allows the dominant coalition to control multiple zones of uncertainty.

Panebianco's overall argument is thus that the more institutionalized a party is, the more autonomous it is with regard to its environment, and the less likely it is to change its 'genetic model' (the original organizational set-up). As an illustrative example, he points to the development of the Conservative Party in Britain. In 1975, the Conservatives democratized their criteria for selecting leaders in the wake of a series of electoral defeats. Suddenly, the leader became 'a hostage of Conservative parliamentarians', which allowed the popular Margaret Thatcher to defeat Edward Heath and William Whitelaw in the leadership election and push the party's policies further to the right (Panebianco, 1988: 251). What this example shows, according to Panebianco, is that if we want to explain changes in parliamentary politics (such as the rise of Thatcherism), we must attend to structural dislocations within the organizational core of political parties and to the external pressures exercised upon this core by different contingency factors.

To systematize this analytical ambition, Panebianco (1988: 58–59) proposes five general indicators of party institutionalization in which institutionalized parties: (1) possess a 'developed central bureaucracy' at the national level, (2) ensure 'homogeneity of organizational structures at the same hierarchical level', (3) secure financing from a '*plurality* of sources', (4) dominate partner organizations such as donors and interest groups, and (5) operate with a close correspondence between statutory norms and the 'actual power structure'. In the next chapter, I will employ these five characteristics to chart the degree of institutionalization across three cases of European movement parties. This will allow me to explore whether connections exist between the administrative structure of the parties, their external environments and their overall success in their respective arenas.

The hegemony of 'the official story'

The conception of a political party as an open system, determined at least partially by environmental conditions, is well aligned with other early contributions to the comparative perspective. One example is Kenneth Janda's (1980) persistent focus on 'autonomy' and 'institutionalization' in his impressive cross-national survey of 158 parties in 53 countries, another is Joseph Schleisinger's (1984: 390) curious characterization of parties as 'forms of organized trial and error', and a third example is Kay Lawson and Peter Merkl's (1988: 5) description of party failure as something that occurs when parties 'do not perform the function they are expected to perform in their society' (see also Lawson, 1994). However, the most notable contribution to this 'comparative-historical' research agenda is, arguably, Richard Katz and Peter Mair's (1994) frequently cited anthology, *How Parties Organize*. Based on data gathered in their 1000-page handbook, published two years earlier (Katz and Mair, 1992), the two authors summoned a group of well-esteemed party researchers with the ambition of deepening our knowledge of the organizational characteristics of political parties in Western Europe. As Mair (1994: 1–2) puts it in the anthology's introductory chapter, while pointing to a number of 'surprisingly evident lacunae' in research on parties:

> The empirically grounded study of parties as organizations, which provides the focus for this volume, has long constituted one of the most obvious of these lacunae. ... Thus while we now know a great deal about parties and their voters, about parties and their governments, and about parties and their competitors, there continue to be severe limits

to the comparative understanding of precisely how party organizations work, about how they change, and about how they adapt.

One of the most groundbreaking decisions made by Katz and Mair (1992) during the course of collecting data for their anthology was to focus solely on what they called 'the official story', meaning that contributors to the project would have to rely only on authorized material produced by the parties themselves. Hence, instead of approaching parties through a selection of both formal and informal data, as so many party researchers had previously done, the contributors would only consider formal rules and statutes, official budgets and membership statistics, as well as 'other party reports and documents' (Katz and Mair, 1992: 7). The rationale behind this was that official data tends to reflect the current balance of power within party organizations, and that changes in this balance will eventually manifest themselves in rules and regulations. Although acknowledging that the 'official' story is not necessarily the 'real' story, Katz and Mair thus refute Duverger's (1954) and Panebianco's (1988) warnings about not relying too heavily on authorized material as being 'fundamentally wrong in its emphasis'. The official story, they contend, provides a useful starting point for understanding the organization of political parties and offers an 'incomparable source of reasonably hard data that can be used in the analysis of party organization across both time and space' (Katz and Mair, 1992: 8).

The methodological principles spelled out in the work of Katz and Mair has had unparalleled impact on the contemporary party organization literature (Gauja and Kosiara-Pedersen, 2021a). In fact, most studies of party organization today rely almost exclusively on 'the official story', albeit often without referring to their approach as such. One example of this trend is Wolfgang Müller and Kaare Strøm's (1999) anthology, *Policy, Office, or Votes?*, which is concerned with explaining the behaviour of leaders in different types of parties. The common framework that runs through the book is that parties can be differentiated in terms of whether they focus on maximizing the impact of their policies ('policy-seeking' parties), maximizing their control of the executive body ('office-seeking') or maximizing electoral support ('vote-seeking'). Although the editors recognize that parties are complex organizations and that probing the behaviour of party leaders would require analysts to peek inside the 'black box' (Strøm and Müller, 1999: 12), none of the volume's contributors seriously meets that ambition. Sticking firmly to the official story, they all set out to explain organizational behaviour based on authorized material produced by the parties themselves.

A more recent example is Susan Scarrow and colleagues' (2017) anthology, *Organizing Political Parties*, in which a number of high-profile scholars update debates about structures, resources, and representative strategies in present-day parties. Unlike the above example, the editors of this volume (Scarrow and Webb, 2017: 13, emphasis added) explicitly embrace the official story approach, noting that:

> This choice was made in full knowing that formal structures do not tell the complete story about actual power relations. *The alternative would have been to collect expert judgements concerning these issues.* We reject this approach in part because it would have required us to enlist a far greater number of willing volunteers in a project that is already large, not to mention that expert surveys raise their own set of issues about *validity, accuracy and comparability.*

This passage captures nicely the spirit of the comparative perspective on party organization. First, it illustrates the departure from the methodological principles guiding particularly the work of Michels and Ostrogorski, but also Duverger and Panebianco. Methods that were instrumental for both the classical and the configurational perspective – participant observation, personal communication and other informal strategies for collecting data – are not considered legitimate in more recent studies. All that counts are official documents and, if necessary, expert judgements. Second, it shows how the research strategy has shifted from inductive reasoning and theory building to deductive reasoning and formal comparisons across time and space. In that sense, the comparative perspective combines the classical perspective's interest in party organization with the configurational perspective's focus on systematism, but abandons the ambition of qualitatively understanding 'the inner life of the party' (Barrling, 2013). Later, I will briefly discuss three main areas of concern for the comparative perspective and highlight how I intend to use these in my analysis of Alternativet, Podemos and the Icelandic Pirate Party.

Members and staff

One of the central discussions picked up by Katz and Mair's comparative project is the question of whether parties are in decline; that is, whether their role in representative democracy has diminished over time. In this book's preface, I presented a brief history of political parties as an organizational form. The basic point was that parties have had a hard time reflecting demands for increased participation and deliberation, and that this, alongside several additional factors, has contributed to the heavy decline in party memberships that we have witnessed since the middle of the 20th century (see Ignazi, 2017). While Katz and Mair recognize this development, they refute the proposition that parties as such are in decline, citing evidence from their impressive research project. Their most basic point is that we need to abandon the notion of the party as a unified actor.

Instead of perceiving parties as single entities, they should instead be seen as organizations consisting of three bodies or faces: the party *in public office* (MPs), the party *in central office* (national leadership and staff) and the party *on the ground* (members and loyal voters). Their contention is that only the latter face of the party is in decline (in some countries), while the two others are thriving (Katz and Mair, 1993). This is the situation that has given rise to the 'cartel party' thesis (Katz and Mair, 1995), as discussed in Chapter 4.

This distinction between politicians (in public office), staff (in central office) and members (on the ground) spawned a renewed interest in comparative studies of party developments across all three faces. For instance, building on longitudinal data from the original research project, Mair (1994) shows how membership decline occurred in eight out of ten countries in Western Europe from 1960 to 1990, with countries like Great Britain, the Netherlands, Finland and Denmark experiencing the most dramatic drops. At the same time, however, parties in all ten countries grew in terms of salaried staff – sometimes even by more than 300 per cent. Denmark clearly experienced the most severe drop in party memberships, with 21.1 per cent of the electorate being registered as party members in 1960 and only 6.5 per cent in 1990. Notably, however, Danish parties saw their staff numbers grow by a staggering 112 per cent during the same period (Bille, 1994).

The same research interest can be observed in Russell Dalton and Martin Wattenberg's (2002) project on *Parties Without Partisans*, in which a team of scholars explore developments across 'advanced industrial democracies' such as Australia, Britain, France, Germany and the United States. Instead of using Katz and Mair's distinction between politicians, staff and members, the contributors to this particular project follow VO Key's (1942) tripartite focus on parties *in the electorate* (how parties provide a link between people and parliament), parties *as organizations* (how parties organize internally) and parties *in government* (how parties manage governmental affairs), but the objective is more or less the same: to clarify whether and how it makes sense to talk about party decline as a general tendency. The overall conclusion that Dalton and Wattenberg arrive at is that parties are *changing* rather than necessarily *declining*; adapting to new conditions and altering their modus operandi as well as their organizational structure – much like Panebianco (1988) proposed with his comparative-historical theory.

The comparative perspective has also yielded several studies exclusively focused on party members. One of the most frequently cited in this regard is Ingrid van Biezen and colleagues' (2012) account of declining party membership across 27 European countries. Their main conclusion is that 'party organisations have reached such a low ebb that the formal organisational level is itself no longer a relevant indicator of party capacity', which leads them to call for a broader understanding of party membership that might also include supporters and sympathizers (van Biezen et al,

2012: 24). In France and the UK, for instance, less than 2 per cent of the population today are registered as party members; in Poland and Latvia, that number has even fallen below 1 per cent. Similar conclusions are reached by Paul Whiteley (2011) who sets out to find an explanation for the decline in party memberships in representative democracies. Whiteley tests two prevalent hypotheses: (1) that the falling numbers are caused by the cartel-like relationship between party and state, which ultimately stifles voluntary activity at the grassroots level, and (2) that the availability of new modes of political participation associated with new media and creative forms of activism have rendered party memberships superfluous and irrelevant. Using survey data from 36 democracies around the world, (Whiteley, 2011: 36) finds evidence for the first hypothesis, but not for the latter, concluding:

> As parties get closer to the state and become more professionalized, they find it easier to ignore their volunteers, while at the same time expecting them to take on more regulatory burdens. Party leaders have little incentive to recruit and retain new members if the taxpayers pick up the costs of running the party organization. The data suggest that there is a generational dimension to these trends, with the recruitment of new age cohorts being problematic everywhere, but particularly so in high-regulation countries. Thus, the state itself may be smothering party activity.

Such explanations clearly support the 'cartel party' thesis, as they detail the decline of the party on the ground and relate this decline to increased state regulation, but they say little about the associated development of the party in central office. In fact, as Paul Webb and Dan Keith (2017: 40) proclaim, growth and decline in terms of party staff is 'one of the most under-researched fields in the study of political parties'. However, several recent studies within the comparative perspective have sought to investigate this dimension of party organization by looking at official data, submitted by parties themselves. One example is Webb and Keith's own empirical investigation, which relies on data from yet another major research project known as the Political Party Database (PPDB) project that charts party developments across more than 250 countries worldwide. When it comes to party staff, however, the researchers were only able to acquire data from 15 countries. This testifies to the parties' reluctance in terms of submitting information about employees and speaks to the general limitations inherent to the 'official story' approach. Nonetheless, Webb and Keith are able to paint a relatively coherent picture with the data at their disposal, concluding that the average European party employs approximately 43 people in its central office (0.12 employees per 1,000 party members) and around 26 people in parliament (2 employees per MP).

In terms of longitudinal developments, Luciano Bardi and colleagues (2017) use the same database to show that the total number of salaried staff working in party headquarters has increased by more than 21 per cent since 1970 but has declined a little since 1990. On the other hand, a huge increase in parliamentary staff can be observed during the same period. In 1970, the average European party had seven people working full-time in parliament. In 1990, that figure had risen by 200 per cent to 21. In 2010, the average number of salaried staff was 22. Overall, it therefore seems fair to conclude that the staff/membership ratio is developing in a direction that clearly favours staff over members and parliament over central office. Hence, the cartel party thesis seems confirmed once more by the most recent numbers available. The following chapter explores whether this trend also applies to the three movement parties, and what that might say about the parties and their institutional context.

Income and spending

The rapid decline in memberships that most parties experienced during the 1970s and 1980s presented them with a thorny problem, since the loss of members curbed the parties' ability to engage voters at a grassroots level through voluntary activism and diminished their most important source of income: membership subscriptions. As we saw in Chapter 4, this caused especially large centrist parties to turn to the state for resources, thereby forging a cartel-like relationship between the two. However compelling this explanation is, it lacks nuance and overlooks other ways in which parties can acquire resources without relying on membership subscriptions. At least, this is the argument advanced by Jonathan Hopkin (2004) in an article that delineates three additional strategies that parties have historically employed as a response to the loss of membership-driven income. The first is the 'clientelistic mass party'. It represents a situation where a party attempts to boost its membership base by offering members 'selective incentives' (a term borrowed from Panebianco) such as jobs or welfare benefits on behalf of the state. According to Hopkin, this strategy is most prevalent in countries with an underdeveloped state bureaucracy 'susceptible to party infiltration' (Hopkin, 2004: 632). The second strategy is the 'externally financed elite party', and the name is rather revealing. This represents a situation where an external donor supplies the party with funds in return for certain policies. Although relatively prevalent around the world, the US system is particularly suited to such relationships between party elites and 'super PACs'. The third strategy is the 'self-financing elite party', and it signifies a situation akin to the one just described, but where the main donor is an insider rather than an outsider. Unsurprisingly, this strategy is primarily employed by business firm parties. (For an even more nuanced review of funding strategies, see Scarrow, 2007.)

The very existence of these non-cartelization strategies reveals that not all parties rely exclusively nor even primarily on public funding. Some parties are funded by external donors, others by internal donors. Most European parties, however, do receive a substantial promotion of their income from the state (Falguera et al, 2014), with British and Swiss parties as the possible exception. Drawing on data from the PPDB project, Ingrid van Biezen and Petr Kopecký (2017: 87) provide an overview of the sources of income that parties in European countries generally rely on, noting that 'in the majority of countries, the relative importance of state subsidies to the total party income is clearly quite pronounced'. For instance, while the average European party receives approximately 56 per cent of its income from the state, in countries such as Hungary and Spain, that figure is almost 80 per cent. In other countries, private donations account for a much larger share of the overall income. Parties in the UK, for instance, receive 44 per cent of their financial resources from private donations. Surprisingly perhaps, in a strong welfare state like Denmark, that figure is 38 per cent (but unlike the UK, state subsidies are still relatively large in the Danish context). Finally, in countries including the Netherlands and Germany, parties primarily rely on membership fees. Table 6.2 represents a simplified version of that supplied by van Biezen and Kopecký, which focuses on a limited number of countries. The highest number in each category is in bold.

The PPDB project also contains information about the financial strength of parties across a number of European countries. Webb and Keith (2017) summarize the most important findings and provide an overview of income and spending at a country-specific level. In terms of overall income, the authors find that parties in countries such as France and Germany are much better off than parties in countries such as Belgium and Portugal. While the former have an average income of approximately €60,000,000, the latter only have around €5,000,000 at their disposal. One caveat here is, of course, that these numbers reflect the size of the economy as a whole. This is arguably also why parties in large countries (France, Germany, Spain) are much wealthier than parties in smaller countries (Belgium, Portugal, Israel). As such, if one takes the size of the nation's economy into account, the picture changes substantially. In the category called 'mean party income per billion euros of GDP', parties in Portugal are twice as wealthy as parties in France and Germany. These figures say something about the monetary value attributed to parties in different countries, with Portuguese parties soaking up a relatively large chunk of the country's overall wealth. In fact, Portuguese parties are only surpassed by Spanish and Czech parties when it comes to overall income in relation to the nation's GDP. It is also worth noting that UK parties are among the poorest in all of Europe, especially if

Table 6.2: Parties' income sources at country level

Country	State subsidies	Private donations	Membership fees
Denmark	46.1%	38.0%	10.6%
France	43.6%	23.6%	13.0%
Germany	31.6%	12.3%	41.7%
Hungary	79.3%	9.6%	8.0%
Netherlands	29.2%	1.8%	**42.9%**
Spain	**79.8%**	2.0%	13.5%
UK	11.3%	**44.0%**	14.9%

Note: The highest number in each category is in bold.

Source: Adapted from Van Biezen and Kopecký (2017)

one takes into account the size of the UK economy. In fact, only parties in the Netherlands are less well off in that respect.

Another way of measuring a party's financial resources is by focusing on expenditure. For instance, how much money do parties in different countries typically spend on election campaigns? The cost of participating in campaigns is generally rising each year, leaving smaller parties in a difficult position when it comes to reaching voters and competing for attention. This has led countries such as the UK and France to implement 'campaign spending ceilings' that legally limit how much money a party can spend on election campaigns (Clift and Fisher, 2004). However, as Webb and Keith note, vote-maximizing and office-seeking parties 'will inevitably direct as much of their financial resources as possible (and sometimes more) into paying for electoral efforts', which makes campaign expenditure 'a valid measure of organizational strength' (Webb and Keith, 2017: 38). As such, the authors once again draw on the PPDB project to provide an overview of campaign expenditure across a number of European countries. On the one hand, the level of expenses generally matches the income level, in the sense that parties in Spain and Germany spend the most on election campaigns, while parties in Portugal and Hungary spend much less. On the other hand, a couple of unexpected observations can be made. For instance, parties in the UK are among those with the highest campaign expenditure, which might come as a surprise given their modest income levels. Similarly, although Czech parties are the undisputed top-earners when their income is compared with the size of the national economy, they spend remarkably little on election campaigns. In absolute numbers, they spend 23 times less than Spanish parties (the European top-spenders). When adjusted for the size of the national economy, the figure is even higher (35 times less). This testifies to the importance of taking the national context of parties into account when comparing them on a formal basis, which is precisely what I will try to do in the following chapter.

Participation and representation

A final theme that should be considered when it comes to the comparative perspective is intra-party democracy (IPD); that is, the participatory structure of the parties themselves. The scholarly interest in the ability of parties to structure their own organizations in a democratic manner dates back to the earliest texts on party organization (Ostrogorski, 1902; Michels, 1915; Follett, 1918), which seems logical, given the central role that parties play in making representative democracy work and the historical scepticism of partisanship in general (see Chapter 1). Building on Elmer Eric Schattschneider's (1942: 1) famous and perhaps controversial assertion that representative democracy is 'unthinkable' without political parties, William Cross and Richard Katz (2013: 1) motivate the interest in IPD by saying: '[I]f state-level democracy cannot flourish save for parties, the questions inevitably arise of whether parties themselves must be, should be, and are internally democratic with respect to their own decision-making practices and distributions of authority or influence.'

This quote explains why so many scholars share an interest in exploring the level of organizational democracy within parties and it hints at three approaches to the study of IPD: one that is prescriptive (must be), one that is normative (should be) and one that is descriptive (are). The answer to the first issue is relatively straightforward: representative democracy, understood as a system of government that relies on regular elections, clearly works in the instrumental sense without a high-level of IPD. The second issue is less straightforward: should parties be internally democratic and, if so, what does this mean? While such questions are usually addressed by political theorists working within the field of party research (such as Teorell, 1999; White and Ypi, 2016; Wolkenstein, 2016), some scholars working with the comparative perspective have nonetheless ventured into normative territory. One example is Piero Ignazi's (2020) attempt to establish the basic requirements for IPD proper. Noting that parties *should* be internally democratic, because 'no other alternative [than party organization] is palatable for a democratic competitive setting', Ignazi (2020: 17) suggests four principles that must be in operation for a party to be considered democratic: *inclusion* (membership influence on decision-making processes), *pluralism* (protection of minority views), *deliberation* (reasoned and enlightened debate) and *diffusion* (distribution of decision-making power across organizational layers). While many parties prioritize one or two of these criteria – most often inclusion – they tend to ignore or downplay the others. Only truly democratic organizations prioritize all four principles. (For a more technical discussion of IPD indicators, see von dem Berge and Poguntke, 2017.) In the following chapter, I will use Ignazi's (2020: 9) 'four knights of intra-party democracy' to assess the level of internal democracy within Alternativet, Podemos and the Icelandic Pirate Party.

Despite such normative assessments, the vast majority of studies of IPD within the comparative perspective approach the theme in a descriptive manner, in an attempt to answer the questions: *are* political parties democratic, and are *some* parties in *some* regions typically more democratic than others? While some researchers compare parties in a temporal register, exploring how parties evolve in time (for example Loxbo, 2011), most accounts of IPD compare different parties in different institutional contexts (for an early example, see Gallagher and Marsh, 1988). One very prominent example of this research interest that has defined the field of IPD research for more than a decade is Reuven Y Hazan and Gideon Rahat's (2010) comprehensive cross-national survey of candidate selection methods. The authors contend that understanding the methods that parties use to select their electoral candidates is vital if we want to get a grip on the way IPD is practised in real life. To this end, they consider four central aspects of candidate selection methods: (1) candidacy – 'Who can be selected as the party's candidate?' – (2) the selectorate – 'Who selects the candidates?' – (3) decentralization – 'Where does selection take place?' – (4) appointment and voting – 'How are the candidates selected?' (Hazan and Rahat, 2010: 18). In terms of candidacy, the authors distinguish between 'inclusive' parties that allow all citizens to enter the race to become candidates and 'exclusive' parties that only allow certain party members, such as those of a certain age and seniority, to run.

The same distinction applies to the selectorate. Inclusive parties allow all voters to participate in candidate selection processes. Exclusive parties are those where only the leader(ship) decides. In terms of decentralization, the authors develop a vocabulary that resembles Duverger's (1954) when distinguishing between 'social' decentralization (for example when certain demographic groups based on gender or occupation are secured representation) and 'territorial' decentralization (such as when local branches are allowed to nominate candidates). Finally, Hazan and Rahat distinguish between voting and appointment systems. In short, candidates are selected through a voting system if the candidate's votes 'are the sole determinant of their candidacy' and if the voting results are 'used to justify and legitimize the candidacy' (Hazan and Rahat, 2010: 72). If one or both of these requirements are not fulfilled, the selection method is characterized as a matter of appointment. In the following chapter, I will use these four dimensions to chart the process of candidate selection in the three movement parties.

Another interesting example of a descriptive IPD study is Niklas Bolin and colleagues (2017) who, on the basis of information from the Political Party Database, set out to assess the level of IPD across 122 cases of Western parties. They begin by distinguishing between two fundamental types of internal democracy: 'plebiscitary IPD', where policy deliberations are separated from the actual decision-making process (often a simple yes/no vote), and 'assembly-based IPD', where the decision-making process includes an element of deliberation. The main difference is that, in the latter case, 'the act of voting on a proposal is preceded by an exchange of arguments and, normally, by the possibility to amend the proposal' (Bolin et al, 2017: 161). Although a few parties adhere to a restricted version of IPD based on plebiscites, most allow for some level of deliberation prior to the actual decision-making. The Dutch Party for the Animals (a small green party) exhibits the highest level of assembly-based IPD, while the Italian Northern League (a large right-wing party) displays the lowest level. In fact, these two parties illustrate a more general tendency: that green parties are the most democratic 'party family', while right-wing parties are the least democratic. Surprisingly, perhaps, left socialist parties are typically less democratic than liberal parties and social democrats.

In terms of institutional contexts, Bolin and colleagues (2017: 171) find that 'differences between countries explain more of the variance in levels of AIPD [assembly-based IPD] than differences between party families'. Countries such as the UK, Ireland, Norway and the Netherlands score highest when it comes to IPD, while Spain, France, Italy and Austria score lowest. In some countries, however, there are considerable variations. In Denmark, for instance, the authors find some parties to be very democratic, while others are very oligarchic. In fact, the Red-Green Alliance is in the global top 10 per cent, but the Danish Social Democrats are shown to be the second-least democratic party of all cases in the sample. One variable that significantly influences the level of IPD is the existence of party laws, since such laws tend to impose demands for membership participation on parties (van Biezen and Piccio, 2013). As Bolin et al (2017: 174) note, 'legally binding requirements are indeed an effective way of promoting IPD'. Another significant factor that explains high levels of IPD is high levels of political trust. When citizens trust government institutions and politicians, they presumably also register for political parties and demand influence on decision-making processes, but, as the authors note, the causality could also run in the opposite direction. Furthermore, GDP per capita likewise seems to constitute a significant factor when it comes to predictions of IPD, in the sense that wealthy countries tend to harbour democratic parties; again, one could speculate about the direction of causality. Finally, a couple of party-level factors are shown to be important. Parties with large membership bases generally display lower levels of IPD, while parties with left-leaning ideologies tend to be more democratic than others. Although the former might seem to confirm Michels' (1915) iron law of oligarchy, other factors, such as party age and government experience, which are shown to be insignificant predictors, refute the irreversibility of his thesis.

New trends within the comparative perspective

In a recent review article, Anika Gauja and Karina Kosiara-Pedersen (2021a: 36) discuss what they perceive to be the 'newest trends in party organization research'. In particular, they focus on three novel themes that concern contemporary party scholars: (1) the 'personalization' of party politics, (2) the rise of movement parties, and (3) the alteration of party affiliation. Interestingly, all three themes somehow challenge the conventional understanding of political parties as demarcated entities with clearly defined boundaries. I will go on to briefly consider each of these themes, focusing on the challenges they present to the comparative perspective and the research strategies usually employed within this perspective.

The personalization of politics is a theme that is typically discussed by social movement scholars and researchers working with political participation in relation to digital media. Personalization can be described as a process in which people engage with political issues individually instead of joining forces with others in trade unions, social movements or political parties (Bennett and Segerberg, 2011). While this trend may be described as an integral part of a postmodern and neoliberal society predicated on individuation (Beck and Beck-Gernsheim, 2002), personalization has certainly been intensified and accentuated by the rise of social media, with platforms like Facebook and Twitter affording a shift in political activity from a 'logic of collective action' to a 'logic of connective action' (Bennett and Segerberg, 2012). In party organization studies, the notion of personalization is often linked to a process of 'presidentialization', understood as a 'process by which regimes [political systems] are becoming more presidential in their actual practice without, in most cases, changing their formal structure' (Poguntke and Webb, 2005: 1). Given its informal character, presidentialization can take many forms. In party organizations, however, it usually means that the leader(ship) becomes more prominent at the expense of ordinary members and mid-level candidates. In 'presidential' parties, the leader is relatively unaccountable to the party with respect to policies, campaigns, appointments and so on. The level of presidentialization varies from one country to another, given the impact of constitutional structures on such processes (Samuels and Shugart, 2010), but the party's own organizational structures have been found to play a significant role as well. According to Gianluca Passarelli (2015), the 'genetic' features highlighted by Panebianco (1988) – the relationship between core and periphery, the possible existence of a financial sponsor and the level of charismatic leadership – are particularly important in terms of curbing or accentuating the process presidentialization.

The rise of (digital) movement parties in Europe and Latin America has also caught the attention of several scholars working within the comparative perspective (including della Porta et al, 2017; Anria, 2019; Gerbaudo,

2019). In a sense, the following chapter is an attempt to add another layer to this growing research interest. Chapter 4 discussed the main properties of movement parties, defined by Herbert Kitschelt (2006: 280) as 'coalitions of political activists who emanate from social movements and try to apply the organizational and strategic practices of social movements in the arena of party competition'. In Kitschelt's view, movement parties are characterized as relatively structureless organizations that lack methods for aggregating interests and engage in both parliamentarian and extra-parliamentarian activities. Based on the cases of Alternativet and Podemos, I argued that only the latter properly characterizes present-day movement parties, although there is clearly something to be said about the problems associated with structurelessness in such formations. While contemporary movement parties are much more aware about the importance of formal structures, the advent of digital technology has provided them with extraordinary means for aggregating interests in an instant and accurate fashion. In that sense, movement parties might be best characterized as 'hybrid' entities (Chironi and Fittipaldi, 2017) that attempt to strike a balance between the horizontality of social movements and the verticality of parties, while dealing with the difficult dilemmas that emerge from this ambition (della Porta et al, 2017).

The final trend that Gauja and Kosiara-Pedersen observe is the general alternation of party affiliation, which may be seen as a consequence of the two former trends. Within the last decade, several comparative scholars have begun to explore new ways that citizens relate to political parties, and what that might mean for our understanding of party membership in general (for example Bale et al, 2019). As Gauja (2015) notes, several parties now offer citizens different modes of affiliation. The Conservatives in the UK, for instance, allow people to join the party in three ways: as a 'Friend', 'Member' or 'Donor' (Gauja, 2015: 243). Similarly, as we saw in Chapter 5, Alternativet allows citizens to tailor their membership to individual preferences, with fees varying from approximately €2.50 per month to approximately €80 per month. However, some parties have stopped recruiting rank and file altogether. The Dutch Freedom Party, headed by Geert Wilders, operates entirely without ordinary members, while Nigel Farage's Brexit Party (now called Reform UK) relies solely on online support. This has given rise to criticism regarding the lack of organizational and political rights enjoyed by online supporters who donate money to the party without becoming members. However, the overall trend is clear. Parties are increasingly abandoning traditional models of party membership, based on demographic groups and fixed subscriptions, in favour of individualized modes of affiliation that cater to electoral markets rather than predefined social segments related to class, gender, or geography. As Susan Scarrow (2015: 206) explains:

The new partisan models define organizational aims in terms of accountability to electoral markets. They prioritize the mobilization of individuals, not of self-identified social groups. In this new environment, parties are experimenting with ways to boost loyalty and partisan interest among key supporters, including, but not limited to, traditional party members. These initiatives may create new conflicts within party organizations, not least because the new forms of affiliation are often layered on top of traditional membership structures.

Picking up on the last part of this quote, we might also ask how these new modes of party affiliation challenge core assumptions within the comparative perspective. At the very least, they raise some thorny questions about how to properly measure and analyse developments in party membership. Gauja (2015: 244) suggests that 'party member surveys will need to move away from formal, state-based conceptions of membership, and incorporate ... individual perceptions and organisational adaptations of membership'. This ambition not only represents a break with the theoretical categories employed in comparative research on party membership, it also constitutes a challenge to the methodological principles that this perspective typically relies on. Most importantly, how is it possible to supplement the 'official story' approach that has dominated comparative research for decades with alternative data sources that allow us to interrogate changes in 'individual perceptions and organizational adaptations of membership'? Will this push comparative scholars to abandon their somewhat stubborn resistance to unofficial and qualitative data? The jury is still out, but it certainly seems like the official story has reached its limits.

Comparative contributions to organization studies

Unlike party research, organization and management studies are rarely comparative. While the vast majority of party scholars today prefer to explore organizational developments across cultural and institutional contexts based on large-n samples, contemporary organization scholars typically immerse themselves in single (or perhaps a few) cases. There are, of course, exceptions and specialized subfields are dedicated to comparative organizational research (such as Peterson and Søndergaard, 2011; Hotho and Saka-Helmhout, 2017). However, such subfields have been characterized as suffering from 'an excess of simple empirical reportage' as well as 'weak' theory building (Redding, 1994: 323) and they do indeed represent exceptions to the rule that the most influential organization studies typically prioritize depth over width and quality over quantity (Stablein, 2003). This is, at least, the case in the European context.

It was not always like that. In fact, many classical organization and management studies were comparative and derived their legitimacy precisely from analysing organizational characteristics across a large number of cases. Examples include Fredrick Herzberg and colleagues' (1959) account of job satisfaction, Joan Woodward's (1965) work on the structuring role of production technology in industrial organizations, Paul Lawrence and Jay Lorsch's (1967) study of differentiation and integration in complex organizations and Geert Hofstede's (1980) study of the relationship between national cultures and work-related values. In fact, the whole premise of classical research traditions like contingency theory and – to some extent – neo-institutional theory could be said to rest on the perceived value of comparisons. One way to look for insights about the importance of systematic comparisons, formal data and large-n case samples is thus to revisit some of these contributions and contemplate their methodological dispositions, but, given that this book represents an attempt to introduce organization scholars to party research, it might be more rewarding to look at party-specific justifications for employing a comparative perspective and then reflect upon these.

In another recent paper, Gauja and Kosiara-Pedersen (2021b) discuss the current state of party research and offer a number of important observations about the hegemony of 'the official story' and the almost exclusive focus on quantifiable data. The authors' main argument is that the turn away from inductive reasoning, qualitative research and theory building and towards a more 'heterogeneous, specialized and quantified' type of research has (Gauja and Kosiara-Pedersen, 2021b: 124):

> enabled party scholarship to find impact and relevance through the provision of technical advice to parties and policymakers. On this basis, scholars are able to affect how parties organize and provide the essential linkage between people and elected representatives. However, while political party researchers have been able to engage audiences outside academia with this specialized and technical advice, the sub-discipline has shifted away from some of the 'bigger picture', normative questions surrounding the role of parties in modern representative democracies.

In other words, the research strategies that undergird the comparative perspective have allowed party scholars to become more relevant in the eyes of practitioners and policy makers, thereby strengthening the real-world impact of their findings. However, this hard-won impact comes at a price, in this case a diminished focus on theory building and normativity, both of which are virtues clearly associated with the classical perspective – normativity – and the configurational perspective – theory building – as well as organization and management studies – in particular, subfields such as critical management studies.

The impact agenda also permeates organization and management studies. Here, however, the notion of impact seems to translate into a focus on journal metrics and citations rather than public dissemination and policy advice (deGama et al, 2019). This myopic focus on institutionalized indicators of impact has yielded a number of critical responses from authors, voicing calls for organization scholars to start 'writing differently' (Pullen et al, 2020), and it has led to fierce debates within organization and management studies about how best to engage with practitioners. One such debate arose a decade ago under the heading 'critical performativity'. It began when André Spicer and colleagues (2009) published an article in which they problematize the 'oppositional' attitude that has characterized critical management studies for many years. In their view, organization scholars are too content with a non- or anti-performative research strategy that allows them to critique existing power structures and practices without getting their hands dirty, since one of the primary objectives of such research is to create knowledge that is not instrumental, in the sense that it cannot be inscribed in means–end calculations (see Fournier and Grey, 2000). In contrast, the authors argue for a more engaged and 'useful' type of research that 'involves active and subversive intervention into managerial discourses and practices' (Spicer et al, 2009: 538). Instead of being anti-performative, they encourage organization scholars to be *more* performative; to find a way of strengthening the practical impact of their research.

The call for critically performative research was immediately met by harsh critique from many 'critical' organization scholars. While some focused on what they perceived as a desperate and corrupting pursuit of 'relevance' (Spoelstra and Svensson, 2015), others pointed to the uncontrollability of research and the unlikeliness of performativity actually succeeding (Fleming and Banerjee, 2016; Knudsen, 2017). Some also deconstructed the theoretical foundation of critical performativity as a concept and questioned the somewhat exclusive focus on managers as agents of change (Cabantous et al, 2016), while others suggested that only particular organizations should qualify as worthy of critical intervention (Parker and Parker, 2017). In the end, these critical responses to the idea of a new research agenda led Spicer and colleagues (2016) to specify their argument and sketch out a path forward. Their idea was to abandon the fierce 'intra-academic debates' and 'theoretical policing' that characterize some strands of organization studies and focus instead on issues of public importance that matter to non-academic groups. In particular, they advocate an approach to issues selection that prioritizes questions seen as 'important or pressing for constituents that are beyond their own narrow disciplinary debates', regardless of the fact that 'these may be relevant to a fairly narrow public – such as a locality, a particular occupational field, an industry, a union or a particular organization' (Spicer et al, 2016: 234).

For a project that explicitly rejects overly abstract theorizing, the authors' practical advice for maximizing such real-life relevance is, ironically, to engage in a type of 'dialectical reasoning' that explores 'tensions between two opposite concepts' without necessarily resolving them (Spicer et al, 2016: 235). Here, one could be excused for wondering whether practitioners actually care about dialectical reasoning and inter-conceptual tensions. It seems fair to assume that few do. As such, one might argue that organization scholars committed to the critical performativity agenda could learn something from comparative party research and its approach to the notion of impact. There are, in my view, at least three elements that make comparative studies of political parties relevant to practitioners working in or with party organizations.

First, the themes that comparative party scholars find interesting often overlap with themes that party practitioners find interesting. This chapter has outlined three main research themes: membership, finance and intra-party democracy. All of these are clearly matters of concern for people working in parties, given their importance for the proper functioning of such organizations (Scarrow et al, 2017). Gauja and Kosiara-Pedersen (2021b: 130) note: 'Political parties themselves are very well aware of the changing conditions in which they work and see how the conditions for e.g., financing, membership and candidate recruitment changes.' In that sense, party scholars inadvertently heed Spicer and colleagues' (2016) call for research that addresses issues of public concern by focusing on what actually matters to those they study.

Unlike party researchers, however, organization scholars (including myself) often prioritize issues that are too complex and esoteric for practitioners to genuinely care about. In the words of Signe Vikkelsø (2014: 418), organization scholars 'are increasingly preoccupied with general theoretical, or philosophical, starting points, their mutual incompatibility or combinatory potentials and their analytical freshness; and less interested in the practical relevance and usefulness of the empirical analyses they bring about'. This is perhaps why so relatively few organization scholars, compared with party researchers, are called upon by governments, companies, NGOs, think tanks or the media to address what Spicer calls 'substantive questions' of public concern (Spicer, 2014: 724). As a remedy for this lack of relevance, Vikkelsø advocates a return to the notions of 'task' and 'purpose' as primary research interests for organization scholars. This would, in her view, lead organization scholars to address questions of practical relevance. How does the organization currently handle its task? What are the challenges? What solutions have been tried? How did they work? For whom? What are the costs? Who is to pay for them? And so on. Interestingly, these are precisely some of the core questions guiding the comparative perspective on political parties.

Second, the focus on quantification makes it easy for practitioners to comprehend empirical insights because numbers lend themselves more easily to generalizations (Justesen and Mik-Meyer, 2012). It is, of course, true that many important things are 'beyond measure' and that quantifications always rest on simplifications that naturalize otherwise contingent matters (Butler et al, 2020), but numbers do offer an easy way of getting a message across and stimulating action (Mazmanian and Beckman, 2018). If critical organization scholars truly want to be relevant and subvert managerial discourses and practices, quantification is perhaps one – overlooked – tool that could be utilized for both academic and activist reasons.

Numbers alone are rarely enough, however. After all, what makes the comparative perspective unique is the comparisons. It is interesting to trace organizational developments over time, such as how membership has declined in a particular party, but comparisons help relativize these changes. Is a particular development unusual or common? Does it constitute a paradigmatic example or perhaps a black swan? What contingency factors might help us understand it, and what type of action does it call for? Such questions will often be of great interest to practitioners, not only those working with political parties but those working with organizations in general (see Caiden, 1989). To answer them, however, researchers need a great deal of data – or, rather, data from different contexts. Such data is not easy to generate. It requires time, skills, and access, perhaps especially when working with parties. Collating the data included in the next chapter, for instance, took more than a full year. This is why party researchers often establish cross-national research teams and share data on open-access platforms. The aforementioned PPDB project is one example; others include: the Manifesto Project (a database that contains political programmes from more than 1,000 parties in more than 50 countries), the MAPP Project (a database with membership statistics from parties in 32 countries), the ParlGov Project (a database of election data about approximately 1,700 parties, 1,000 elections and 1,600 cabinets) and the PartyFacts Project (a website that links different types of party-related dataset). Imagine what could be achieved if organization scholars collaborated in this fashion, compiling comparable data from similar organizations in different contexts. New findings would surely be generated, and another level of real-life impact would quite possibly be realized.

7

Alternativet in Comparative Perspective

Introduction

The previous chapter unfolded the comparative perspective on party organization, based primarily on the conceptual framework of Angelo Panebianco (1988) and a wide variety of empirical studies of political parties in Western democracies (including Katz and Mair, 1994; Müller and Strøm, 1999; Scarrow et al, 2017). This perspective has a dual focus on the structural characteristics of political parties and the institutional environments in which they operate, but the overall ambition is always to draw out conclusions based on cross-contextual comparisons. There are no limits to what can be compared, but five themes tend to recur: genetic models (decision made in the party's past), environmental factors (party systems in particular), popular support (voters and members), finances (income and spending) and levels of intra-party democracy (membership participation and rules for candidate selection). Empirically, the comparative perspective relies heavily on what has become known as 'the official story', understood as authorized material produced by the parties themselves (see Katz and Mair, 1992; Scarrow et al, 2017). Scholars working with the comparative perspective almost exclusively focus on official sources of information such as manifestos, statutes, budgets and membership statistics, based on the premise that information derived from such sources constitutes an 'incomparable source of reasonably hard data that can be used in the analysis of party organization across both time and space' (Katz and Mair, 1992: 8). If no official information is available, scholars working with the comparative perspective tend to rely on expert statements (Scarrow and Webb, 2017).

This chapter compares Alternativet with two relatively similar parties in relation to the five themes just mentioned, based on official material produced by the parties themselves, as well as several secondary sources such as journal articles and expert statements from researchers who have studied the parties in question.[1] The two additional parties are the Spanish party Podemos and the Icelandic Pirate Party (also called Píratar). The main reason for choosing these two is that they can be characterized as European movement parties in the sense that they consistently try to transfer the organizational principles of social movements to the electoral arena (della Porta et al, 2017). Additional reasons are that all three parties were founded within a period of under two years and they have all experienced a trajectory of rapid success followed by rapid decline. A final reason is that the three parties operate in fairly different institutional environments. While Podemos exists in a historically stable and essentially hostile electoral system, Píratar inhabits a very liberal and surprisingly turbulent environment. By comparing Alternativet with these two parties, it will be possible to see more clearly the contingent nature of the party's organizational set-up.

I begin by recounting the origin story of the three parties, highlighting the intertwined nature of European movement parties in general. I then unfold the genetic models of the three parties and their institutional environments. This leads me to consider developments in popular support, in terms of voters as well as members, going back to the parties' formative phase and moving up to the present. Next, I dig into the financial side of the three parties, outlining developments in income sources and expenditures. Finally, I explore the level of intra-party democracy in each case, focusing on the four elements spelled out in the previous chapter. I close the chapter by drawing a handful of conclusions across the different sub-analyses, concluding that Alternativet could learn something from both Podemos and Píratar in terms of maintaining popular support and achieving political impact.

A brief history of three European movement parties

Social movement scholars often talk about three 'waves of protest' that, since the late 1990s, have washed over large parts of the world (for example Funke and Wolfson, 2017). What connects the three waves is their anti-establishment character, their claim to universal representation of 'the people' and their reliance on digital technology for mobilization and coordination purposes (Gerbaudo, 2012). The first wave is usually associated with the Global Justice Movement – or the 'movement of movements' – which emerged from the 1999 World Trade Organization (WTO) protests in Seattle and morphed into a global network of interrelated groups united around events such as the World Social Forums and the Global Days of Action (della Porta, 2007). The second wave is represented by the many 'square protests' that arose in the aftermath of the financial crisis in 2008 and 2009 such as the Arab Spring, Occupy Wall Street, and the 15M movement in Spain (Prentoulis and Thomassen, 2013). These movements all followed a logic of occupation, in which the amalgamation of physical bodies in high-profile city squares was seen as an expression of resistance to the powers that be. These movements hardly ever articulated specific political demands, since their physical presence *was* the demand and because their claim to represent 'the people' or 'the 99%' was too universal to be translated into particularized demands for change (Husted and Hansen, 2017).

The no-demand tactics employed by the Global Justice Movement and the square movements failed to result in serious social change. Although the Arab Spring successfully sparked progressive change in Tunisia, most other countries experienced considerable backlashes in terms of human rights, civil liberties and youth employment in the wake of the protests (Robinson and Merrow, 2020). Similarly, Occupy Wall Street appears to have had 'little assessable impact' on electoral politics, except for a few unauthorized co-optations by politicians such as Al Gore and Nancy Pelosi (Malone and Fredericks, 2013). This lack of impact understandably frustrated some movement actors. For instance, co-initiator of Occupy Wall Street, Micah White (2016: 38), has characterized the movement's refusal to articulate demands as a 'naïve mistake' and called for new progressive initiatives to target state institutions once again (see also Dean, 2016). Such frustration paved the way for the third wave of protests. This wave is associated with a range of movement parties, including Podemos in Spain, Movimento 5 Stelle in Italy and Syriza in Greece, that all seek to transfer the organizing principles of previous protests to electoral politics (della Porta et al, 2017). To understand the many European movement parties that emerged in the years following the fall of the square protests is thus to take their organizational and political legacy into account.

Píratar

The three political parties analysed in this chapter were all founded during the course of only 15 months, from late 2012 to early 2014, but one of them has a somewhat longer history. The first Pirate Party was established in Sweden in 2006 by a software engineer called Rick Falkvinge as a prank reaction to the judicial takedown of the file-sharing website Pirate Bay. However, the party quickly matured into an international coalition of parties focused on much more than just internet freedom and copyright laws. The Swedish party's first major achievement came in 2009 when, perhaps as a reaction to the imprisonment of the founder of Pirate Bay, it quadrupled its membership base and earned more than 7 per cent of the votes in the European elections, thus gaining two seats in the European parliament (Almqvist, 2016). The international success of the pirates was further confirmed when the German Pirate Party in 2011 secured almost 9 per cent of the votes in the Berlin regional elections (Ringel, 2019). Since then, national divisions of the International Pirate Party have been established in more than 30 countries across the world, all of them sharing a focus on issues like direct democracy, government transparency, freedom of speech and copyright laws.

The Icelandic chapter of the Pirate Party – Píratar – was founded in November 2012 by poet and politician Birgitta Jónsdóttir with internet activists such as Smári McCarthy. Before establishing Píratar, Jónsdóttir had previously been an MP for the Citizens' Movement (a single-issue party focused on government reform in the wake of the financial crisis). However, towards the end of 2012, Jónsdóttir started to focus exclusively on setting up Píratar, with the aim of competing in the 2013 national elections (Southwell and Pirch, 2021). The pirate project was different from some of the other initiatives Jónsdóttir was involved in because, she claimed, it would not revolve around her as a person (Tulinius, 2012). Instead, Píratar would be based on collective leadership, and internal decision-making processes would be anchored in principles of direct – digital – democracy, meaning that 'every policy proposal, elected position within the party, and party primaries before local and general elections are decided by an online vote, in which every party member can participate' (Ómardóttir and Valgarðsson, 2020: 847). At the 2013 elections, Píratar secured 5.1 per cent of the votes, thereby winning three seats in the Icelandic parliament (Althingi) in constituencies in and around Reykjavik. The party's vote share almost tripled in 2016, resulting in ten Althingi seats, although Píratar actually polled over 40 per cent around the infamous 'Panama papers' leak, just six months before the elections. This impressive result meant that Píratar became 'something of a poster child for the international pirate movement' (Sigurdarson, 2021: 145) and that proponents of 'digital parties' increasingly looked to Iceland for inspiration (Gerbaudo, 2019). However, success was short lived, as the party lost four seats in the premature 2017 elections, but it has since managed to maintain six seats in parliament.

Alternativet

One month after Píratar first entered the Icelandic parliament, Uffe Elbæk and Josephine Fock launched Alternativet in Denmark. Since much of this book has already been dedicated to unfolding the party's genesis (see Chapters 3 and 5), I will simply say a few things about the relationship between Píratar and Alternativet. Although few formal links presumably exist between the two parties, it is safe to say that Elbæk and his collaborators were inspired by the Icelandic experiment. For instance, the official spokesperson for the Danish Pirate Party (a very small organization that does not compete in elections) was heavily involved in establishing Alternativet, and he eventually decided to leave the pirates and run for parliament as an official Alternativet candidate (he maintained his pirate identity and sometimes campaigned dressed as a pirate). Moreover, in Elbæk's (2018a) manifesto *The Next Denmark* (see Chapter 3), he explicitly mentions Píratar's groundbreaking idea of adding interest rates to natural resources, which testifies to the inspirational relationship that exists between the two parties. Jónsdóttir has likewise stated that Píratar is inspired by Alternativet in their attempt to increase the level of intra-party democracy. As she notes: 'We often compare ourselves to Alternativet in Denmark. I think the energy there is around Alternativet, and their focus on involving citizens, is very similar to us' (Knudsen, 2016: np).

Podemos

That said, Southern Europe was always a more significant source inspiration for the founders of Alternativet (see Alternativet, 2016c). Although the party was formally launched a few months before Podemos, political projects like Syriza and Movimento 5 Stelle figured prominently in internal debates within Alternativet during its first years of existence (the latter more than the former, given Syriza's explicit left-wing stance). But once Podemos was established, ties between Denmark and Spain started to emerge, with representatives from both parties visiting each other and sharing ideas for how to re-articulate the progressive agenda in 21st century Europe. Representatives from Alternativet were particularly infatuated with Podemos' use of digital tools such as AppGree and Agora to increase the level of membership involvement in decision-making processes, but were less easy about the strong antagonistic discourse that representatives from Podemos initially employed as well as their unapologetic claim to be a 'populist' party (see Errejón and Mouffe, 2016).

Podemos was established in January 2014 as an attempt to unite the many disparate voices that emerged from the famous anti-austerity and pro-democracy movement known as 15M. It was not intended as a political party – in fact, the initial manifesto called *Making a Move* explicitly rejects the party as a viable organizational template – but the project nonetheless morphed into a formal party organization within the span of merely four months. This curious turn of events has led scholars like Cristina Flesher Fominaya (2020: 222) to characterize Podemos as an 'unintended consequence' of 15M. Ironically, one of the main slogans used by members of the 15M movement was *No nos representan* (They don't represent us), and it was employed precisely to distance the movement from representative institutions such as political parties (Antentas, 2022). Nonetheless, after a comprehensive participatory process, the first Citizen Assembly (known as Vistalegre 1) decided to establish Podemos organizationally as a political party and elected a political science professor called Pablo Iglesias as its secretary general with almost 90 per cent of the votes.

Prior to the first Citizen Assembly, Podemos competed in the 2014 European elections and won a surprising 8 per cent of the Spanish votes. Iglesias was one of five Podemos candidates to enter the European parliament, but he resigned his seat a year later to focus on the 2015 national elections in Spain. Here, Podemos achieved one of the most impressive results in contemporary Spanish politics by winning no less than 20.7 per cent of the votes and 65 seats in parliament, with particularly strong support from electoral districts around Barcelona and Bilbao. Partly because of Podemos' success, none of the traditional parties managed to secure a majority, which created an extremely fragmented situation that eventually resulted in a repeat election just six months later. In the meantime, Podemos decided to forge an alliance with several left-wing parties, including the United Left, under the name Unidos Podemos (meaning United We Can). At the 2016 national elections, Unidos Podemos increased its vote share by almost three percentage points, thereby gaining a total of 71 seats. This gave the alliance an important seat at the table, but it was presumably not enough to enter a governmental coalition. At the 2019 elections, the alliance changed its name to the feminine Unidas Podemos, to indicate its commitment to the feminist agenda, but ultimately lost 29 parliamentary seats. Once again, no party succeeded in forming a government, and repeat elections were once again announced. Although Unidas Podemos lost seven additional seats at the second 2019 election, reducing its total to 35, it nonetheless managed to form Spain's first coalition government with the Spanish Workers' Party (PSOE). Iglesias was appointed deputy prime minister and minister of social rights, while Irene Montero (who happened to be Iglesias' wife) was made minister of equality.

Podemos' success in the 2015 elections, and its subsequent decision to enter an electoral alliance and later a governmental coalition, arguably marks the height of the contemporary European movement party era, perhaps only surpassed by Movimento 5 Stelle's impressive win at the 2018 elections in Italy. While support for most European movement parties has declined in recent years, Podemos has nonetheless managed to translate the powerful political energy invested in the 'third wave of protest' into tangible political results. In particular, the party has been heavily involved in securing major health-care investments and guaranteeing better rights for women. The following sections compare internal and external contingencies in relation to the three parties to say something about the conditions for this achievement, and whether it might be possible for other movement parties to achieve what they have managed to do in their respective countries.

Genetic models and institutional environments

In this section, I will analyse the relationship between the 'genetic models' of the three parties and their institutional environments. To this end,

I will use the analytical strategy outlined by Panebianco (1988) but focus predominantly on environmental conditions. So, I will refrain from engaging in a comprehensive analysis of the administrative structure of Podemos and Píratar, but will briefly consider the elements that Panebianco highlights as important in terms of assessing the genetic models of political parties in general: (1) the relationship between core and periphery, (2) the possible existence of an external sponsor, and (3) the level of charismatic leadership. In terms of the environmental conditions, I will likewise use Panebianco's own points of observation: (1) the level of environmental complexity, (2) the level of environmental stability, and (3) the level of environmental hostility.

Alternativet

As highlighted in the previous chapter, Panebianco approaches the question of internal factors in a somewhat unique fashion. Panebianco's idea is to focus on the 'genetic model', which refers to a political party's original organizational set-up, but this approach deviates tremendously from the way that someone like Duverger describes the 'anatomy' of party organizations (see Chapter 4). As pointed out by Anria (2019), the genetic model can be thought of as a 'historical cause' – as something that relates to the party's past – whereas the environmental factors can be thought of as a set of 'constant causes' that continuously change and force the party to adapt.

First, in the case of Alternativet, the relationship between core and periphery is clearly characterized by what Panebianco (1988: 50) calls 'territorial penetration' (rather than 'territorial diffusion'). The party initially emerged and grew as a result of the national party establishing local branches across Denmark. As explained in Chapter 3, Alternativet was officially launched at a press conference in the Danish parliament, and regional chapters were then later established as a way of enrolling members and engaging them in the process of developing the party's first political programme. One might argue that some kind of spontaneous germination took place in the years and months leading up to the launch, with different activists meeting and discussing the possibility of joining forces, but the formal birth of the party was a centralized act of creation.

Second, Chapter 5 briefly considered the role of external sponsors in Alternativet, including one particular donor, philanthropist and businessperson Ross Jackson, who donated several hundred thousand euros to the party in its first years of existence. However, as we shall see, Alternativet's primary source of income derives from state subsidies and membership subscriptions. As a large donor, Jackson clearly endowed the project with some level of organizational stability and external legitimacy, but, given his lack of high-profile status in the Danish public sphere and the one-off nature of his donations, it is safe to say that Alternativet is predominantly characterized by internal legitimation. Alternativet has also collaborated with NGOs such as Amnesty International, ActionAid Denmark and the British pressure group Compass, but they too remain marginal in terms of the party's overall legitimation to constitute proper 'sponsors' in Panebianco's sense of the word. This means that the party's overall 'license to operate' primarily derives from principles and practices conceived by members of the organization itself.

Third, when it comes to the level of charismatic leadership, it seems fair to conclude that Alternativet owes a lot to its co-founder Uffe Elbæk, who served as minister of culture in Denmark for a short period prior to the launch of the party. When the news broke in late 2013 that a new political party was being launched, the headlines read 'Uffe Elbæk establishes a new party', 'Elbæk returns with a new party', 'Elbæk's new party intends to challenge the culture in parliament' and so on. This indicates that, from the outset, the identity of the party was closely connected to Elbæk as a person. Numerous interview respondents for my own studies similarly acknowledge that Elbæk's reputation as a creative and innovative politician was one of the main reasons for joining the party. Furthermore, when Elbæk eventually decided to leave the party in 2020, Alternativet immediately experienced a drop in the opinion polls, and even more members discontinued their subscriptions as a consequence. In many ways, Elbæk personified Alternativet from 2013 to 2020. He was the face of the party, and many looked to him for direction when things turned sour in the wake of the 2017 local elections. As such, the level of charismatic leadership is easily characterized as relatively high during those years, but it has since decreased significantly as other people have assumed the role of political leader.

Turning to Alternativet's external conditions, we might say that the party operates in a *simple* and *stable* environment. Denmark is a small and homogenous country where significant political shifts are rare (Green-Pedersen and Kosiara-Pedersen, 2020). Electoral turnout is generally high (Hansen, 2020), and the range of political themes in election campaigns are typically limited to a few main issues such as economy, health and, more recently, immigration (for example Mansø and Svendsen, 2022). This makes election processes relatively predictable, and parties can therefore easily position themselves in political debates without having to prepare for sudden institutional jolts. Some parties are furthermore seen as 'owning' certain issues (Hjorth, 2017), and voter movements usually take place at the centre of the political spectrum, which once again stabilizes the electoral process (Lolle and Borre, 2007).

These environmental conditions might be seen as disadvantageous to a new 'challenger party' (De Vries and Hobolt, 2020) like Alternativet, but other institutional factors enable party innovations within the formal political system. For instance, the electoral threshold stands at a mere 2 per cent, which is one of the lowest in the world (Bormann and Golder, 2022). On top of that, only around 20,000 signatures are required for a political party to enter the electoral competition (the precise number of signatures amounts to 0.57 per cent of the total number of votes cast at the previous election). The electoral system in Denmark might thus be described as 'open yet stable', which indicates favourable or *liberal* conditions for new parties to emerge and win representation in parliament (Green-Pedersen and Kosiara-Pedersen, 2020). This is arguably one reason why the national elections in 2022 saw no less than 13 parties on the bill, including five established within the last ten years.

Before turning to the next case, it makes sense to briefly consider the level of institutionalization achieved by Alternativet. As mentioned in the previous chapter, the level of institutionalization depends on five separate factors (see Panebianco, 1988: 53). For the sake of simplicity, I will combine them here to assess the extent to which Alternativet can be said to live an autonomous existence with regard to its external environment. One of the main factors determining a party's level of systemness (the institutionalization of its organization) is the development of a central bureaucracy. As we saw in Chapter 5, Alternativet has recently experienced an increase in bureaucratization compared with its early years. New regulation has been accepted, new administrative roles have been invented and defined, and operational transparency has been substantially improved. There is now also a significant degree of homogeneity in terms of the organizational structures at the same hierarchical level, meaning that different branches operate according to roughly the same principles and procedures. All of this indicates a high level of systemness.

Moreover, as we shall see, the party attracts funding from a 'plurality of sources' (Panebianco, 1988: 59), which also contributes to the process of institutionalization in the sense that it makes Alternativet less vulnerable to sudden environmental shifts, such as voter volatility. That said, the party has recently lost a substantial number of members and voters – and hence funding – which not only makes Alternativet more dependent on the state but also influences its ability to maintain a developed central bureaucracy. Significant fluctuations in the number of salaried staff members testifies to this dynamic. In late 2019, Alternativet had what amounts to 18 full-time employees. Three years later, that figure had decreased to only six full-time positions. This indicates that the party's level of overall institutionalization is now somewhat lower than before.

On the positive side, however, the actual power structure in Alternativet today tends to mirror the official statutes. As described in Chapters 3 and 5, this has not always been the case, but recent organizational developments have ensured a closer correspondence between statutory norms and real-life practice (Husted and Mac, 2022). In sum, Alternativet can be characterized as an institutionalized party, but more success in future elections is probably required to maintain this status. (See Arter and Kestilä-Kekkonen, 2014, for a more comprehensive definition of party institutionalization that also includes the voter base.)

Podemos

Unlike Alternativet, Podemos was established through a process of 'territorial diffusion', in which different movement actors joined forces by establishing an electoral organization to represent them in parliament. As mentioned earlier, it all began with the anti-austerity movement that swept through Spain in 2011 (known as 15M or Los Indignados), which represented a multiplicity of heterogeneous political demands and united these demands in common opposition to the country's political-economic elite (what would later be known as La Casta). Podemos was initially conceived as a 'tool' or a 'participatory method' for decision-making in electoral politics, intended to unite various anti-austerity forces on the Spanish Left (Fominaya, 2020: 221), but quickly ended up as a separate entity, partly as a consequence of the established left's hostility to the idea of a joint political project (Iglesias, 2015).

Although this origin story clearly indicates that Podemos is a product of bottom-up processes, the idea of creating a political party was initially conceived by a small group of intellectuals, based at the Universidad Complutense de Madrid, who had previous experiences with constituent processes in Latin America (Pavía et al, 2016). Inspired by the work of Ernesto Laclau in particular, this group understood how to draw up political imaginaries and articulate new political frontiers, but they also appreciated the importance of allowing these articulations to crystallize around some kind of singularity; that is, a political party or even a political leader (see Laclau, 2005: 100). As such, a certain degree of centralization or 'penetration' was indeed involved in the birth of the party. However, it would be a mistake to credit Iglesias and his associates with the sole responsibility of giving life to one of the most successful movement parties in contemporary European politics, since many other important actors were involved in giving life to Podemos (Lisi, 2019).

In terms of external sponsorship, Podemos has consistently refused to accept large donations from private actors such as corporations or foundations, preferring instead to rely on crowdfunding and 'microcredits' (small civic loans with no interest rates) from individual members and supporters, which are paid back once the Spanish state reimburses the party's electoral expenses (Lupato et al, 2023). Moreover, as we will see further below, a large chunk of Podemos' income derives from crowdfunding initiatives where individuals are encouraged to aid the party in preparing for electoral campaigns. No member is allowed to donate more than €10,000, which is a way for Podemos to ensure that it does not become dependent on a large private donor or even on banks. As such, it seems safe to conclude that Podemos, perhaps even more than Alternativet, is based on internal legitimation. Several important actors have supported Podemos in its quest to challenge the conventional political system in Spain and therefore endowed the party with legitimacy, but none of these can be considered a proper external sponsor.

Finally, there can be little doubt about the significance of charismatic leadership in terms of the initial success of Podemos. In fact, Pablo Iglesias has himself written extensively about the strategic use of himself as an object of identification for those participating in or sympathizing with the 15M movement. As he notes, the point of his participation in various TV shows was to let viewers know that 'the guy with the ponytail' was competing in elections, regardless of whether they knew anything about the party (Iglesias, 2015: 190). Hence, the role of Iglesias and other central figures such as Íñigo Errejón can hardly be underestimated. Paolo Gerbaudo (2019) even describes Iglesias as a 'hyperleader', in the sense that he assumed the role of a talisman who embodied the true spirit of the party instead of serving as the day-to-day leader who makes tough administrative decisions (see Husted, 2019). Other researchers have similarly characterized Iglesias as a 'highly mediatic' leader because of his ability to exploit the affordances of social media platforms like Twitter or Instagram for political purposes (Suau-Gomila et al, 2020).

These points suggest a relatively high level of charismatic leadership in Podemos. Notably, however, opinion polls only decreased slightly when Iglesias decided to leave the party in the wake of the disastrous regional elections in May 2021. This may indicate that the party's new leader, Ione Belarra, has been able to maintain a high level of charisma across the organization or, as Marco Lisi (2019) argues, that charismatic leadership does not play an important part after all.

Turning to the external conditions, we can say that Podemos operates in a *complex* but, at least until recently, *stable* environment. For more than three decades, the Spanish electoral system was characterized by a level of political stability that is almost unheard of in multi-party systems (Bosch, 2020). Despite the introduction of proportional representation after the fall of the Franco regime in the late 1970s, two parties have historically been dominant: the Spanish Workers' Party (PSOE) and the Christian-Democratic Popular Party (PP). From 1982 onward, the two parties took turns in running central government, sometimes in collaboration with small regional parties (Lago, 2020). That all changed, however, in 2015 when Podemos successfully challenged their hegemony by winning more than one fifth of the votes and 65 seats in the Congreso (the lower house). This institutional jolt has arguably made Spanish politics more volatile in recent years, with new contenders and new coalitions continually emerging. The most recent coalition government with representatives from PSOE and Unidas Podemos, which itself is a coalition of three parties, is an example of this trend.

The Spanish electoral system can also be described as *complex* because it is based on an idiosyncratic and somewhat 'disproportional' method where rural constituencies are positively discriminated in a way that clearly favours the two largest parties. Proportionality in electoral politics usually refers to the relationship between the overall share of votes and the share of seats in parliament. The Spanish system is structured so that rural districts elect far more representatives per capita than urban districts, but many districts elect fewer than five representatives (Bosch, 2020). These two factors are almost always beneficial to the two largest parties, since small districts get to elect a disproportional number of representatives, but rarely enough to allow third parties to win representation, and third parties are more popular in the big cities. Hence, as Agustí Bosch (2020: 394) notes, third parties 'are the clear casualties of the electoral system'.

The Spanish electoral system was set up in this manner to avoid what the constitution explicitly refers to as 'inconvenient fragmentation' (Bosch, 2020: 390). During the country's transition to democracy, the incumbent centre-right government had to ensure political stability to guarantee support from central actors in the old Franco regime such as the church and the army. This attempt to introduce an extremely stable version of democracy resulted in one of the most disproportional systems in all of the OECD (Bosch, 2020). That said, the electoral threshold in Spain currently stands at 3 per cent, which is relatively low compared with similar countries, though not as low as in Denmark. Moreover, the number of signatures required for a new party to run for parliament is also on the lower end of the spectrum, but these favourable conditions are all overshadowed by the disproportional nature of the electoral system. The Spanish political context can thus be described as stable and complex but also *hostile* towards small, progressive, urban parties like Podemos.

Before moving on to the final case, we need to briefly assess Podemos' level of institutionalization. In terms of bureaucratization, Podemos has clearly evolved a centralized administrative structure throughout its years of existence, although less money has recently been spent on wages and salaries for staff. As mentioned, the party started out as a very decentralized network of relatively autonomous 'circles', but quickly turned into a more hierarchical administrative unit (Lisi, 2019). The party is still more democratic than most traditional parties, not least given its use of participatory digital technology (Gerbaudo, 2019), but decisions regarding political strategy and other key issues are today made by the party leadership and its staff (Rodríguez-Teruel et al, 2016). According to Panebianco (1988), this indicates a high degree of systemness. On the other hand, given the autonomous nature of the circles – and since Podemos operates entirely without formal branches – structural differences clearly exist between administrative units at the same hierarchical level. This could potentially weaken the level of systemness, but the deliberative (rather than decisional) character of the circles arguably prevents this from happening.

Furthermore, as we shall see, Podemos attracts funding from a plurality of sources. This again indicates a high level of systemness, although the party has become more dependent on the state in recent years. Finally, while accounts of life inside Podemos suggest that statutory norms are not always realized in practice, there nonetheless seems to be a relatively close correspondence between rules and real life (for example, Lisi, 2019; Fominaya, 2020; Kioupkolis, 2016). In sum, Podemos can clearly be described as an institutionalized party that is organized in way that allows it to operate in a stable but hostile environment (Paneque, 2023) without entirely surrendering its movement-like identity.

Píratar

Like Alternativet, and unlike Podemos, Píratar was founded through a process of territorial penetration. As mentioned, the party was established by a handful of activists, including Birgitta Jónsdóttir, who was previously elected as one of four representatives from the Citizens' Movement. Jónsdóttir was also involved in several other political initiatives in the wake of the 2008/2009 financial crisis and achieved worldwide notoriety in 2010 for her involvement in the making of the 'Collateral Murder' WikiLeaks video (see Pilkington, 2013). As such, she was a very well-known figure in Icelandic politics prior to the formation of Píratar, despite her activist stance and somewhat fringe character. According to Jónsdóttir, the motivation for launching an Icelandic version of the Pirate Party was to enhance the public's understanding of technology in contemporary society, and to use this improved understanding to promote democratization within the formal political system (Sigurdarson, 2021). Once the party had been established, local branches were created across the country, which allowed Píratar to compete in the 2013 elections. This sequence of events is clearly indicative of territorial penetration. There are, clearly, elements of diffusion in Píratar's origin story. Most importantly, the party was founded on the back of the Pots and Pans Revolution that hit Iceland in 2009, and it could therefore be seen as that movement's parliamentary arm (Ómardóttir and Valgarðsson, 2020).

In financial terms, Píratar has no external sponsor, and – like the two other parties – it must therefore be considered a case of internal legitimation. In fact, as we shall see, Píratar has consistently received more than 90 per cent of its income from state sources. However, unlike Alternativet and Podemos, Píratar was initially part of a large cross-country network: the International Pirate Party. Although Píratar officially resigned its membership of the network in 2015 (Sigurdarson, 2021), this international alliance arguably played a crucial role in terms of endowing the party with legitimacy from the beginning (Southwell and Pirch, 2021).

As indicated already, charismatic leadership certainly played a role in propelling Píratar to success. Jónsdóttir was particularly instrumental in that regard. As Hallur Thor Sigurdarson (2021: 144) notes, with a reference to the impressive result achieved by the party in the 2013 elections: 'There is a consensus, both generally and amongst the interviewees [party members consulted for Sigurdarson's study], that such a result could not have happened without Jónsdóttir's popularity.' As such, it seems fair to conclude that Píratar resembles Alternativet and Podemos in terms of charismatic leadership. However, certain aspects of the Icelandic party differentiate it from the two other movement parties. First, Jónsdóttir was not actively employed to promote Píratar in the way that Pablo Iglesias was used to promote Podemos. Unlike Iglesias, she never occupied any kind of formal leadership position within the organization, and she never performed the role of a 'hyperleader' (Gerbaundo, 2019). Furthermore, her departure before the 2021 elections did not cause Píratar to collapse in the same way that Elbæk's departure from Alternativet did in 2020. These elements indicate that charismatic leadership plays a slightly lesser role in Píratar compared with the two other parties.

In terms of the external environment, Píratar operates in one of the world's oldest assembly democracies, first established in 930 AD some 45 kilometres east of present-day Reykjavik. Iceland was, however, occupied by Norway and then Denmark between 1262 and 1918, which effectively curbed the development of the country's formal political system. As such, the current electoral system dates back to 1843 when the Danish King 'declared that Iceland should have its own constitutional assembly, which was to be known as Althingi' (Helgason, 2010: 3). Despite its young age, the electoral system in Iceland was, for a long time, relatively stable, with the liberal–conservative Independence Party governing the country permanently for 80 years from 1929 (Ómardóttir and Valgarðsson, 2020).

After Iceland's economic collapse in 2009 and the subsequent Pots and Pans Revolution, in which frustrated citizens took to the streets and used social media platforms to force the government to step down (Castells, 2012), Icelandic politics has been 'extremely turbulent' and characterized by high voter volatility (Önnudóttir et al, 2022: 1). At the elections in 2009, the Independence Party failed to win for the first time, leaving the prime minister's office to the Social Democratic Alliance, and a crowdsourced constitutional process was launched to re-establish the legitimacy of the political system (Popescu and Loveland, 2022). The draft for the new constitution, despite being accepted by popular vote, was rejected by a parliamentary majority as 'undemocratic' (because the political parties were excluded from the process), which reignited the frustration that many citizens felt towards the political system (Thorarensen, 2014). Since the elections in 2009, six new parties have entered parliament, which is significant for a country with a very small population (Önnudóttir et al, 2022). Moreover, large parties, such as the Social Democratic Alliance, have been surpassed by new contenders, such as the Left-Green Movement, the People's Party and Píratar. One could therefore argue that the electoral system in Iceland is currently *unstable* (Ómardóttir and Valgarðsson, 2020), especially compared with the Danish and Spanish context.

The Icelandic electoral system might be unstable, but it is also relatively *simple*, in the sense that members of the unicameral legislature are elected from a total of only six constituencies. Each constituency elects nine representatives. Nine additional MPs are chosen based on a proportionality principle, meaning that the Althingi consists of only 63 members, making it one of the smallest national assemblies in the Western world (the Danish Folketinget has 179 members, Spain's Congreso has 350 members). The electoral threshold is 5 per cent, but with a population of only 390,000 and approximately 200,000 voters, this must be considered a low entry barrier. Furthermore, the number of signatures required to run for parliament is 30 times the number of seats in a particular constituency, which normally means approximately 300 (1,890 signatures are required if a party is competing in all six constituencies). Once again, this must be characterized as a very low entry barrier, even for a small country. As such, the Icelandic electoral system can be classified as very *liberal* or open to new challenger parties such as Píratar.

The level of institutionalization achieved by Píratar is, in many respects, limited when compared with the two other parties. In fact, as Silja Ómardóttir and Viktor Valgarðsson (2020: 848) argue, it is 'surprising that the Pirate Party has survived this long, having such different internal ideologies, repeated inter-personal conflicts, and a shaky, non-hierarchical institutional structure'. Added to this, the number of salaried full-time positions in the party's central bureaucracy has decreased since the peak of Píratar's success. The party now employs what amounts to 2.5 full-time positions, which represents a relatively sharp decrease from 2019, when the party employed 4.5

Table 7.1: Internal and external contingencies across Alternativet, Podemos and Píratar

	Penetration or diffusion	External sponsor	Charismatic leadership	Stability or instability	Complexity or simplicity	Hostility or liberality
Alternativet	Penetration	Low	High	Stability	Simplicity	Liberality
Podemos	Diffusion	Low	High	Stability	Complexity	Hostility
Píratar	Penetration	Medium	Medium	Instability	Simplicity	Liberality

full-time positions. These numbers might seem insignificant in themselves, but, for a small organization like Píratar, they are anything but trivial.

According to Panebianco (1988), some of the internal conflicts encountered by Píratar in recent years may paradoxically have been caused by the liberal environment in which the party operates. As he notes, 'environmental hostility produces environmental uncertainty, and uncertainty encourages organizational cohesion' (Panebianco, 1988: 206). In other words, the more liberal the environment, the more room for what Ómardóttir and Valgarðsson (2020) call 'different internal ideologies', which then quickly leads to 'repeated inter-personal conflicts'. Regardless of whether this is strictly true or not, it is nonetheless interesting that Podemos, which operates in a hostile environment, for a long time managed to maintain a fairly high level of internal cohesion, despite its multifarious heritage, while both Píratar and Alternativet, which operate in liberal environments, have been plagued by tensions and conflicts from the get-go. In fact, it was only when Podemos eventually established itself as a force to be reckoned with that internal disagreements really broke out (Paneque, 2023). See Table 7.1 for an overview of internal and external contingencies across the three parties.

Voters and members

Since the peak of their successes in 2015 and 2016, the three movement parties have all experienced significant setbacks across the two parameters that we consider in this section: their overall vote share has decreased, and their membership base has been substantially reduced. There is, however, an exception to this bleak picture. Píratar has successfully expanded its membership base throughout its ten years of existence, from just over 2,000 members in 2015 to more than 5,000 members in 2021. This 150 per cent increase is indeed impressive, and it may tell us something about the conditions for success for movement parties in general. In what follows, we consider developments across the three parties in terms of voters and members.

Voters: declining support across all three parties

The most common way of assessing the overall success of political parties is simply to look at their electoral performance. This factor tells us something about one of three 'organizational faces', outlined by Richard Katz and Peter Mair (1993), namely 'the party in public office', but it tells us little about what they call 'the party in central office' – the administrative leadership – and 'the party on the ground' – members and supporters. It nonetheless remains one of the most important ways of assessing party success or failure. Electoral performance may have direct impact on the two other faces and vice versa, but that is not always the case (for example Fisher et al, 2006;

Andrews and Jackman, 2008; Pedersen and Schumacher, 2015). Indeed, the findings presented in this chapter further support the argument that there is a difference between the party 'in public office' and the party 'on the ground', in the sense that declining electoral performance does not always lead to a loss of members (as in the case of Píratar) and vice versa (as in the case of Alternativet).

As suggested by Figure 7.1, all three parties have experienced significant setbacks when it comes to electoral performance, both in terms of vote share (percentage of votes in national elections) and seat share (percentage of seats in national parliament). While Podemos has experienced the most severe setback in percentage points, losing 8.3 points and 36 parliamentary seats during the course of only three years (from 2016 to 2019), Píratar has experienced a comparable decline percentagewise by losing almost 40 per cent of its votes in national elections from 2016 to 2021. Alternativet has never enjoyed a large vote share, and its overall loss of electoral support is therefore comparatively smaller. The party lost 1.8 percentage points and 4 seats from 2015 to 2019, but then managed to regain an extra seat (and 0.3 percentage points) in the 2022 elections.

In terms of electoral performance, Alternativet is thus the only party who has so far managed to stop and reverse the downward spiral. While both Podemos and Píratar's electoral performances can be characterized as inverted U-curves (the latter more than the former), Alternativet delivered a surprising result in the 2022 elections by managing to increase its vote share, thereby staying above the electoral threshold. Alternativet's electoral performance in 2022 was surprising because several opinion polls close to election day suggested that the party would be eliminated or at least prevented from gaining representation in parliament. However, partly due to successful alliances with minor green parties such as the Vegan Party and Momentum, and partly due to Franciska Rosenkilde's popularity as a leader (see Chapter 3), Alternativet successfully preserved its parliamentary presence.

There are several ways of explaining the decline in electoral support experienced by Podemos and Píratar and there are a few common denominators that may help us unpack the development. First, both parties came extremely close to joining governmental coalitions with other centre-left parties in the wake of their impressive 2016 results, but neither managed to negotiate agreements with the bigger parties. This may have left some voters disillusioned with the parties' perceived unwillingness to 'get their hands dirty' and achieve tangible political impact. At the same time, the level of intra-party democracy in both parties has declined significantly. In the case of Podemos, the importance of the 'circles' has diminished as a consequence of the party entering parliament, and they currently seem to have very little influence on key policy issues (Paneque, 2023). In the

Figure 7.1: Electoral performances of Alternativet, Podemos and Píratar

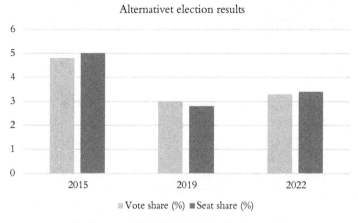

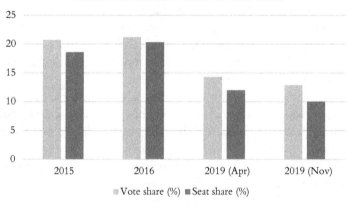

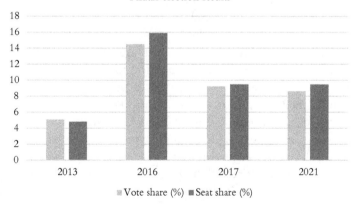

case of Píratar, persistent speculations about the oversized influence of the certain MPs – Jónsdóttir in particular – have led observers to criticize the party for not delivering on its collective leadership ideals (Ómardóttir and Valgarðsson, 2020). As we saw in Chapters 3 and 5, similar developments can be observed in Alternativet, with the watering down of the 'open-source' approach to policy making. The combination of low impact and low membership participation may easily have led many voters to seek representation elsewhere (for example Sanches et al, 2018).

Second, both parties have been plagued by internal conflicts. Within Podemos, disputes concerning the overall political strategy led prominent figures such as Íñigo Errejón to leave the party for of a new political platform called Más País, which entered parliament in 2021 as a rival party. In Píratar, internal disputes between Jónsdóttir and the chairman of the party's executive council broke out in 2016 over whether Píratar could genuinely claim to represent libertarian interests. Jónsdóttir publicly stated on Facebook that the party was not for libertarians, which presumably led many such voters to disengage from the pirate project (Ómardóttir and Valgarðsson, 2020). Again, as outlined in Chapter 3, similar tendencies can be observed in Alternativet, with the party's official leader position changing twice in just one year due to internal conflicts.

However, the main factor determining the three parties' declining electoral performance is arguably a change in political discourse (Mondon and Winter, 2020; Gerbaudo, 2021b). The parties initially rode the wave of popular uprisings, which pitted 'the people' against 'the elite' and created favourable conditions for leftist movement parties that sought to overturn the political system. However, these uprisings have since faded, and new political currents have taken hold in the public debate. In all three countries, new right-wing forces have recently gained momentum (Vox in Spain, Danmarksdemokraterne in Denmark and the Centre Party in Iceland), thereby forcing Podemos, especially, to reposition itself as an anti-fascist party instead of anti-elite party. This has arguably led many working-class voters to abandon the party for political formations that maintain an uncompromising anti-elite rhetoric, such as the new right-wing parties. As Gerbaudo (2021c: np) notes in relation to Podemos: 'A focus on anti-fascism turned out to be not that different from many causes célèbres of the Left: ethically indisputable and highly popular with core supporters, but a hard sell for the general public.' The same could arguably be said about Alternativet and Píratar. The political discourse in Denmark and in Iceland has once again shifted from a focus on democracy, sustainability and social welfare to immigration, crisis management and austerity. Only time will tell whether the three parties are able to adapt to the new political climate and to thrive in conditions that are perhaps less favourable to leftist movement parties.

Members: only one party with consistent growth

As already hinted at, the development in registered memberships across the three parties is curious when compared with their electoral performance. While two parties have experienced a rapid increase followed by a sharp decline, one has consistently expanded its membership base. This is not necessarily odd. The curious element is that the party that keeps expanding its membership is the party that has experienced the most dramatic decline in voter support from one election to the next, namely Píratar. As shown in Figure 7.2, Píratar's membership count has increased at a steady pace from approximately 2,100 in 2015 to 5,200 in 2021. The increase is sharpest in the successful years from 2015 to 2016, but the party has somehow kept adding members, even in the wake of the disastrous 2017 elections. One explanation could be that Píratar does not remove inactive members from its membership registration system, but it is nonetheless remarkable that people continue to enlist despite disappointing electoral results. Another explanation could be that membership fees in Píratar are voluntary (members do not *have* to pay anything), which gives members less of an incentive to resign their subscription.

Podemos' membership model is fairly similar to Píratar's. As is the case for most 'digital parties' (Gerbaudo, 2019), becoming a member is essentially a matter of signing up on a website and takes very little effort (valid ID is required but no more than that). Unlike Píratar, Podemos recently added a €3 fee to its membership model. This was decided at the second Citizen Assembly (Vistalegre 2) in 2017 and was one of the reasons why several high-profile figures decided to leave the party. Podemos distinguishes between 'active' and 'inactive' members, with inactive members being those who have not logged in to the online platform Participa for more than a full year. If inactive members are included, Podemos is by far the biggest membership party in all of Spain, with more than half a million registered users on its online platform (Biancalana and Vittori, 2021). If inactive members are excluded, Podemos is still one of the biggest parties in membership terms, peaking at almost 300,000 in 2017. That said, the party has seen a fairly sharp decline in membership since 2019, with more than 50 per cent of its active members becoming inactive during the course of only two years.

Nonetheless, Podemos continues to be a very large membership party both in national and international terms. For comparison, the Spanish Workers' Party (PSOE) has fewer than 200,000 members (Vittori, 2017), and Movimento 5 Stelle in Italy (the other big European movement party) has approximately 130,000 members (Biancalana and Vittori, 2021). Both Píratar and Alternativet are much smaller than Podemos. This has much to do with the sizes of their countries, but Podemos' achievements in terms of membership subscriptions are still impressive, even if the numbers are

Figure 7.2: Registered or active members of Alternativet, Podemos and Píratar

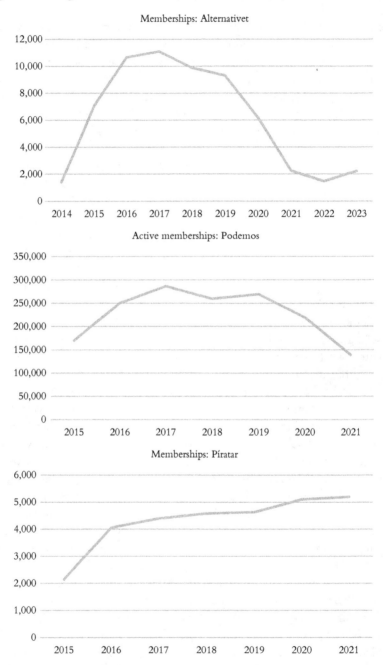

adjusted for country size. While Podemos in 2017 managed to enrol almost 1 per cent of the total Spanish electorate (almost 1.5 per cent if inactive members are included), Alternativet 'only' enrolled 0.25 per cent of the Danish electorate. Píratar is a special case here, since Iceland only has around 250,000 registered voters, meaning that the party effectively enlists more than 2 per cent of the total electorate.

In real numbers, Alternativet is the smallest of the three parties. Although it once had more than 10,000 registered members, making it the third largest membership party in Denmark, it now has just over 2,000 members. The events leading to this dramatic decline are detailed in Chapter 3, but the remarkable fall was also caused by Alternativet deciding in early 2020 to remove members who did not pay the subscription fee. As mentioned in Chapter 5, Alternativet's membership model is based on a tailor-made system in which members can decide for themselves what to pay each month. The minimum level is DKK20 (approximately €2.50), the maximum level is DKK600 (approximately €80). Despite this low minimum level, Alternativet has nonetheless lost almost 90 per cent of its members in just four years, which must be considered a devastating decline, regardless of the party's success in terms of retaining parliamentary representation. It not only means that there are fewer people to fulfil the organizational roles required to run a modern party organization, it also means that Alternativet has lost one of its main income sources. We shall see, however, that Alternativet – like the two other parties – now relies extensively on state subsidies for survival, thereby lowering the importance of having a large membership base.

Income and spending

In some ways, the three parties have very different budgets. They get their incomes from different sources and spend their money differently. There are also substantial differences between the national contexts in which the three parties operate. For instance, as we saw in Chapter 6, parties in Spain receive substantially more state funds than parties in Denmark, and Danish parties are therefore used to relying more heavily on private funds. Furthermore, Spanish parties often spend more money on election campaigns than Danish – and Icelandic – parties (Jiménez and Villoria, 2018). In fact, Spanish parties are the European top-spenders when it comes to election campaigns (Webb and Keith, 2017). That said, the three parties nonetheless exhibit a couple of similar trends. For instance, as we will see, all three parties increasingly rely on state funding. This does not necessarily mean that the parties today receive more money from the state than previously, but it does mean that the share of their total income deriving from state sources has increased substantially over the years. The three parties are more dissimilar when it comes to expenses. For instance, while Píratar seems to spend the most money – relative to its budget size – on staff wages, Alternativet spends much more on campaign activities than the two other parties.

Income: increased reliance on state funding

In most Western democracies, the level of state funding is positively correlated with electoral performance (Koß, 2010). In other words, more votes mean more state funding. This is also the case in Denmark, where parties each year receive DKK34.50 (approximately €4.50) per vote in national elections. This means that funds are distributed to all parties running for parliament – even to those who do not make it above the 2 per cent electoral threshold. In 2015, Alternativet received 168,788 votes in the national elections, which translated into almost DKK6 million (approximately €800,000). In 2019, the party's total number of votes dropped to 104,287, which meant that Alternativet lost more than 25 per cent of its state-sponsored revenue and had to scale down operations. Alternativet also lost a large portion of its private funding during those years, partly as consequence of rapid member defection. In fact, in 2017, the party received more than DKK4 million in membership fees. Four years later, that figure had dropped to less than DKK1 million. Paradoxically, this means that the total share of revenue coming from the state has increased at a steady pace ever since the party was launched in 2013 (see Figure 7.3). In 2021, no less than 73 per cent of Alternativet's income came directly from the state.

This trend is more or less identical across all three cases. In Iceland, all political parties that receive more than 2.5 per cent of the votes in national elections are entitled to state funding. One part of these funds is allocated directly to party organizations based on electoral performance, while another part is allocated to individual members of parliament. In some cases, such as Píratar, the MPs channel their individual funds back to the party instead of spending the money for their own professional purposes. On top of that, there is a relatively large pool of state funds allocated for election campaigns – approximately €2 million. Somewhat controversially, these funds are distributed based on opinion polls and, in 2016, Píratar thus scooped up 35 per cent of the money, as it topped the polls in the wake of the Panama Papers leaks (Broomfield, 2016). Hence, as Figure 7.3 illustrates, Píratar has always relied heavily on public funding. While all Icelandic parties get most of their revenue from the state or municipalities (GRECO, 2008), Píratar constitutes an extreme case of state-sponsored party organization, with close to 100 per cent of its income deriving from public sources. In real numbers, the party's reliance on the state has also increased dramatically over the years. In 2013, when the party first entered parliament, Píratar received slightly more than ISK11 million in state subsidies (approximately €70,000). Seven

Figure 7.3: Income sources for Alternativet, Podemos and Píratar

Alternativet income, 2014–2021

Podemos income, 2015–2021

Source: Podemos (2023)

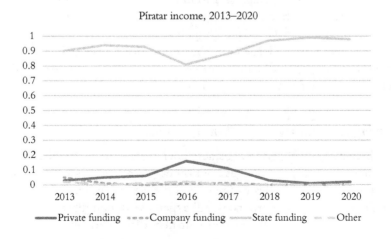

Píratar income, 2013–2020

years later, that number had risen to more than ISK71 million (approximately €500,000).

A similar, yet not so extreme, development can be identified in the case of Podemos. Just like the two other countries, Spanish state funds are distributed to political parties based on their electoral performance (GRECO, 2009). Spanish state subsidies are distributed in the same way as in Iceland, with one part of the money going directly to the party and another part going to the individual MPs. However, only left-wing parties have a tradition for channelling individual funds back to the party organizations (therefore known as 'revolutionary money'). As a party based firmly on the left, Podemos has always followed this model. In Figure 7.3, these two income sources are kept separate for the sake of transparency – one is called 'state funding', the other is called 'MP donations'. The most important development to observe in the case of Podemos is the dramatic increase in the total share of state funding. In 2016, at the height of its success, Podemos received 39 per cent of its income from private sources, such as crowdfunding campaigns and microcredit schemes, and 'only' 60 per cent from public sources – MP donations and state subsidies. In 2021, the share of income deriving from private sources had fallen to a mere 16 per cent, while public funds accounted for 84 per cent of the party's total revenue. Just as for Alternativet, this does not mean that Podemos today receives more money from the state than in 2016. It simply means that the overall share of income stemming from public sources has increased.

Overall, it seems safe to conclude that the three parties would not have been able to achieve the level of success they have enjoyed without substantial public funding. All three countries provide generous grants to political parties that make it across a fairly low electoral threshold (in Denmark, there is no threshold). Spanish parties might receive a little more money than Icelandic and Danish parties, even when the numbers are adjusted for the size of the national economy (Webb and Keith, 2017), but none of the countries restricts access to public funds in a way that resembles the situation in, for instance, the UK or Switzerland (Falguera et al, 2014). As such, one could argue that the generous levels of public funding have successfully assisted the parties in staying afloat despite serious electoral setbacks, and thereby giving them all an honest chance at regaining political momentum.

Spending: different resources, different priorities

The three movement parties considered here cannot be classified as wealthy. Podemos has the biggest budgets, but other Spanish parties are much more resourceful when it comes to finances (Jiménez and Villoria, 2018). That said, Podemos has increased its overall expenses throughout the years, from just over €3 million in 2015 to approximately €16 million in 2019, but that figure has recently dropped to around €11 million. Similarly, Píratar has also increased its overall spending level, from approximately ISK14 million in 2015 (approximately €90,000) to more than ISK82 million in 2019 (approximately €550,000). This represents an almost 500 per cent increase in total expenses. Alternativet is the only party whose expenses have decreased since its parliamentary entry, from around DKK12.5 million in 2016 (approximately €1.7 million), a non-election year, to less than DKK5 million in 2021 (approximately €670,000).

As Paul Webb and Dan Keith (2017) suggest, campaign expenditure is one of the most important ways of estimating the strength of political parties. If this is correct, Podemos is clearly the strongest party of the three, with more than half a million euros going to campaign activities in 2016 – and this is even excluding contributions from the other parties in the Unidas Podemos electoral alliance. When looking at the total share of expenses going to campaign activities, however, Alternativet exceeds both Píratar and Podemos by a wide margin. In 2015 (the first time Alternativet competed in elections), the party spent a staggering 33 per cent on campaign activities. This must have something to do with the work that went into collecting enough signatures to become eligible to run for parliament, as the total share of expenses going to campaign activities dropped in later years, but the figure remains surprisingly high. In 2019 (the second time Alternativet competed in elections), 17 per cent of the party's total expenses went to campaign activities. In comparison, Podemos has consistently spent around 4 per cent of its expenses each year on things like advertisements and social media presence, while Píratar only spends around 3 per cent on those activities. As such, Alternativet seems to spend much more money – relative to its budget size – on election campaigns. That said, it should be noted that Alternativet, unlike Podemos and Píratar, hardly spends any money on such activities in non-election years.

When it comes to expenses, the biggest general post is, by far, wages and salaries for staff members. This goes for all three parties, although Píratar seems to spend a little more on staff costs. In 2019, the pirates spent no less than 63 per cent on wages and salaries. In comparison, Alternativet and Podemos spend around 50 per cent each year on such matters. In fact, in 2021, that figure dropped to only 40 per cent in the case of Podemos. Considering the overall increase in spending, this may be one indication that the level of 'systemness' (Panebianco, 1988) currently achieved by Podemos is now lower than usual. The opposite could perhaps be said about Píratar, although other factors seem to curb the degree of institutionalization in the Icelandic case, as discussed earlier.

Participation and representation

There can be no doubt that the three parties value membership participation highly. In fact, their primary ideological framework is perhaps most accurately described as 'participationism', (Gerbaudo, 2019: 81). Only secondarily can Podemos, Píratar and Alternativet be characterized as socialist, anarchist or green. This means that all three parties are much more democratic than traditional European mass parties, in terms of both decision-making and deliberation. This is no surprise given that green and left-leaning parties usually prioritize intra-party democracy much more than right-wing and centrist parties (Bolin et al, 2017). However, as we saw in Chapter 6, other non-ideological factors tend to predict high levels of intra-party democracy. For instance, parties with small membership bases are usually more democratic than parties with large ones, and parties in countries with high GDP per capita are similarly more committed to participation and deliberation than parties in other countries (Bolin et al, 2017).

When these factors are taken into consideration, Podemos stands out as a black swan. The party has a very large membership base, it operates in a country with a relatively low GDP per capita (at least in a Western European context) and it clearly belongs to the 'left socialist' party family, which tends to exhibit surprisingly oligarchic traits. Nonetheless, the party continues its commitment to intra-party democracy, although recent years have seen a decline in the actual influence of ordinary members. In what follows, I will use the framework spelled out by Piero Ignazi (2020) to assess the level of intra-party democracy in the three parties. So, I will consider the level of *inclusion, plurality, deliberation* and *diffusion*. At times, the four factors will not be discussed equally, due to a lack of available information.

Participation: the four knights of intra-party democracy

Alternativet has always prided itself on being a very democratic party. The party's bottom-up (or open-source) process of policy making clearly represents the clearest expression of its commitment to membership participation. The process consists of three steps. First, any party member can organize a political laboratory where members and non-members meet and discuss a particular policy issue, such as tax, health or education. Second, the outcome of these discussions is then summarized in a written template and turned into a policy proposal that is uploaded to the Dialogue digital platform . Here, more members can help the authors qualify the proposal, but only the authors can edit its contents. Finally, after three weeks of online debate, the proposal is submitted to the political forum, which consists of approximately 40 representatives. The political forum must decide – in a yes/ no vote – whether to accept or reject the proposal. In most cases, however, a working group is tasked with rewriting the proposal in a way that aligns with the rest of Alternativet's political programme (see Husted and Plesner, 2017).

Recently, the number of political laboratories has decreased to a minimum. This has effectively brought the bottom-up process of policy making to a halt. Almost all proposals today are drafted by the MPs and their staff, although members are frequently consulted via social media. Members can also submit proposals to the Annual Congress, but most policy initiatives are launched by the political leadership. This makes the current level of *inclusion* in Alternativet modest, at least when compared with earlier years. However, as argued in Chapter 5, when it comes to *diffusion*, the local branches are allowed to select candidates independently and launch initiatives without necessarily consulting national headquarters. In fact, Alternativet's organizational configuration might even be described as 'stratarchical' (Eldersveld, 1964) in the sense that local branches are allowed to act autonomously if their actions can be justified with reference to the values and the manifesto. In terms of *plurality* and *deliberation*, Alternativet is still very much committed to its values and debate principles. As we shall see in Chapter 8, the values and principles are created to foster enlightened debate and ensure that no members feel marginalized. That said, the gradual discontinuation of the political laboratories means that today there are fewer spaces for enacting the type of pluralistic debate that initially made Alternativet famous in Denmark and abroad.

Podemos' model of policy making was initially very similar to Alternativet's. Instead of political laboratories, Podemos has circles where members and non-members can deliberate on policy issues. The circles were often territorial, and grounded in a particular local context, and seen as vital to the party's claim to represent the spirit of the 15M movement because they were leaderless and based on consensus (Pavía et al, 2016). Initially, the circles could propose policy changes by submitting them to the Citizen Assembly, but the circles have recently been reduced to discussion groups without serious decision-making power, and the party's executive body, the Citizen Council, today administers the activities of the circles (della Porta et al, 2017). As Andreu Paneque (2023) notes, Podemos has undergone a process of institutionalization and centralization in which the lower levels of the organization have been stripped of autonomy and decision-making power. This essentially challenges the party's movement-like identity. Nonetheless, Podemos continues to use digital tools such as AppGree and Agora (the infrastructure behind Participa) to allow ordinary members a voice on important decisions (Biancalana and Vittori, 2021). Hence, Podemos must be considered less democratic than Alternativet in terms of *diffusion* because the latter maintains a higher degree of 'local decentralization' (Duverger, 1954: 56), but more democratic than Alternativet in terms of *inclusion* due to the frequent use of digital tools for intra-party plebiscites. Podemos should also be considered more democratic than Alternativet in terms of both *pluralism* and *deliberation*, since the circles, unlike the political laboratories, are still functioning, albeit at a reduced scale and frequency.

Píratar has no fancy name for what Alternativet calls 'political laboratories' and what Podemos calls 'circles', but the party essentially relies on the same organizational model. Ordinary party members can, at any time, call a meeting on a given topic. After the meeting, members can write up a policy proposal and submit it to a digital vote on Píratar's official platform. In some ways, this resembles Podemos' and Alternativet's policy-making process, but there are important differences. First – and most significantly – the process is still in use. Unlike the two other parties, Píratar has not yet scaled down its commitment to intra-party democracy, so bottom-up policy making is therefore still a thing in the Icelandic case. Second, all members can participate in all formal decision-making processes. Ideally, no decision about policy or strategy is made without the inclusion of ordinary members. Finally, all votes count equally, which means that MPs or board members have no higher standing or veto rights when it comes to deciding on the political direction of Píratar. Some informal decisions are made by the MPs on a daily basis, and the frequency of meetings and votes has decreased over the years, but Píratar nevertheless takes the prize as the most democratic party of the three. Not only are more people *included* in decision-making processes, the power to decide is also *diffused* evenly across organizational layers. Furthermore, the principles of *plurality* and *deliberation* are preserved through the continued use of meetings where members and non-members can discuss matters of concern in the absence of formalized hierarchies and rigid party discipline. This does not mean that Píratar's policy-making process is perfect from a democratic point of view, but it does represent a relatively pure expression of the 'participationist' ideology (Gerbaudo, 2019).

Representation: a few words on candidate selection

The three parties are somewhat alike when it comes to candidate selection, and I will therefore only briefly consider this aspect. In the case of Alternativet and Píratar, local branches are allowed to select parliamentary candidates, and all candidates are listed according to a principle of equal ranking, rather than prioritized. All members with more than 90 days seniority are allowed to run. In Alternativet, they cannot be members of other parties while running for parliament. Podemos' circles used to be responsible for candidate selection, but that procedure changed with the second Citizen Assembly in 2017. Today, the local circles only express their preferences for certain candidates, while the party's executive body, the powerful Citizen Council, makes the final appointments.

Using Reuven Hazan and Gideon Rahat's (2010) framework, we can say that Alternativet and Píratar are more inclusive when it comes to candidate selection than Podemos. All members can be selected as candidates (criteria 1), ordinary members select the candidates (criteria 2), the selection process takes place at a local level (criteria 3) and the candidates are selected based on voting rather than appointment (criteria 4). In Podemos, all members can run, but the political leadership eventually appoints the parliamentary candidates. As Manuela Caiani and colleagues (2022: 411) note: 'This structure ensures that the secretary general ... has nearly full control over the party.' In that sense, Podemos has actually become a fairly hierarchical organization that in many ways resembles a traditional mass party. In fact, the secretary general of Podemos currently wields more formal power than the political leader of the social democratic PSOE (Carvajal and Sanz, 2017). This may seem paradoxical, given the party's consistent claim to represent the democratic spirit of the 15M movement, but it has been deemed necessary by members as well as leaders to realize the idea of turning Podemos into a *maquina de guerra electoral* (Carvajal and Sanz, 2017; see also Paneque, 2023).

As such, we can once again conclude that Píratar remains the most democratic and inclusive party. Alternativet is almost as inclusive when it comes to candidate selection, but less so for ongoing deliberation and decision-making. Podemos is, by far, the most exclusive party in terms of the candidate selection, but arguably more inclusive than Alternativet with respect to everyday membership participation due to its firm reliance on digital polling tools. This might mean that Podemos endorses a 'plebiscitarian' type of participation (Gerbaudo, 2019), where members vote on predefined yes/no questions instead of discussing political issues in a reasoned and enlightened manner, but it nonetheless represents one way of giving ordinary members a voice in an otherwise large and complex organization.

Insights across the cases

At least three conclusions can be derived from our discussions so far. First, based on the analysis of institutional environments, we can say that Iceland arguably represents the most hospitable environment for movement parties since the country's electoral system is not only simple and liberal but also politically unstable, which provides an opportunity for challenger parties to gain a foothold. Furthermore, generous public funding schemes are available to political parties (some are even distributed according to opinion polls rather than electoral performance) and the Icelandic electorate is generally very engaged in politics. In fact, in 2010, more than 40 per cent of the population were members of a political party (Önnudóttir et al, 2022). These factors have arguably contributed to allowing a seemingly non-institutionalized party such as Píratar to survive and make an impact politically despite numerous internal challenges. Conversely, the Spanish context can perhaps be described as the least attractive institutional environment. Public funding for political parties is generous, but other factors, such as a disproportional election system, make it difficult for new contenders to break the mould.

This makes Podemos' achievements over the last ten years seem even more impressive, and it perhaps explains why the party has found it necessary to transform itself into a centralized electoral machine.

Second, while all three parties have lost voters since 2015 and 2016, Píratar and Alternativet have recently managed to stop the bleeding. In both cases, it appears that the personal and political conflicts that occurred between 2017 and 2020 have largely been resolved. At least, it no longer seems as if these conflicts cause voters to disengage. The decrease in voter support is likewise reflected in the membership statistics of Alternativet and Podemos. While the former lost 90 per cent of its members in just a few years, the latter has seen a dramatic decline in active members. In both cases, this may have something to do with the diminished level of intra-party democracy. It is worth noting that Píratar – the only party that still commits unequivocally to the participationist agenda – has managed to expand its membership base despite electoral setbacks.

Third, in terms of income sources, we have seen that all three parties increasingly rely on public funding for survival. This has always been the case for Píratar, but the two other parties now also receive around three quarters of their income from the state. This makes the parties extremely sensitive to electoral setbacks, since state funding in all three cases is positively correlated with electoral performance. Looking at the evolution of funding for Podemos and Alternativet, it is safe to say that the parties were politically strongest in periods when they received funding from what Panebianco (1988) calls a 'plurality of sources'. This is inevitably a chicken-and-egg situation, since a strong political presence might incentivize people to donate money, but it seems safe to conclude that a diverse funding strategy is preferable to the overwhelming reliance on state funding that we see today.

Comparing Alternativet with Podemos and Píratar has taught us that movement parties struggle across Europe. Since the heyday in 2015 and 2016, popular support for left-leaning formations that rely on participationist ideologies has declined at a rapid pace. While some parties, such as Podemos, have responded by centralizing the organization to transform it into an electoral war machine, capable of striking compromises with opposing forces and entering governmental coalitions, other parties, such as Píratar, have maintained their commitment to democratic ideals. At the time of writing (late 2023), Píratar is the only party of the three that is polling above its last election result. This may have a lot to do with Píratar's opposition status, but it is nonetheless telling that the most democratic party is also the most successful in terms of popular support. And perhaps this is the main lesson. Maybe movement parties must retain the democratic spirit, upon which they were initially founded, to offer people a proper alternative to the current state of affairs.

8

The Cultural Perspective

> In liberal representative systems, parties are voluntary organisations made up of individuals who have chosen to contribute financially and, in many cases, through their work and participation. They attract members who identify, to various degrees, with the collective and work together for its electoral success. ... They follow largely self-imposed rules and produce narratives. In fact, each party within a polity functions as a mini society, with its distinctive rules, ideas and practices that persist through time as institutions. Observers sometimes talk derogatorily about parties as 'tribes' but why not take this quip seriously?
>
> Florence Faucher (2021: 56): 'An anthropology of contemporary political parties'

Introduction

The previous chapters have all been aimed primarily at organization studies, encouraging scholars within this academic field to develop an interest in the internal orchestration of political parties; not only because parties have been surprisingly overlooked as relevant study objects but also because they offer a window to dynamics that are present in most organizations but often concealed by the seemingly non-political façade of traditional business firms and other 'ordinary' organizations (Husted et al, 2022). In that sense, the first seven chapters represent an attempt to bring the established literature on party organization, which generally belongs to the realm of political science – and comparative politics more specifically – into dialogue with organization studies. This chapter, however, reverses the flow of that conversation by drawing on hallmark contributions to organization studies to enrich the established literature on party organization. More precisely, the aim of the chapter is to develop what I call a 'cultural perspective' on party organization. Although some of the other perspectives that I consider in this book likewise claim to address cultural dynamics – mostly the classical perspective – none of them seriously allows the notion of culture to take centre stage. This chapter is therefore meant as an addition to the literature on party organization.

To be sure, some scholars have indeed conducted studies of organizational cultures in political parties. One noteworthy example is Myron Aronoff's (1977) account of the Israeli Labor Party, in which he shows the organizational culture of the party to mirror the national culture of Israel, with its complex composition of diverging norms and values. A more recent example is Florence Faucher-King's (2005) ethnographic study of party conferences across four British parties, in which she uncovers the symbolic value of these theatrical events. An interesting aspect of the two studies, conducted almost 30 years apart, is that the first chapter in both books is dedicated to establishing the legitimacy of anthropological research strategies as opposed to quantitative methods and comparative strategies. To me, this says a lot about the dominance of the comparative perspectives in party research and the literature's persistent unwillingness to consider 'that which cannot be measured' (Eriksen, 2021: 21). As Aronoff (1993: 3) puts it in an updated version of his book: 'Although various forms of structured and unstructured interviewing with open and closed questionnaires have been employed … I could not find a single case in the literature where sustained participant observation over a long period was the main research method.' Today, not much has changed (Faucher, 2021). As such, it seems to me that more must be done to convince party researchers about the value of studying the organizational culture of political parties through qualitative methods that help us uncover 'the hidden aspects of organizational life' (Yanow et al, 2012: 331).

Etymologically, the word culture derives from the Latin verb *cultūra*, which signifies the act of cultivating land or plants. The notion of culture therefore points to something that grows organically from the soil of a nation, a community or an organization. Culture is a spontaneous, somewhat uncontrollable, phenomenon that can be cultivated but not necessarily controlled. In common parlance, culture is understood as 'the way we do things around here', but, in academic writing, it is usually given a more precise meaning. A classical definition describes culture as man-made 'webs of significance' (Geertz, 1973: 5) that condition everyday experiences of people in a particular social space. A more recent definition that builds on this view characterizes culture as 'a system of shared values (that define what is important) and norms that define appropriate attitudes and behaviors for organizational members' (Chatman and O'Reilly, 2016: 160). What seems to recur in most substantial definitions of culture is an emphasis on values and norms (Alvesson, 2011). While values provide valuations – they represent what is perceived as particularly important in a given context – norms guide behaviour through formal and informal codes of conduct (Korte, 2009).

There are, however, several ways of approaching the study of organizational culture. Three approaches are usually highlighted (Martin et al, 2004). One approach – 'integration' – views culture as a pattern of underlying assumptions shared by all members of an organization and focuses on the ability of managers to shape those assumptions (for example Schein, 1985). Another approach – 'differentiation' – views culture as a source of conflict and focuses on the possible existence of mutually opposing subcultures within an organization (for example Kunda, 1992). The final approach – 'fragmentation' – views culture as an ambiguous phenomenon and focuses on the ways in which individuals make sense of cultural symbols and artefacts (for example Parker, 2000). In this chapter, I will review all three approaches and settle for a 'multifaceted' approach that takes integrative, differential and fragmentary aspects into account. Towards the end of the chapter, I consider how cultures can work as control systems and discuss the implications of this insight for studies of political parties.

Three approaches to organizational culture

The scholarly concern for organizational culture is typically dated back to the 1980s, where a strong interest in 'Japanese-style' management suddenly emerged as a consequence of Western corporations losing ground to companies like Toyota, Sony and Honda, which all emphasized culture as the key to successful business administration (Schultz, 1995). Theoretically, the interest in organizational culture was propelled by a number of high-profile publications that focused on culture as a previously overlooked variable that could explain why some companies outperformed others. One oft-cited example of this trend is Tom Peters and Robert Waterman's (1982) bestseller, *In Search of Excellence*, which surveys the presumably excellent culture of 43 top-tier US firms. Based on extensive interviewing and a great deal of consultancy buzz, the authors arrive at eight principles that seem to guide all high-performance enterprises. While several of the companies highlighted by Peters and Waterman later experienced severe setbacks, the idea that managers could espouse a particular cultural philosophy to achieve high employee commitment and then scale-back on expensive bureaucratic structures had taken hold in the worlds of both academics and practitioners (Kunda, 1992). After that, there was no turning back. Cultural management suddenly appeared to offer a smarter and cheaper way of organizing a business compared with old-school theories of command-and-obedience (for example Deal and Kennedy, 2000).

Despite this sudden infatuation with culture, organization scholars have always had an eye for the intangible aspects of organizations. As Martin Parker (2000) shows, founding figures like Max Weber and Frederick W Taylor were likewise preoccupied with topics closely related to organizational culture. While Taylor (1911) placed great emphasis on the importance of instigating a 'mental revolution' among both workers and managers in order to avoid 'systematic soldiering', Weber (1922) not only dealt with issues pertaining to occupational ethics and value rationality, he also advocated a type of *interpretive* science focused on subjective meanings and motives (Weber, 1949). Nonetheless, these figures have later been portrayed as interested solely in the rational and technical elements of organized life – as proponents of 'one best way of organizing' – thereby serving as convenient strawmen for more 'humanist' research traditions (Parker, 2000). The interest in culture is furthermore mirrored by Taylor and Weber's contemporaries in the field of party research. Robert Michels (1915: 109), for instance, believed oligarchization to be driven by both technical and psychological factors and described party leaders as having been 'cultured' into desiring parliamentary influence through intra-organizational leadership training.

However, what characterizes many classical and contemporary accounts of culture is a tendency to view organizations as monolithic entities with one relatively homogenous culture (or perhaps a few). Scholars and practitioners alike frequently refer to *the* organizational culture of a particular enterprise or analyse conflicts between two otherwise harmonious subcultures. Furthermore, a number of studies privilege managers as the inaugurators or transformers of a particular organizational culture. This tendency is even more pronounced in popular business literature. It is not uncommon here to find headlines such as 'How managers create high-performance cultures' or 'How every manager can create a culture that works'. In this view, managers are cast as heroic figures, capable of singlehandedly instituting a consistent set of values and norms in an organization. Similar observations could easily be made about the presumed role of party leaders in popular discourse. For instance, Jeremy Corbyn was recently charged with instigating a 'toxic culture of chaos' in the British Labour Party prior to its 2019 electoral defeat (Robinson, 2020) and, as we shall see in the following chapter, Uffe Elbæk was often described as the very embodiment of Alternativet's colourful culture during his time as party leader.

This monolithic and managerialist view of organizational culture characterizes an approach that Joanne Martin (1992) calls 'integration'. In the following sections, I first outline the integration approach and the core assumptions that guide this way of thinking about culture. Then, I outline two additional approaches (differentiation and fragmentation) and describe how I intend to use them in the analysis of Alternativet's organizational culture.

Integration

According to Martin (1992), three elements characterize the integration approach to organizational culture: consensus, consistency and clarity. First, as mentioned, authors who follow an integrationalist line of inquiry often assume that all members of an organization agree about its culture. They can easily describe the culture and they know how it materializes and who initially invented it. They also know what purpose their culture serves and how it is connected to their own professional identity. In short, there is a broad cultural consensus. At the centre of this approach is one of the most influential organization theorists of all times, Edgar Schein. Schein rose to prominence in the 1980s with the publication of his book *Organizational Culture and Leadership* (now in its fifth edition and cited almost 65,000 times), in which he spells out a theory of organizational culture based loosely on the work of symbolic anthropologists like Clifford Geertz (1973) and social psychologists such as Chris Argyris and Donald Schön (1978). Schein (1985: 9) famously defines organizational culture as:

a pattern of shared basic assumptions that was learned by the group as it solves its problems of external adaptation and internal integration, that has worked well enough to be considered valid and, therefore, to be taught to new members as the correct way to perceive, think, feel in relation to those problems.

A number of observations can be made about this definition. The first thing to note is that culture is said to constitute a 'pattern of shared basic assumption'. This idea goes back to Geertz' (1973: 5) reading of Weber and his contention that 'man is an animal suspended in webs of significance he himself has spun' and that cultural analysis, accordingly, should be understood as the interpretation of the exact meaning of 'those webs'. The notion of shared basic assumptions points to an additional feature of Schein's theory, namely the fact that culture is said to materialize in three distinct levels. The surface level is 'artifacts'. This consists of all those things that can be readily observed: buildings, logos, paintings, clothing, office supplies, technology, slogans, jingles and so on – but also everyday language, emotional displays, rituals and ceremonies; all that one 'sees, hears, and feels when one encounters a new group with an unfamiliar culture' (Schein, 1985: 25). These are phenomena that are easy to experience but hard to understand since they are said to represent deeper meanings. This brings us to the second level: 'espoused values'. This consists of the organization's official beliefs. One may encounter these beliefs on web pages, in advertisements, at seminars or during ceremonial speeches. This is where managers proclaim that their organizations are profitable, accountable, responsible, sustainable, democratic, collaborative, data-driven or transparent. Such values are typically espoused for purposes of internal cohesion and impression management. Hence, they may often reveal more about what people claim to do than what they actually do, although such 'aspirational talk' can indeed have performative effects for organizations (Christensen et al, 2013).

However, if, at some point, espoused values 'have worked well enough to be considered valid' – if they achieve what Schein calls 'social validation' – they gradually become embedded in the unconsciousness of organizational members as shared basic assumptions. This third level represents the cultural DNA of an organization. This is, according to Schein, the level that observers must understand in order to comprehend the exact meanings of artefacts. One can only fully understand the significance of a particular type of clothing or ceremony when one has identified the shared basic assumptions that add meaning to these artefacts. As such, there will always be consistency between artefacts and assumptions. The espoused values, however, might easily contradict both assumptions and artefacts.

The task for the researcher following the integration approach is thus to identify artefacts and values, uncover assumptions and then investigate whether there is consistency or conflict between the three cultural levels. In the case of disharmony, it is the manager's job to reintroduce consistency because only managers are capable of instigating cultural transformations. This can be done by altering the espoused values in a way that reflects the shared basic assumptions, but most managers will probably start by 'imposing their own beliefs, values, and assumptions about how things should be done on their followers and employees' through so-called embedding mechanisms (Schein, 1985: 235).

As a proponent of the integration approach, Schein neatly illustrates what Martin means by *consensus*, *consistency* and *clarity*. Every organization has one – and only one – culture.[1] The culture is consistent in the sense that artefacts and assumptions are intimately linked and there is clarity about the exact meaning of cultural artefacts. These three elements are all challenged by the differentiation approach. Here, focus is on possible conflicts between organizational subcultures, predicated on the conviction that 'consensus' always represents the triumph of dominant voices and the violent marginalization of minorities. As Martin (1992: 68) puts

Figure 8.1: Schein's iceberg model of organizational culture

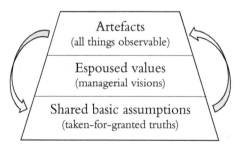

it: 'Integration studies contribute to a vicious hegemonic cycle whereby this research serves the interest of members of dominant groups, while ignoring those who see things differently.' In the following chapter, we shall see how a dominant culture of inclusivity and open-mindedness is established in Alternativet and how it ironically marginalizes actors that 'see things differently'.

Differentiation

Like the integration approach, the differentiation approach rests on three central elements: *inconsistency, subcultural consensus* and *relegation of ambiguity to the periphery* (Martin, 1992). Let's consider each of these in turn. First, the emphasis on inconsistency is paramount to understanding the differentiation approach. It almost goes without saying that a focus on consensus and consistency prevents the researcher from observing the equivocal nature of artefacts and values – and that is precisely what researchers committed to differentiation are seeking. Martin (1992) highlights three general types of cultural inconsistency that researchers often look for: action-based, symbolic and ideological. Action-based inconsistency occurs if the values espoused by management are incongruent with the practices of the organization. For instance, a company might espouse values such as responsibility and fairness, but hide profits in tax havens. This could lead certain parts of the organization and its environment to question the integrity of the management team and its commitment to the official values. Symbolic inconsistency occurs if disharmony exists between the espoused values and the artefacts of the organization. For instance, a company might espouse values such as egalitarianism and horizontality, but provide only managers with large offices on the top floor. Again, this may lead observers to charge the organization with hypocrisy. Finally, ideological inconsistency occurs if espoused values conflict with each other. For instance, a company might claim to promote sustainability or biodiversity, but also pride themselves on having an economic-growth mindset.

The focus on inconsistency is an important element of the differentiation approach because it allows researchers to show that norms and values are open for interpretation and that this openness often spawns conflict between different parts of an organization. In that sense, it is a more polyphonic approach that gives voice to those who are silenced by the hegemony of an official, managerial, perspective, thereby adding nuance to the slightly one-sided picture painted by the integration approach. However, the attention given to conflict means that the differentiation approach is predicated on binaries and oppositional thinking. Whereas the integration approach tends to privilege the managerial point of view, and assumes that this view is consensual, the differentiation approach tends to emphasize the view of a relatively homogeneous subgroup such as 'workers', 'women' or 'foreigners' who are usually portrayed as suppressed or marginalized.

The differential view of culture is likewise visible in Gideon Kunda's (1992) celebrated study of 'normative control' in a Silicon Valley corporation pseudonymized as 'Tech'. In this account, the software engineers of the corporations are pitted against senior management. The former have traditionally dominated the organization: the corporation is frequently described as an engineering firm (or an 'engineering sandbox'), and most low-level managers are trained as professional engineers. In fact, managers that have a background in business tend to downplay it and are encouraged to spend their weekends obtaining an engineering degree. The business perspective is, however, gradually gaining traction with senior management. This causes conflicts between the two occupational groups and leads the managers to promote a sophisticated type of self-management centred on autonomy and employee empowerment. Paradoxically, this lack of rules and formal requirements is exactly what makes the software engineers work longer and harder than anyone else. As one manager notes (Kunda, 1992: 5): 'You can't *make 'em* [the engineers] do *anything*. They have to want to. So, you have to work through the culture. The idea is to educate people without them knowing it.'

The antagonisms between different subgroups are even more pronounced in John van Maanen's (1991) equally celebrated account of Disneyland as a workplace. Here, the upper-class Tour Guides are seen as the most privileged subgroup alongside the Ride Operators, whereas the Food and Concession Workers are at the bottom of the social hierarchy. Uniforms play a major role in distinguishing one group from another, since wages are relatively similar, but there are also behavioural differences. While the lower-level workers are expected to carry out their daily duties without much theatrical display, the Tour Guides and the Ride Operators are tasked with playing roles that exhibit the childlike happiness of the Disney universe. Supervisors and management representatives conduct regular checks to see that the 'Disney way' is being performed in a satisfying manner. As such, what van Maanen shows is that cultural differentiation can occur between management and workers and between different employee subgroups.

Both Kunda's and van Maanen's studies illustrate an important point about the differentiation approach: there is always internal cohesion within the respective subcultures. In Kunda's case, the software engineers are treated as a homogeneous group that works according to the same basic assumptions, and, in van Maanen's case, the Ride Operators and the Tour Guides are portrayed as responding similarly to the type of emotional management that exists at the 'Smile Factory'. This means that cultural ambiguity is relegated to the periphery, beyond the boundaries of the respective subgroups. For instance, in Kunda's account, we only briefly learn that the Wage Class 2 workers (mostly secretaries and clerks) have a less consistent interpretation of the Tech culture. In fact, many of the workers are described as being 'in the background or on the sideline' and as having an 'ambiguous' or 'incongruent' attitude towards the company culture (Kunda, 1992: 205). Hence, equivocality is clearly recognized in the differentiation approach, but it is understood as existing outside or underneath internally unambiguous subcultures. In the next chapter, we shall see how two distinct subgroups can be identified within Alternativet and how they enter a conflict about the precise meaning of the party's values.

Fragmentation

Unlike the two former approaches, the fragmentation approach 'brings ambiguity to the foreground, rather than excluding it or channeling it outside a realm of cultural or subcultural clarity' (Martin, 1992: 130). The point here is to emphasize that, upon closer scrutiny, most cultural manifestations appear ambivalent rather than evident and perhaps even meaningless to members of an organization. Who says that artefacts like uniforms and office buildings represent a consistent set of collectively shared assumptions about life in a particular organization? And, if they do, how are we to know what those assumptions are? Furthermore, while some members may interpret espoused values and artefacts in one way, others may easily have wildly different perceptions. In a sense, it would be strange to assume organization-wide or even group-based consensus in this regard. As Cathrine Hasse (2011) notes, if Kunda had talked to every member of the organization that he calls Tech, the idea about two distinct subcultures would probably begin to fade.

As such, the fragmentation approach highlights the fact that the two other approaches rely on simplifications. With the integration approach, the description of the organization is simplified in the sense that minority voices are silenced or disregarded. With the differentiation approach, one group (for example management) is usually portrayed as superior to another group (such as workers), the consequence being that the superior group is often described in an extremely generalizing manner (for example that management is always looking to increase profits by controlling workers in every way possible). The fragmentation approach seeks to acknowledge that the world is far more complex than the two other approaches assume. Organizations seldom have *one* single culture, nor do they consist of two easily discernible and relatively stable subgroups. The world of organizations is messier than that. This messiness is at the heart of the fragmentation approach.

According to Martin (1992), three elements characterize the fragmentation approach: (1) focus on ambiguity, (2) complexity of relationships between manifestations, and (3) a multiplicity of interpretations that do not coalesce into a stable consensus. There are many ways of taking ambiguity and multiplicity into account. One is to look for tensions, contradictions and paradoxes in relation to cultural manifestations. This approach is taken up by Parker (2000) in his study of British manufacturing company Vulcan Industries. The company's official narrative revolves around the idea of being a family business. It is a family-owned enterprise and it claims to treat its employees as family members: people care for each other and one person's problem is regarded as everyone's problem. This suggests an integrated culture. However, when scratching the surface of the family culture, Parker starts to uncover 'cracks in the picture of togetherness' (Parker, 2000: 131). Most importantly, he observes an opposition between people working at the 'top site' – design, marketing, finance sales – and those at the 'bottom site' – the production unit. Each group appears to follow a distinct mode of operation and regards the other group with fundamental suspicion. 'The Vulcan family was one with two halves', Parker (2000: 135) points out. This observation suggests a differentiated culture. Finally, upon closer inspection, Parker realizes that divides also exist *within* the two subcultures. For instance, at the bottom site, the young engineers seem to regard themselves as distinct from senior engineers (and vice versa), while those belonging to one department appear to rely on different assumptions compared with those working for another department. As Parker (2000: 156) notes 'Top site managers, bottom site managers, new engineers, and so on all had different views on the organization's central tasks and pursued these in a variety of contradictory and divergent ways.' This clearly suggests a fragmented culture.

Similar to researchers working with the differentiation approach focusing on three types of inconsistency, proponents of the fragmentation approach examine three kinds of ambiguity: action based, symbolic and ideological. Action-based ambiguity occurs when confusion arises about the relationship between an organization's espoused values and its actual practices. To revisit an earlier example, a company might promote values of responsibility and fairness, but have an extremely complex tax-compliance policy that makes it difficult to decipher if and how the organization actually contributes to society in monetary terms. Symbolic ambiguity occurs when there is no clear-cut relationship between espoused values and artefacts. A company might claim to operate according to values such as egalitarianism and horizontality, but equip employees with different uniforms without necessarily indicating any kind of hierarchy. This may easily lead members to speculate about the perceived status of the uniforms and invite multiple interpretations of their internal relationship. The fragmentation approach always assumes some level of symbolic ambiguity, but the degree of uncertainty varies (Alvesson, 2011). Finally, ideological ambiguity occurs when there is uncertainty about the relationship between different espoused values. A company might claim to exhibit values like sustainability and biodiversity, but (as often happens) omit a specification of these otherwise 'empty signifiers' (Laclau, 1994).

The fragmentation approach seems to fit the present quite nicely. While the integration approach was developed with inspiration from anthropological studies of small and somewhat isolated communities such as Geertz' (1973) account of cockfighting in a Balinese village, the fragmentation approach has been developed as a response to a postmodern age characterized by individuality, complexity and constant flux (Mills et al, 2001). With the advent of digital technology, the boundaries between organizations and their environments are becoming ever more blurred. Customers now participate actively in the production of goods and services, freelancers are increasingly preferred to employees, and organizations seem to operate independently of time and space constraints (Plesner and Husted, 2019). This makes it difficult, if not impossible, to speak of one or two consistent cultures. What is the organizational culture of Uber, a taxi company that is present in more than 10,000 cities but employs no drivers and owns no vehicles? Who decides where this organization starts and stops, and who can speak on behalf of its members? In such a setting, it simply makes more sense to view culture as a fragmented and fickle network of humans, artefacts, norms and values. The same goes for political parties. The old bureaucratic machines of the industrial age are today giving way to innovative party formations that toy with the boundaries of the organization and frame their ideologies to fit individual concerns (Husted et al, 2022). In the following chapter, we shall see how a fragmentation approach can help shine a light on Alternativet's organizational culture, and how a cultural set-up characterized by 'designed ambiguity' (Kunda, 1992) has worked to the party's political advantage.

Towards a multifaceted approach

The following chapter is dedicated to an analysis of Alternativet's organizational culture, based on the three approaches. Instead of choosing sides, the idea is to explore integrative, differential and fragmentary aspects of the party's cultural manifestations. This is in line with Martin and colleagues' (2004) call to move 'beyond struggles for intellectual dominance' and instead adopt a multifaceted approach. As Martin and Frost (1996: 610) note:

> If any organization is studied in enough depth, some issues, values and objectives will be seen to generate organization-wide consensus, consistency and clarity (an integration view). At the same time, other aspects of an organization's culture will coalesce into subcultures that hold conflicting opinions about what is important, what should happen and why (a differentiation view). Finally, some problems and issues will be ambiguous, in a state of constant flux, generating multiple, plausible interpretations (a fragmentation view).

To carry out such an analysis, I first need to define organizational culture in a way that allows me to move somewhat smoothly between the three approaches. As Jennifer Chatman and Charles O'Reilly (2016) point out in their comprehensive literature review, most researchers accept Schein's (1985) conviction that culture can be explored at three levels (see Figure 8.1), but add 'norms' to the equation to highlight that cultures can work as 'social control systems in organizations' (Chatman and O'Reilly, 2016: 214). We will return to this point shortly. However, accepting Schein's definition of culture comes at a cost. First, it means that we are tasked with unearthing the *unconscious* assumptions that drive members of an organization to act in a certain way. To complete this daunting task, researchers need to employ psychological – if not psychoanalytical – methods to get inside the minds of other people. As Schein (1985: 208) notes, members of an organization must be willing to see themselves as 'clients', and researchers need to think of themselves as 'clinicians' if they are to learn something fundamentally true about the bottom level of the cultural iceberg. Second, accepting Schein's definition of culture also means that we accept that culture is a managerial invention. In his view, only managers can invent and transform cultures because they occupy a privileged position in the organizational hierarchy.

From a differentiation point of view, the latter is unacceptable. The point of this approach is to explore conflicts between opposing subcultures, some of which inevitably contradict managerial beliefs, values and assumptions (Schultz, 1995). In that sense, leadership may be a 'culture-influencing activity' (Alvesson, 2011: 111), but it is certainly not the only input to cultural output. From a fragmentation point of view, however, both premises must be rejected. Managers are no more in charge of cultural change than any other member of the organization. In fact, since cultures are assumed to be deeply ambiguous and therefore wide open for subjective interpretations, it makes little sense to speak of individuals as cultural instigators or transformers. Multiple forces contribute to the game of signification that breathes life into organizational cultures, and researchers must therefore liberate themselves from the idea of the manager as a cultural entrepreneur.

So, the differentiation and the fragmentation approach converge in relation to the anti-managerialist position. However, the latter also abandons the idea of unconscious assumptions as the 'cultural DNA' of an organization (Schein, 1985: 21). It seems patronizing to assume that research subjects suffer from a type of false consciousness that prevents them from identifying their own biases, and it makes little sense to think that researchers can gain access to the realm of the unconscious if only they are able to establish trust relationships with their 'clients'. As Vincent Crapanzano (1986) notes in his forceful critique of Geertz' analysis of Balinese cockfights, ethnographers all too often view themselves as capable of penetrating the deeper layers of cultural manifestations and therefore rarely take the time to provide those inhabiting the culture with an actual voice. This approach easily leads to preconceived and arrogant – if not entirely unconvincing – accounts of organizational cultures that expose little more than the author's own convictions and moral biases.[2]

In many ways, a multifaceted approach resonates with Sara Louise Muhr and colleagues' (2022) framework for studying occupational culture in the Greenland Police Force. Based on an interventionist ethnography, the authors show how culture can be seen simultaneously as a source of integration, differentiation and fragmentation. However, instead of viewing fragmentation as a process that leads directly to organizational disintegration (as the literature commonly does), they show how cultural ambiguity can produce cohesion and unity in an organization such as the Greenland Police. The following chapter picks up on this point and relates it to Alternativet.

Cultural control

At least since the rise of the Human Relations School in the 1930s, the idea that informal conditions significantly affect the inner workings of formal organizations has been at the centre of organization theory and industrial sociology (Muldoon, 2012). For instance, in FJ Roethlisberger and William Dickson's (1939: 554–555) account of the Hawthorne Studies, they describe how covert 'patterns of relations' govern 'both the kind of behavior that is expected of a person and the kind of behavior he can expect from others' at the Hawthorne plant. Based on close observations of shop floor interactions, they argue that factory workers are controlled far more by informal norms – 'the logic of sentiments' – than by the formal ordering of the corporation (Roethlisberger and Dickson, 1939: 564).

In the work of Roethlisberger and Dickson, the logic of sentiments is understood as operating covertly and in opposition to the formal structures of an organization. However, the perceived contradiction between the formal and the informal starts to wane in the 1980s when organization scholars begin to conceptualize informal modes of control as an integral part of the formal organization. For instance, in his 1980 'synthesis of the literature on organizational design', Henry Mintzberg (1980) highlights what he sees as an emerging organizational configuration based on ideology as a coordination mechanism. Seeing this configuration as an extension of the 'adhocracy' – a structure based on informality and mutual adjustment between workers – Mintzberg (1980: 339) describes the emerging organizational form as follows:

> It relies for coordination on socialization – in effect, the standardization of norms; it uses indoctrination as its main design parameter; and its dominant part is ideology ... [it is a] part, in fact, of every organization, representing a pull toward a sense of mission. Perhaps the *Missionary*

Configuration will emerge as the fashionable structure of the post-adhocratic age.

Prophetic or not, Mintzberg's words quickly came to represent a fitting description of a type of organization governed by what Amitai Etzioni (1964: 59) calls 'symbolic control' or 'normative power'. Etzioni suggests that such control mechanisms are most prevalent in political and religious communities, since these typically operate without 'physical' (coercive) or 'material' (economic) control mechanisms at their disposal. This idea was later picked up by prominent scholars such as Rosabeth Moss Kanter (1972) in her account of 'utopian' communities and Joyce Rothschild-Whitt (1979) in her work on 'collectivist' organizations such as worker cooperatives. Through such studies, organization scholars are able to show how political and religious communities are capable of attracting members and coordinating activities in the absence of formal structures and economic incentives by simply relying on carefully selected principles. As Rothschild-Whitt (1979: 515) notes:

> Most bureaucratic workplaces emphasize remunerative incentives and few employees could be expected to donate their services if their paychecks were to stop. Collectivist organizations, on the other hand, rely primarily on purposive incentives (value fulfillment), secondary on solidary incentives such as friendship, and only tertiarily on material incentives. ... [T]his kind of normative compliance system tends to generate a high level of moral commitment to organizations. ... Indeed, work in collectives is construed as a labor of love, and members may pay themselves very low salaries and may expect each other to continue to work during months when the organization is too poor to afford their salaries.

With the work of scholars including Arlie Hochschild (1983), Barbara Czarniawska-Joerges (1988), Dorinne Kondo (1990), and John van Maanen (1991), the focus on normative modes of control was reintroduced to occupational settings. However, it is Gideon Kunda (1992) who is usually credited with placing the concept of normative control at the heart of critical organizational analysis. Through his ethnographic study of Tech, Kunda shows how organizational culture can be employed as an ever-present instrument of control that targets 'the underlying experiences, thoughts, and feelings' of employees and supervisors alike (Kunda, 1992: 11). According to him, normative control can be defined as a way of exercising power that works *through the culture* rather than through bureaucratic procedures and targets the hearts and minds of people in the organization. As he notes, 'under normative control it is the employee's self – that ineffable source of subjective experience – that is claimed in the name of corporate interests'

(Kunda, 1992: 11). It is a highly efficient way of governing behaviour in an organizational setting and is a less expensive control mechanism, and therefore an incredibly attractive source of influence for formal as well as informal leaders.

Since the publication of Kunda's *Engineering Culture*, several studies have explored similar dynamics under headings such as 'concertive control' (Barker, 1993), 'social control' (O'Reilly and Chatman, 1996), 'cultural control' (Wilson, 1999), 'identity regulation' (Alvesson and Willmott, 2002), 'socio-ideological control' (Kärreman and Alvesson, 2004) and 'brand-centered control' (Müller, 2017). A general point that runs through such studies is that the worker's authenticity, his or her true self, is sacrificed in the process of constructing what William Whyte (1956) calls 'the organization man'; that is, an employee identity that obediently conforms to the espoused values of the corporation. For instance, Hochschild (1983: x–xi) defines norm-based 'emotional labor' as 'the pinch between the real but disapproved feeling on the one hand and an idealized one, on the other', while Kunda (1992: 183) highlights 'depersonalization' as a widespread phenomenon among employees at Tech. In these accounts, the organizational self is thus seen as a 'false self' that somehow suppresses the 'true self' (Hochschild, 1983: 194). However, while recent studies have confirmed the inauthentic nature of normative control regimes (for example Casey, 1999; Thornborrow and Brown, 2009; Westwood and Johnston, 2012), others have pointed to developments in the field where authenticity is actively encouraged rather than silently suppressed.

Just be yourself …

As mentioned, the fundamental premise of normative control is that employees are exhorted to identify with potentially appealing but inauthentic 'member roles' (Kunda, 1992) or 'self-conceptions' (Thornborrow and Brown, 2009) that are 'deemed congruent with managerially defined objectives' (Alvesson and Willmott, 2002: 619). While this type of management has significant advantages, in the sense that it is both invisible and inexpensive, it has likewise been shown to foster disbelief and burnout (Fleming and Spicer, 2003). Consequently, in recent years, new management techniques have emerged that focus specifically on the 'search for authenticity' (Hochschild, 1983: 185) as well as more flexible and autonomous work lives (Boltanski and Chiapello, 2005). According to Peter Fleming and Andrew Sturdy (2009), this new trend signals the rise of what they call 'neo-normative' control. Under this 'tailored variant of normative control' (Fleming and Sturdy, 2011: 182), members are invited to collapse the distinction between their 'true' and 'false' self, fusing the two into one harmonious subject (Fleming and Sturdy, 2009: 570):

employees are encouraged to be themselves rather than normatively conform to an externally engineered, homogeneous and organisationally based identity. A key element of this apparent new freedom is having fun at work. This reflects a development in the management of fun from the emphasis on conformity and organisational loyalty associated with normative control, towards one of diversity and instrumentality.

As such, while classical forms of normative control thrive on homogeneity and uniformity, neo-normative control plays on heterogeneity and individualization. Jana Costas describes this as a shift from a metaphorical image of the organization as a 'family', in which members are assigned given roles and positioned in paternalistic relationships (see Fleming, 2005), to a culture of friendship that 'appears more open, egalitarian, and individualistic' (Costas, 2012: 377). Here, workers are not necessarily required to 'love' the corporation itself, as is implied by many normative control regimes (Andersen, 2015); they simply have to love 'being in the company' (Fleming and Sturdy, 2009: 574). With neo-normative control, we thus encounter a 'just be yourself' discourse that shuns uniformity and celebrates difference. One key aspect of this type of cultural control involves an invitation to have fun at work, not least because it is seen as a way of expressing authenticity and resisting the standardizing force of classical normative control (Westwood and Johnston, 2012). As Nick Butler and colleagues (2015: 497) note, 'humour – manifested as parody or sarcasm – serves as a way of distancing oneself from the norms of good corporate citizenship'. However, as they and others point out, humour is an ambiguous phenomenon that is 'not inherently opposed to power' and may even be 'well-suited as a tool for exercising power in the contemporary context' (Karlsen and Villadsen, 2015: 515). In the next chapter, we shall see how humour operates as an integral part of Alternativet's organizational culture and how it serves to stifle critique and reconcile political differences within the party.

Party cultures

As exemplified by Kanter (1972) and Rothschild-Whitt (1979) as well as Etzioni (1964), the concept of normative control applies well to studies of religious and political organizations, which possibly has to do with the ideological nature of such formations (Czarniawska-Joerges, 1988). As a Tech manager in Kunda's account of corporate culture notes, the gist of normative control is that people should 'have the religion and not know how they ever got it!' (Kunda, 1992: 9). However, while plenty of studies have explored normative control in extra-parliamentarian organizations such as NGOs (O'Toole and Grey, 2016, for example), social movements (Osterman, 2006), activist networks (Sutherland et al, 2014) and alternative groups (Reedy et al, 2016), hardly anyone has investigated such dynamics within the realm of electoral politics (for exceptions, see Rye, 2014; Ringel, 2019; Husted, 2021). This research gap is surprising, not only because it is relevant to study how some of the most powerful organizations in contemporary society are governed, but also because normative control seems manifested so evidently in the notion of 'party discipline' (see Willmott, 1993; Rye, 2014). To be sure, plenty of insights can obviously be generated by analysing the organizational culture of social movements, especially in relation to movement parties such as those analysed in the previous chapter (see Fominaya, 2020 for an example), but the overall lack of party-specific accounts is nonetheless striking.

That said, some studies have focused on the organizational culture of political parties while addressing questions of culture-based control more implicitly. One early example is Myron Aronoff's (1977) account of 'power and ritual' in the Israeli Labor Party. Aronoff's objective is twofold. On the one hand, he seeks to illuminate the organizational culture of one of the most significant parties in Israel's political history. On the other, he makes a plea for the (re)introduction of anthropological methods to the study of political parties. In terms of the former, Aronoff's main argument is that the culture of the Labor Party largely reflects the national culture of Israel. Like the state of Israel, the Labor Party was created as a strategic fusion of different political identities, when, in 1968, three centre-left parties (Mapai, Andut HaAvoda and Rafi) decided to join forces to shore up votes in the struggle against growing conservative forces. In Aronoff's view, this heterogeneous heritage created a particular organizational culture, ripe with contradictory norms and values, which often resulted in a silent suppression of contentious issues. To theorize this type of suppressive control, Aronoff draws on Peter Bachrach and Morton Baratz' (1962) conceptualization of 'nondecision-making' and shows how the organizational culture of the Labor Party affords practices of clandestine agenda-setting in relation to unspeakable issues, such as the separation of church and state, since such issues are perceived as threatening the unity of the party. Aronoff makes a compelling case for the use of anthropological methods to expose aspects of party organization, previously overlooked by the established literature on political parties. In particular, he highlights the unparalleled utility of participant observation in relation to the study of rituals and symbols in party organization. As he notes (Aronoff, 1977: 6):

I maintain that it is most difficult, if not impossible, to gather data sufficiently rich in the usage of symbols in different social contexts without the researcher's observing and recording the usage of the symbols in the context of ongoing social relationships. Participant observation is therefore a crucial, if not essential, methodology for the study of key aspects of ideology, as well as various other important aspects of socio-political relationships that I shall discuss.

Unfortunately, the reception of Aronoff's study was not exclusively positive. While some criticized his conceptualization of rituals as symbolic actions where the outcome is decided in advance (Zenner, 1978), others characterized his equation of national culture with party culture as strained, and lamented the level of empirical access in the study (Kahan, 1978). Perhaps for that reason, few researchers initially followed in Aronoff's footsteps. In fact, as outlined in Chapter 6, the dominance of the comparative perspective (which, methodologically as well as theoretically, can be viewed as diametrically opposed to the cultural perspective) continued to grow throughout the 1980s and 1990s.

David Kertzer's (1996) account of the Italian Communist Party (PCI) represents a rare exception. Building on Aronoff's interest in symbolism, Kertzer chronicles the story of how the party dealt with the fall of communism in 1990 by renaming itself the Democratic Party of the Left, changing its logo from hammer and sickle to a large oak tree and reframing the official interpretation of the past. Prior to the collapse of the Soviet Union, the party relied heavily on a romanticized version of a glorious past, in which communists were seen as history's main protagonists who courageously defeated Germany and liberated Europe from the totalitarian grip of fascism. After the fall of the Berlin Wall, however, that narrative no longer seemed legitimate, and the party therefore embarked on a process of redefining its own identity and organizational culture. This involved an intense struggle between the party's reformist majority and a small traditionalist minority still wedded to communism as an ideological framework. Against Aronoff's somewhat static definition of rituals, Ketzer's argument (1996: 129) is that the old communist rituals (such as the constant use of 'comrade') served as a means of reconciliation between the reformists and the traditionalists:

> By participating in ritual, people achieve a sense of oneness. ... Less well appreciated is the fact that ritual produces such solidarity without presupposing that the people involved actually interpret the rite in the same way. Communist Party members and sympathizers who assemble in a central piazza, wave red flags, and sing revolutionary songs thereby strengthen their bonds of solidarity with one another and reinforce their sense of identification with the party. While some see the rally as a step toward bringing about the end of capitalism, others view it simply as a pleasant way to spend an evening.

This argument clearly resonates with the basic gist of the fragmentation perspective in the sense that it brings ambiguity to the forefront by illustrating how cultural manifestations do not signify the same thing for all members of an organization. In fact, one of Kertzer's main arguments is that Achille Occhetto, the PCI leader in charge of the transition, succeeded in modernizing the organization by relying heavily on ambiguous symbols that meant different things to different people. However, Ketzer's account of the PCI is mostly differential. It pits two subcultures – the reformists and the traditionalists – against each other and associates particular symbols and values with each camp. Each subculture is characterized as culturally consistent, and the battle for the soul of the party is construed as a struggle *between* these two subcultures rather than a more general struggle over the meaning of symbols. Kertzer exemplifies this dynamic through an in-depth examination of party congresses, which he describes as 'the PCI's holiest rite' (Kertzer, 1996: 137). Focusing on the 19th congress in November 1989, he shows how the reformist majority actively employed cultural artefacts to signal the transition to a post-communist position. The venue in Bologna was decorated in traditional red colours, but the word 'communism' was entirely absent, and the hammer and sickle symbol 'was shrunk to practically microscopic size' (Kertzer, 1996: 140). To counter this symbolic attack on the party's identity, the traditionalist minority used every occasion to invoke communist iconography and sang hymns such as 'Bandiera Rossa' and the 'Internationale'. Only by carefully embracing these symbols (excluding the infamous hammer and sickle) was Occhetto able to win the support of both the reformist and the traditionalist camps.

Such descriptions clearly illustrate the value of using party congresses as windows to the inner life of an organization. At these events, 'internal struggles about programmes and procedures are often fought in plain sight and passionately covered by various media outlets' (Husted et al, 2022: 1334). This is perhaps why the relatively limited literature on party cultures tends to focus precisely on party congresses (or conferences, as they are often called). One particularly noteworthy example is Florence Faucher-King's (2005) impressive study of conferences in four British parties: Conservative, Labour, Liberal Democrat and Green. With an exceptional attention to detail, Faucher-King examines different elements of the party conferences through an anthropological lens, sensitive to the critical role played by rituals in terms of conferring legitimacy on the event as well as the organization as a whole. For instance, she analyses how conferences help to constitute parties as 'imagined communities' (Anderson, 1991), tied together by a normative commitment to ideologies or values that few people can actually define, and how the ritualized nature of conferences helps to reinforce affective bonds between party members ('brothers and sisters' in the case of Labour) who otherwise have very little in common. She also details how the conferences reflect different understandings of leadership and authority. While the Greens and Labour are highly suspicious of leadership, and therefore perform a number of democratic rituals at their annual conferences, the Conservatives and Liberal Democrats are much more comfortable with the idea that some people occupy privileged positions within the organization. (For an interesting comparison of 'green party culture' in France and Britain, see Faucher, 1999.)

Recently, a handful of organization scholars have embraced the idea of studying political parties from a cultural perspective. This has led to interesting analyses that help shine a light on intra-party dynamics otherwise ignored by the established literature on party organization, but it has also pushed the boundaries for how to study organizational politics more broadly. One example is Leopold Ringel's (2019) account of the German Pirate Party. Through ethnographic methods, Ringel exposes a culture of secrecy among the party's newly elected politicians that, in many ways, runs counter to the official ideals of full transparency that have made the pirates respected and admired around the world. To be successful in parliament, the politicians are required to keep some things confidential, including agreements with other parties, which leads them to oscillate between 'open' frontstage behaviour and 'secret' backstage behaviour. While this strategy obviously violates the official pirate ideology, it nonetheless provides the politicians with room for manoeuvre and allows them to strike deals that are clearly in the interest of the party's constituents.

In another example, Paresha Sinha and colleagues (2021) explore what they call the 'dramaturgical resistance leadership' of Jeremy Corbyn during his successful campaign to become leader of the British Labour Party in 2015 and 2016. Building on Victor Turner's (1974) framework for social drama analysis, the authors detail how Corbyn relies on a particular type of narrative to foster a culture of resistance to the political establishment while simultaneously blurring the boundary between the organization – Labour – and affiliated activists, such as Momentum. This combination of narrative elements creates a fertile environment for mobilizing internal support for Corbyn's political project and help Labour rise to new heights in British politics. While Corbyn succeeded in winning the leadership contest, the party failed to win the general election in 2017. In a follow-up study, the authors therefore examine the party's process of dealing with loss, focusing on political parties as unique resources of hope in the face of defeat (Smolović Jones et al, 2021).

Such analyses expose internal processes and inter-personal dynamics that the other three perspectives fail to illuminate but which are nonetheless vital to any comprehensive understanding of party organizations. They explore how party cultures are enacted in practice and exemplify how political parties can be used as magnifying glasses that help us understand organizational dynamics related to power, identity, control and commitment (Husted et al, 2022). Hence, in the following chapter, I will utilize the cultural perspective to understand the role of symbols, rituals and dramas in the case of Alternativet. I will focus on political laboratories and annual conferences in an attempt to show how the party is held together by symbolic practices that allow members to develop affective bonds to the organization and fellow members.

Cultural contributions to party research

In a methodology chapter for a handbook on US politics, Hans Noel (2010: 58) suggests that political parties are extremely difficult study objects for at least two reasons. First, parties are 'informal and sometimes extralegal organizations', meaning that they rarely appear in national constitutions and that the legal framework governing their activities is minimal as a consequence. Second, they 'permeate many different domains of politics' – government, parliament, civil society and so on – which makes it difficult for scholars to assess when, where and how to collect meaningful data about these organizations. We might add that parties are very sensitive and extremely cautious organizations that rarely allow researchers to sneak around unrestricted and seldom submit undisclosed information for scientific purposes. While these factors curb the ability of researchers to study parties in general, they render the study of party *organization* particularly difficult.

Noel's solution to this predicament is for scholars to work with social network analysis to explore how party members are connected and how they maintain relations with stakeholders such as consultants, lobbyists and activists. This is an interesting proposal, but it encourages us to completely abandon the ambition of studying the 'inner life of the party' (Barrling, 2013), since this takes place deliberately 'out of the public eye' (Noel, 2010: 63). My ambition with this chapter has been to show what we might learn from observing what goes on in that 'ill-defined domain', in which party activists operate on a daily basis (Noel, 2010: 63). In my view, the best way to illuminate this otherwise sealed-off territory is to work with the concepts and theories that I have grouped under the 'cultural perspective' heading. I shall highlight here at least three lessons that the established literature on party organization, which is dominated by configurational and comparative research, could learn from engaging more comprehensively with the cultural perspective.

First, the cultural perspective exposes the ways in which political parties are enacted in practice. Instead of focusing on static phenomena like programmes, budgets, membership statistics or representational structures, the cultural perspective focuses on what goes on *inside* the party machine – in the 'lived spaces' (Lefebvre, 1991) inhabited by those involved. Like all organizations, parties must be enacted constantly through ongoing interactions between different actors: agendas must be announced, policies must be developed, activities must be coordinated, events must be organized, meetings must be held, members must be engaged, voters must be mobilized and so on. Without such interactions, organizations become inactive and gradually wither away (for example Hernes, 2014). History is replete with examples of political parties that have suffered this fate. The cultural perspective directs our attention to the micro-level interactions that sustain party organizations as living organisms.

Second, the cultural perspective allows us to analyse phenomena that cannot be measured in any straightforward sense. By focusing on interactions between a multiplicity of both human and non-human actors, scholars working with this perspective try to make 'the invisible visible' (Eriksen, 2021: 21) through 'thick descriptions' (Geertz, 1973) of everyday life in party organizations. By focusing on the norms and values that govern life inside party organizations, scholars working with the cultural perspective are able to expose unwritten rules and customs that may exercise much greater influence on membership behaviour than formal regulations (Roethlisberger and Dickson, 1939). While the integration approach directs our attention to common norms and values, shared by most if not all party members, the differentiation approach alerts us to the fact that party organizations may harbour a number of mutually contradictory subcultures. Finally, the fragmentation approach allows us to zoom in on the individual experience of party members and expose the fact that rituals and symbols may mean very different things to different people.

Third, the cultural perspective is the only perspective that seriously challenges the hegemony of 'the official story' (Katz and Mair, 1992). As mentioned in Chapter 6, the official story approach maintains that it is sufficient for scholars to study formal rules and other authorized documents because they tend to reflect informal power dynamics within the organization. Proponents of the classical and the configurational perspective are similarly suspicious of this assumption in the sense that they believe the most important information to reside in the informal rather than the formal part of the organization, but they nonetheless seem to believe that the official story *ideally* reflects organizational reality. For them, the problem with the official story has to do with inconsistency: there is often an observable discrepancy between representation and reality, as observed by Robert Michels (1915) in relation to SPD party conferences or by Maurice Duverger (1954: xvi) through his conviction that the organization of parties is 'almost entirely a matter of custom'. Proponents of the cultural perspective push the critique of the official story one step further. They do so by bringing ambiguity to the forefront and by emphasizing that formal representations like statutes and regulations are equivocal; they lend themselves to multiple interpretations and are therefore appropriated in different ways by members. Hence, for cultural researchers, the trouble with the official story is not (only) a problem of inconsistency but of *ambiguity*. As RAW Rhodes (2011: 3) notes in his celebrated book *Everyday Life in British Government*, in which he unfolds the virtues of observing government institutions through an interpretivist lens:

> Institutions [parties, for example] are said to take a concrete, fixed form; that is, they have operating rules or procedures that govern the actions of the individuals. This notion is unacceptable. It leads political scientists to ignore effects of contingency, internal conflict, and the several constructions of actors in an institution. If we think of institutions in this way, we do not interpret what institutions mean to the people who work in them. Rather we assume the allegedly objective rules prescribe or cause behaviour.

Taken together, these three points make the cultural perspective a valuable addition to the established literature on party organization. They help us appreciate that political parties are living organisms, that they are governed by cultural norms, and that formal representations of parties are characterized by fundamental ambiguity. The logical result of this realization is that we must probe the subjective understandings of party members and try our best to describe the cultural dynamics that shape these understandings. To do so, however, we need to employ methods and research strategies rarely used in studies of party organization. Hence, the cultural perspective pushes us to study dynamics that the other perspectives overlook and challenges us to update our methodological toolbox and go beyond 'the official story' to explore the seemingly invisible and immeasurable aspects of party life.

9

Alternativet in Cultural Perspective

Introduction

In the previous chapter, I discussed and unfolded what I call the 'cultural perspective' on party organization, based primarily on the work of organization scholars such as Edgar Schein (1985) and Joanne Martin (1992). At the overall level, this perspective focuses on culture as an empirical phenomenon but takes related topics such as identity and power into consideration. This means that the perspective allows for the notion of culture as a gateway to understanding what goes on inside party organizations and seeks to expose the informal dynamics that constitute these collectives on a daily basis. In that sense, the cultural perspective differs substantially from the three other perspectives considered, since none of them offers a comprehensive, in-depth understanding of life inside the party machine. That said, there are certain overlaps between the classical and the cultural perspective. For instance, they both focus on internal power dynamics and the taken-for-granted assumptions that govern interactions within parties. However, the two perspectives differ in their understanding of power, with the former adhering to a Weberian view of authority, and the latter committing to a view of power based on norms and identity. They also differ in terms of analytical strategies. While the classical perspective focuses on inconsistencies between formal rules and actual practices, the cultural perspective takes informality as the starting point for any in-depth investigation and explores how party organizations are talked and enacted into being.

The purpose of this chapter is to apply the cultural perspective to the case of Alternativet. In doing so, I will follow what I have previously referred to as a multifaceted approach to cultural analysis, which seeks to combine insights from the integration, differentiation and fragmentation approaches. For practical purposes, I conduct three separate analyses, each based on one of the three approaches. However, the three analyses turn into a coherent exploration because each of them builds on insights generated by the others. I start by analysing Alternativet's culture as a homogenous set of norms and values that govern actions and interactions within the party. My argument here is that this cultural set-up has helped Alternativet rise to prominence in Danish politics because it encourages members and supporters to read their own preferences into the overall project, but simultaneously prevents them from marginalizing or excluding people with different views. Having established this point, I move on to expose inconsistencies and conflicts between different interpretations of Alternativet's core values and cultural artefacts, focusing particularly on the dramatic local elections in 2017. Finally, I expose the limits of the integration and the differentiation approach by illustrating the fragmented and deeply ambiguous nature of the party's cultural configuration. In the end, I argue that this type of 'designed ambiguity' functions as a subtle and sophisticated type of party discipline within Alternativet, which allows the party to find unity in difference. Hence, my overall argument is that a potential reincarnation of Alternativet as a political project rests on the party's ability to recreate ambiguity and foster political polyphony in a strategic but also disciplining manner.

A new political culture

As recounted in Chapter 3, Alternativet was launched in 2013 as a direct response to the perils of the 'old political culture', which the party sees as characteristic of Danish politics. The old political culture is described as a way of conducting politics that centres on 'mudslinging, tactics, and media spin', and where proper political deliberation has given way to negative campaigning and populist rhetoric (Alternativet, 2014a: 8). Because of this 'old' culture, politicians allegedly fight each other for influence but seem to have forgotten all about the many 'real challenges' facing contemporary society, most notably climate change and environmental degradation. In a debate piece published shortly after the launch of Alternativet, Uffe Elbæk (2014a) characterizes electoral politics in Denmark as a 'theater' where politicians vie for attention and resort to simplistic us-and-them rhetoric to win votes instead of participating in an edifying dialogue about the future of the nation. In another debate piece he unfolds his – and, by extension, Alternativet's – view of the old political culture that permeates the Danish parliament (Elbæk, 2014b: 2):

> I care dearly about Christiansborg [the Danish parliament] and my colleagues, but I also know that we could do much better if only the political culture was different. My workplace has a significant dark side consisting of big egos, lots of gossip, ambushes, collective bullying, loneliness, personalized conflicts, fierce competition, power dramas,

and not least, the urge to be on display whenever the media is around – and they are always around at Christiansborg. It is immediately visible to all those who know what underpins a good organizational culture that such a workplace does not bring out the best in employees. On the contrary, it brings out the most childish and emotional sides of us. … [T]he culture at Christiansborg promotes certain organizational and managerial values and thereby a particular identity and moral codex for politicians. We have created a political culture that curbs reflexive self-criticism, mature self-insight, and sincere curiosity across the parties and between individual members of parliament.

According to Alternativet, one important consequence of this seemingly toxic culture of competitiveness, gossip, bullying and egoism is that it widens the chasm between people and parliament. People want their politicians to discuss important matters and are likely to resent the institutionalized practices of pursuing (personal) power at all costs. Another consequence of such a culture is that it allegedly fosters a cynical approach to politics where citizens become disengaged and therefore uninterested in what goes on in parliament. In the political programme and elsewhere, Alternativet references nationwide surveys that show politicians to be among the least trusted occupational groups in Danish society, alongside journalists and second-hand car dealers. The party notes that: 'The low trustworthiness of politicians and the media's tendency to portray politics as a tactical game gradually worsens the political climate. It damages citizens' desire to participate in politics and can ultimately ruin our ability to address society's real challenges' (Alternativet, 2014a: 8).

To counter the *old* political culture, Alternativet has always ambitioned to create and represent a *new* political culture. Unlike the current condition, this new culture is characterized as revolving around elements such as dialogue, transparency, honesty and public participation. In the political programme, Alternativet therefore highlights several initiatives that are said to promote such virtues within the party itself. One such initiative is an internal ombudsman's council, consisting of four experts in political communication: a university professor in rhetoric, an associate professor in journalism, a professional communication adviser and a journalist. These four experts are meant to assess whether Alternativet actually meets its own standards for political communication. As a member of the board puts it in a press release concerning the ombudsman's council (Alternativet, 2014b: 2):

It is paramount that Alternativet complies with its own goals: that we are transparent, that we are curious, and that we recognize that others might view the world differently. And that we see heterogeneity as the fuel of democracy. We have therefore decided to have independent and insightful people closely monitor us – to correct and encourage us whenever we fail.

The council only released one report, in which it argued that Alternativet, based on a few selected examples, did indeed comply with its own standards for political communication (Alternativet's Ombudsman's Council, 2015). After that, the council gradually dissolved, as the party's focus shifted to the everyday business of running a professional political party. A few attempts were made to resurrect the council, but it has nonetheless been inactive since 2015. While some lamented the dissolution of the ombudsman's council, others pointed to additional and, perhaps, more effective procedures for cultivating a new political culture within Alternativet. One such procedure is the set of 'debate principles' (Alternativet, 2013d), which consist of six almost Habermasian rules for how to engage in political discussions internally as well as in public:

1. We will openly discuss both the advantages and the disadvantages of a certain argument or line of action.
2. We will listen more than we speak, and we will meet our political opponents on their own ground.
3. We will emphasize the core set of values that guide our arguments.
4. We will acknowledge when we have no answer to a question or when we make mistakes.
5. We will be curious about each and every person with whom we are debating.
6. We will argue openly and factually as to how Alternativet's political vision can be realized.

Each principle is followed by a short explanation of its exact meaning. Quite a few of these descriptions centre on the virtue of *listening* or being attentive to others. For instance, the text that follows Principle 2 reads: 'Good solutions can only be reached jointly. That's why it is crucial that we listen to each other – especially when we disagree. Only when we put ourselves in each other's shoes can we debate meaningfully and constructively.' Similarly, the text for Principle 5 says: 'We will always display curiosity about and respect for our opponents with whom we are otherwise in disagreement.' The act of listening therefore quickly became a cornerstone in Alternativet, and members frequently refer to the importance of being attentive to others during debates.

As such, the debate principles have always played a crucial role in Alternativet's political project. They appear in written material and are referenced in speeches and during party-related meetings and workshops. They are often printed on large posters and clearly displayed at political laboratories. This forces participants to acknowledge the existence of the principles and it clearly shapes the type of dialogue that takes place at these events. During one particular laboratory, a party member had written the gist of each principle on the palm of his hand to remind himself not to get carried away during heated discussions. However, despite the instrumental role of the debate principles, other elements have had bigger impacts on the organizational culture of Alternativet. Arguably, the most important element in this context is the party's six core values.

Values, not ideology

One of the most fascinating aspects of Alternativet's political project is that it, initially, was based on little more than six somewhat lofty values. There was 'no grand party bible on the shelf', as Elbæk and Fock proudly proclaimed during the press conference that marked the official launch of the party (Alternativet, 2013e). Instead of publishing an elaborate political programme or specifying a number of key campaign issues, Alternativet started out by highlighting these six values as a foundation for building an unconventional political community from the bottom up. Tangible policies and campaign issues would be developed later through a process known internally as 'open-source politics' (see Chapter 2 as well as Husted and Plesner, 2017). Like the debate principles, the values were supplemented by a short description intended to specify their exact meaning:

1. Courage. Courage to look problems in the eye. But also courage about the future we share.
2. Generosity. Everything which can be shared will be shared with anyone interested.
3. Transparency. Everybody should be able to look over our shoulders. On good days and on bad.
4. Humility. To the task. To those on whose shoulders we stand. And to those who will follow us.
5. Humour. Without humour there can be no creativity. Without creativity there can be no good ideas. Without good ideas there can be no creative power. Without creative power there can be no results.
6. Empathy. Putting yourself in other people's shoes. Looking at the world from that point of view. And creating win–win solutions for everyone.

The primary function of the values is to govern everyday life within Alternativet, but the six words were also instrumental to the party's initial success. Because the values were wide open to interpretation (who knows what words like generosity and humility really mean?) and because they could not immediately be associated with any kind of well-defined ideology (politically charged signifiers like solidarity or freedom were strategically absent), they helped Alternativet mobilize support from across the political spectrum. While some interpreted the values as supporting a liberal, market-oriented world-view, others saw them as fundamental to a socialist way of thinking. One respondent noted: 'It might be that we have 8,000 different definitions of courage, but at least we reflect on our praxis, and then that can be our point of departure.' The weakly defined nature of the values and their ability to attract people with remarkably different backgrounds is illustrated by members describing the values – rather than actual policies – as their primary point of attraction. The values were thus instrumental to creating one of the most heterogeneous political communities in Danish politics, which was precisely what the founders wanted to achieve; because they believed in diversity as a democratic force and they recognized the strategic importance of not being pigeonholed on a classic left/right scale. Elbæk later explained (Alternativet, 2016a: np):

> Apparently, we did something that makes sense for a lot of people. Instead of being tied to an ideology, we are tied to values. This means that people who are former members of socialist parties and people who used to be members of liberal [parties] suddenly unite because the values tie them together. It's not a specific history or a particular understanding of system or class – it's the values.

The pursuit of a non-ideological position is far from novel in politics (Freeden, 2006). However, as several scholars have shown, it is a quest bound to fail. For instance, Laclau (1997: 304) argues that ideologies are nothing but discourses structured around signifiers that have been emptied of meaning in an attempt to represent what he calls 'the absent fullness of the community'. The point is that the critique of ideology depends on the possibility of finding a place external to ideology, which would be the same as trying to find an extra-discursive point of observation – and that is not possible. Hence, values-based politics cannot be seen as a non-ideological type of politics, but as an ideology that pretends to be something else. In fact, as Slavoj Žižek (1989: 2) notes, with a reference to Louis Althusser, 'the idea of the possible end of ideology is an ideological idea par excellence'. Crucially, however, the practical implications of invoking values rather than ideologies are very different. Not least because, as Terry Eagleton (2007) observes, ideologies are most effective when invisible. As we shall see, the explicit rejection of ideology not only allows Alternativet to mobilize support from across the political spectrum, it also installs a certain type of self-management in the individual 'alternativist' (see Husted, 2018).

Alternativet's six core values are espoused in multiple ways. For instance, they almost always figure during meetings, workshops and public events. Similarly, at the end of board meetings, members often spend time contemplating which values characterized the meeting. A third way in which the core values are espoused is through merchandise. At public events, such as televised speeches or demonstrations, leading members of Alternativet are often seen wearing T-shirts or jumpers with one of the six core values printed on them. At one point, Elbæk made it his trademark to wear such clothing, which often provided him with an opportunity to highlight the importance of value-based politics. Furthermore, through the party's official web shop, members of Alternativet can purchase the shirts alongside other merchandise that displays the values, such as badges and fridge magnets. Throughout the interviews conducted for this study, respondents described how they felt that Alternativet and the party's values represented them in a way they had never experienced before. Some respondents even characterized themselves as being one with the values:

> 'What tie us together are our values. I've never experienced that anywhere else – and I've worked with values a lot. But I must say that in all those workplaces I've been, even though values are taken seriously and people are involved in selecting the values, it's always difficult to work according to a set of values. But in Alternativet, we are our values. We've all got the values under our skin. That is what's most extraordinary, I think.'

In the following sections, I shall attempt an analysis of the role played by the values and other cultural manifestations in terms of affording a particular cultural set-up in Alternativet. To that end, I will use the multifaceted framework developed in the previous chapter. I will start by analysing *the* organizational culture of Alternativet and focus on the most common interpretation of the values and other artefacts. This is in line with the integration approach. I will then proceed to a differential analysis and focus on conflicting interpretations of the culture. More specifically, I will focus on the cultural conflict between political representatives (mostly the MPs) and the rest of the organization. Finally, I will analyse the fragmentation of the party's culture and focus on the role played by 'designed ambiguity' in constituting Alternativet as a political project.

Integration: harmony in Alternativet

In an article published in the journal *Culture and Organization*, I take inspiration from studies in organizational psychology and divide Alternativet's core values into two overall categories: vision values and humanity values (see Husted, 2020). Vision values promote creativity and openness to change. Such values typically encourage idea-generation and personal initiative, based on the perception of freedom to think and act independently (for example Finegan, 2000; Abbott et al, 2005). Humanity values, contrary to vision values, promote courtesy and cooperation. Such values typically encourage a benevolent approach to other people, which means that those who share these values are inclined to cancel or disregard differences that usually separate people, such as race, religion or political convictions (for example Finegan, 2000; Abbott et al, 2005). In short, humanity values tend to foster what Schwartz (2007) calls 'moral inclusiveness', understood as a willingness to take opposing views into consideration. Values like courage and humour are often classified as visionary, while values like empathy, humility and generosity are classified as humanitarian. The following (integration) analysis is therefore divided into two parts: one that focuses on vision values, and one that focuses on humanity values. A short ethnographic vignette introduces each part and illustrates a central point in the analysis.

Vision values

Vignette 1: Alternativet's first annual meeting

On a sunny Wednesday morning in June 2014, I found myself in a small village hall in a small town on the northern tip of the island of Bornholm. Throughout the morning, people had arrived from all corners of Denmark to participate in the second part of Alternativet's first annual meeting. While this part of the meeting concerned Alternativet's legal statutes, the first part, held two weeks earlier in the city of Aarhus, concerned the party's political programme. Upon my arrival, I immediately sensed that the Aarhus meeting had been a discouraging and somewhat tiresome experience. As one person said: "Believe me, it was a thoroughly terrible day." According to several participants, the meeting had dragged out for hours because of a seemingly never-ending list of proposed amendments, submitted by participants wanting to push the political programme in different directions. With this experience looming in the back of everyone's mind, the second part of the annual meeting commenced. Before launching into the official agenda, however, a board member took the stage and asked everyone (myself included) to pick one of the six espoused values and reflect on how we intended to bring that particular value to life during the meeting. Having done so, we were then asked to share these reflections with our neighbour. I was paired with an elderly man and I told him that I had chosen courage because I thought that contemporary politics needed some bravery and determination on the part of politicians and voters alike. The man smiled sympathetically, then paused and said: "I have chosen humour because without humour we're never getting anywhere."

One heavily espoused value in Alternativet is courage. Members are frequently seen wearing shirts with 'courage' printed on them and, during events, people will often remind each other to be courageous when debating politics. Courage also figures prominently in the party's manifesto, where it is explicitly stated that 'Alternativet *is* courage' (Alternativet, 2013c, emphasis added). Furthermore, in a popular Facebook video, Elbæk proclaims that 2017 should be 'the year of courage'. In a remarkable attempt to lead the way, the video is recorded in one of the most terrifying rides in the Tivoli Gardens in Copenhagen. Elevated some 60 metres above the ground, Elbæk (2016b), who is said to suffer from acrophobia, explains:

> I believe we need to be much more courageous in general, as citizens and as a society. We should be courageous when we face our problems, and we should be courageous in terms of our curiosity towards each other; courageous in relation to creativity; courageous in terms of stating what we really believe in.

According to Elbæk, courage is thus a matter of believing in oneself, being explicit about one's preferences and facing the problems that one encounters. Particularly the notion of facing problems or 'looking problems in the eye' is a recurrent theme that appears in several of Alternativet's texts, and it is often used to highlight the pressing need for action in relation to climate change. In a newspaper article, published in connection with the Facebook video, Elbæk elaborates on the need to be 'fucking courageous' (Elbæk, 2016b: np). The article begins with a reference to Franklin D Roosevelt's famous quote about fearing fear itself, which allows Elbæk to invoke a dichotomy between courage and fear. Throughout the article, this distinction is repeated, especially in relation to the issue of terrorism (France, Germany, Belgium and Turkey experienced horrible terrorist attacks in 2016). While fear is associated with passivity and retreat, courage is linked to initiative and progress. More importantly, however, courage is associated with the practice of realizing oneself instead of being subdued by those who terrorize (Elbæk, 2016b: np):

> I feel like giving a damn about terror. I feel like giving a damn about those idiots who spoil it for everyone else. I feel like giving a damn about all that and all those who tear things down instead building them up. I feel like we should give each other the opportunity to realize the best version of ourselves instead of denigrating others. And the best version of me is when I'm courageous.

Even though Elbæk and other official representatives often speak of courage in more general terms, ordinary members of Alternativet are quick to translate the value into practice. For instance, one respondent explained how he used courage as a value to remind himself to overcome his fears in a variety of situations. When hosting workshops for Alternativet, he regularly plays the guitar and sings songs to create a warm atmosphere, but playing guitar often makes him nervous to the point where he will consider not doing it. Upon remembering to be courageous, however, he always overcomes. As he puts it: "Damnit, we've got a value called courage!" In this sense, courage connotes self-confidence and willpower, as my own reasoning at the meeting on Bornholm also testifies to. But as Elbæk's video presentation shows, courage is likewise associated with curiosity, collaboration and creativity.

Another very popular value, in terms of merchandise and more broadly speaking, is humour. Like curiosity, humour could easily have been categorized as a humanity value, but, as several official accounts illustrate, humour is more often connected to notions of creativity and initiative. In the official value statement, for instance, humour is framed as the main driver of creativity and good solutions: 'Without humour there can be no creativity. Without creativity there can be no good ideas. Without good ideas there can be no creative power. Without creative power there can be no results' (Alternativet, 2013e).

As such, both of these vision values are in some way connected to notions of creativity, ideation, initiative and progress. The value of humour is particularly telling in this regard. As illustrated by my own experience at the Bornholm meeting, humour promotes a kind of progress that is different from courage. At the meeting, I chose to focus on courage because I believed in the need for determination and willpower, while my neighbour preferred humour as a means of progression. Of course, one can only speculate about incentives and motivations, but, in hindsight, it struck me that the man's propensity for humour might have been motivated by his experience in Aarhus where conflicting interests prolonged the meeting and created an atmosphere that many members associated with the 'old political culture'; that is, an atmosphere characterized by confrontation, combativeness and dogmatism.

Hence, the difference between courage and humour, at least within Alternativet, seems to be that the latter promotes an approach to politics that is more concerned with creating a multiplicity of new ideas rather than clinging dogmatically to one set of ideas. This can be observed not just in Alternativet but in many other contemporary organizations. For instance, in his study of Tech, Kunda (1992) argues that the notion of 'fun' constitutes an important part of the company's corporate culture, where virtues of entrepreneurship and creativity are highly valued. Fleming and Sturdy (2009 and 2011) extend this argumentation by associating the notion of organizational fun with a culture of differentiation and individualization. In the case of Alternativet, the exhortation to be humorous tends to promote an approach to politics where creativity is prioritized. Instead of conforming to other people's views, humour encourages members to be unique and to allow themselves the freedom to explore their own ideas. As one respondent put it: "When we have a value called humour, I dare more."

Summing up, the vision values seem to serve relatively similar purposes. While courage stimulates self-confidence and willpower, humour encourages creativity and uniqueness. The common denominators that connect both values are the notions of ideation and progress based on the power of personal initiative and creative thinking. Through these values, members of Alternativet are thus encouraged to pursue their own ideas and to take initiative in realizing them. But what happens when mutually opposing ideas emerge within the party? In other words, what happens when antagonistic views collide? These are moments when Alternativet's humanity values set in.

Humanity values

Vignette 2: Expelled from Alternativet

Alternativet initially attracted members with remarkably different backgrounds. Some had previously been engaged in leftist parties such as the now-defunct Left Socialists, while others came from more liberal environments. A handful of people even told me that they used to vote for far-right parties, but that they now regarded this as part of a distant past. However, the majority of members had never been engaged in party politics prior to enlisting, which made Alternativet an even motlier crowd. Despite this extreme political diversity, it nonetheless came as a shock for most members when a man called Klaus Riskær Pedersen applied for membership. Pedersen was known to one section of the public as a skilful entrepreneur. The others considered him a criminal. Convicted several times for fraud in Denmark and abroad, Pedersen had served jail time for a few years. Added to this, he had previously been a member of the European Parliament for the biggest centre-right party in Denmark. In many ways, Pedersen thus seemed to represent all that Alternativet was not: corporate and personal greed and old politics. Nonetheless, due to the inclusive attitude of the party, Pedersen was initially accepted. Immediately after enlisting, however, Pedersen began talking to the press. He proclaimed that he believed in Alternativet, but that some of the worst 'fantasies' and 'illusions' had to be rooted out. His job, Pedersen argued, was to get things 'back on track'. After a few days of media frenzy, the central board decided to expel Pedersen from the party on the grounds that he had 'worked against Alternativet's overall idea and basic values' (Alternativet, 2015b). This was the first time someone was expelled from Alternativet. Later, an ordinary member told me her private opinion on the matter: "He was probably courageous and had a sense of humour, but he was definitely not humble; he was not transparent; he was not generous; and he wasn't particularly empathetic either."

Whereas the general role of Alternativet's vision values is to promote ideation and initiative, the humanity values ensure that members remain morally inclusive towards people with different views. The most influential value in this regard seems to be empathy. In fact, the political leadership regularly frames Alternativet as a response to a 'crisis of empathy' in contemporary society, which allegedly has made people incapable of listening to one another without prejudice (for example Alternativet, 2016d). In the official value statement, empathy is described as the act of 'putting yourself in other people's shoes' and 'creating win-win situations for everyone' (Alternativet, 2013e). Being empathetic within Alternativet is thus a matter of being courteous and paying attention to other people's ideas instead of just trying to win an argument or to push one's own agenda. As one respondent explained:

'Empathy can make us listen to each other … it can make us listen to each other on a deeper level. We're supposed to listen to one another, where the other's coming from … or, I can't really remember how we put it exactly, but, you know, we need to pay attention to where the others are coming from.'

An interesting thing about this quote is that it not only illustrates how members of Alternativet translate empathy into action, it also reveals the espoused nature of the six core values. The last part of the quote is particularly telling: "We're supposed to listen to one another", followed by, "I can't really remember how we put it exactly". Such utterances tie in with much literature on the use of values in organizations, especially literature that attempts to answer the question: where do values come from? The most common answer seems to be that values (at least the espoused ones) are those parts of an organizational ideology displayed to the public through, for instance, websites or mission statements (Jaakson, 2010). As such, espoused values are those that leaders find useful, which means that they often end up constituting informal and indirect tools of organizational control (Schein, 1985). Hence, a value such as empathy, while probably shared by most members, likewise serves as a guiding principle that, in the absence of direct supervision or explicit rules, encourages ordinary members to manage themselves according to the idea of listening to one another.

Two other humanity values – generosity and humility – serve similar purposes. They inspire people to listen to one another and they likewise discourage members of Alternativet from engaging in marginalizing behaviour. At least, it becomes extremely difficult to marginalize other people's ideas while maintaining a generous and humble stance. As one respondent explained with reference to what is commonly known within Alternativet as 'a new political culture', a term constructed as the negative image of the established political culture:

'Part of what I really like about the new political culture is that we express ourselves in positive terms – that we don't spend our time attacking each other. It's actually something that I've practised for many years, but I've become even better at it since I joined Alternativet. Because sometimes, when I happen to post [on social media] something just a little bit critical of something, someone will say: "Is that really new political culture?" And I'm actually happy to be reminded in that way ... I'm used to being the most progressive in that area, but it's nice not to be the only one any more.'

As this quote implies, the values of empathy, humility and generosity are generally translated into an obligation to be morally inclusive towards others and to abstain from unproductive criticism ('attacking each other'). Crucially, this also goes for people with opposing views. An illustrative example of how this kind of self-management works in practice was observed at a spontaneously organized political laboratory in June 2015, held at a bridge in central Copenhagen. Here, the workshop facilitator approached passers-by with a simple question: "What is the most important political question for you?" When people responded, the facilitator would always nod his head approvingly and write the answer on a whiteboard. When I asked him how he managed to be so approving of everyone's answers, he showed me the back of his hand where he had written 'yes, and ...' with a black pen. This, he explained, was to remind himself not to engage in the usual 'yes, but ...' type of argumentation, which, according to him, was a far less productive way of deliberating. When asked about why antagonistic views do not clash within Alternativet, another respondent elaborated on the link between the humanity values and the focus on inclusiveness:

'I don't think there's a need for it [clashing]. ... Maybe things are carried by some of those beautiful values about generosity and humility. ... Some of these values intentionally dismantle all those traditional mechanisms of fear. Or, how should I put it, they dismantle the traditional impulse to manifest oneself and to puff one's feathers.'

As illustrated by this quote, a by-product of the focus on moral inclusiveness seems to be a dismounting of personal egos (puffing feathers), which is a translation of the values likewise espoused by the political leadership. This brings us back to the story of Klaus Riskær Pedersen that opened this section of the analysis. While Pedersen seemed to share most of the vision values – he was courageous and had a sense humour, as one respondent noted – he never exhibited any of the humanity values. His worst offence, however, was his attempt to marginalize people with different views from his own. At least, this seems to be the case judging from the official press release. Here, it is described how the expulsion of Pedersen was based on a series of utterances in which, as mentioned earlier, he articulates a desire to 'root out the worst fantasies and illusions', get 'things back on track' and ensure the project does not 'capsize' and fall down 'the abyss' (Alternativet, 2015b: 1–2). Such proclamations are simply not tolerated within Alternativet. In fact, marginalization seems to go directly against the very idea of the party. To say, 'I am alternative; you are not' is the antithesis of what it means to be alternative within Alternativet. As one respondent explained:

> 'This is where I think we really have a job to do internally. We announce these six core values and claim that they permeate everything we say and do. It's probably kind of impossible, but if you do that, then it's really important to walk the talk internally. ... This means that we have to figure out how we talk to and about each other, and, in that sense, I certainly do not believe that marginalizing anyone is appropriate.'

Summing up, like the vision values, Alternativet's humanity values serve relatively similar purposes. While empathy encourages members to listen to one another and to create win-win situations for everyone, generosity and humility are generally translated into an obligation to remain morally inclusive towards different or even antagonistic views. The most important role of the humanity values, however, seems to be to discourage members from engaging in marginalizing behaviour. In fact, the act of marginalization seems to run counter to the very purpose of Alternativet, which, according to the manifesto, is to represent all those 'who can feel that something new is starting to replace something old' (Alternativet, 2013c). Hence, the combination of vision values and humanity values is of utmost importance to Alternativet as a political organization. While the party's vision values encourage members to pursue their own ideas and to take initiative in realizing them, the humanity values discourage people from 'puffing their feathers' by stressing the importance of moral inclusiveness. This combination was neatly summarized by one respondent: "I usually say, 'Everyone's right, but only partially.' Explore the two per cent of truth in what you're saying instead of rejecting things consistently. ... It's far too definite to say, 'This is how it should be!'"

By encouraging people to explore their own 'two per cent of truth' rather than consistently rejecting things, Alternativet allows antagonistic views to co-exist within the party. Since 'everyone's right, but only partially', Alternativet avoids losing support from members who would otherwise feel marginalized by the emergence of dominant ideas. Ultimately, this is what allows an irreconcilable crowd to endure despite fundamental differences.

Differentiation: conflict in Alternativet

The analysis so far has followed the logic of the integration approach and its view of culture as a network of values (the six core values), norms (for example thou shall not marginalize others), humans (such as party members) and artefacts (merchandise, posters and so on). It also complies with Schein's (1985) understanding of culture as something produced by managers, since Elbæk and his associates initially conceived the notion of a new political culture as well as the six core values. Finally, the analysis adheres to the idea that culture is a functional phenomenon; something that is produced as a consequence of ongoing problem-solving. The problem facing Alternativet is what I have previously called the 'problem of particularization' (Husted and Hansen, 2017): a gradual process of ideological specification that easily leads to the marginalization of members who no longer see their own ideas and interests reflected in the party. The apparent solution to this problem is the new political culture or, more precisely, its combination of vision values and humanity values. While the former encourages members to read their own ideas and interests into the party, the latter discourages members from trying to hegemonize their own ideas and interests at the expense of other people's ideas and interests. Because of Alternativet's new political culture, the party can continue to mobilize support from across the political spectrum despite the project's ideological specification (see Husted, 2020).

So far, so good. If you scratch the surface, however, things suddenly appear less harmonious than at first. Cultural inconsistencies and conflicts usually become visible in times of crisis (Martin, 1992). As long as things are running smoothly, heterogeneity is uncontroversial and perhaps even desirable for political organizations such as parties. However, moments of crisis usually turn heterogeneity into a source of conflict, with members fighting over the appropriate interpretation of cultural manifestations such as values or artefacts. These are moments where the differential approach to cultural analysis is particularly useful precisely because it seeks to unearth and illuminate the conflicts that occur between opposing subcultures within an organization (Alvesson, 2011).

In the autumn of 2017, around the time of the local elections, Alternativet encountered its first real crisis. It all began with a leaked email from a member and candidate who expressed, in no uncertain terms, her dissatisfaction with the local leadership in Copenhagen. In the email, she announced her decision to withdraw her candidacy because of a cultural shift that she had observed over the past year. In her view, Alternativet started out as an organization that welcomed critique and edifying dialogue about the party's political and organizational set-up but had recently turned into an organization that 'no longer manages to constructively and reflexively accommodate critical voices'. She then went on to argue that 'all strategically important decisions are made in opaque processes where local democracy clearly has been influenced by other parts of the organization, and where a sly organizational fox such as myself always has been able to predict the outcome in advance'. In her view, the leadership – the national board, the MPs and the leading candidate in Copenhagen – was to blame. She recounted how, on numerous occasions, critics had been silenced and asked to show trust instead of 'gossiping' and 'picking holes in the project' (Helles, 2017: 1):

> I have seen Alternativet's beautiful values and debate principles used repressively to make people fall in line rather than as a foundation for a common constructive-critical and learning-oriented conversation. (The comparison to Orwell's newspeak and the type of language censorship that occurred under certain totalitarian regimes is striking – but those kinds of literary and historical references are frowned upon in Alternativet, although they should inspire reflection). I realize that the election in Copenhagen is – and should be – of strategic importance to the party, but the fact that the political leadership and the secretariat constantly choose to interfere directly with democratic processes to get the desired result is so close to what our hopeful members call 'old political culture' that I am no longer able to tell the difference.

In addition, the member accused the leading candidate in Copenhagen of advancing his own policy agenda at the expense of others, thereby fundamentally violating the basic purpose of the humanity values. 'This', she concluded, 'is an organizational culture that I neither can nor will be part of'. The email and its sweeping critique of Alternativet's leadership would probably have been insignificant had it not been for subsequent events.

At the local elections three months later, Alternativet performed extremely well, especially in Copenhagen where the party earned more than 10 per cent of the votes. Besides gaining important influence at city hall, the result meant that Alternativet could place its leading candidate in one of the city's six mayor positions (in Copenhagen, each administration has its own mayor). Consequently, the party now had to decide which administration and policy area to prioritize. Without much hesitation, the party's leading candidate in Copenhagen chose the often-overlooked and less-prestigious Culture and Leisure Administration. To him, the choice was easy. After all, Alternativet was founded by the former minister of culture as a 'cultural voice' working towards a 'new political culture' (Alternativet, 2013a). However, the decision to prioritize culture and leisure over policy areas that intuitively seemed weightier, such as employment or integration, sparked an unprecedented wave of criticism from dissatisfied members. Opinion pieces were published in newspapers, pictures of resignation forms were posted on social media, and members appeared on national TV accusing Alternativet of betraying its original purpose. Some even circulated pictures on social media of the party's leading candidate in Copenhagen with an added speech bubble: 'Let them eat culture' – a reference to the infamous rebuff of starving peasants attributed to Marie Antoinette.

At the municipal elections, a decision had to be made, but not just any kind of decision. While previous decisions had involved little ideological demarcation, in the sense that choices about including various policy proposals in the political programme did not marginalize other proposals, this decision established a hierarchical relationship between different ideas and interests. The prioritization of 'culture and leisure' over 'employment and integration' thus convinced many members that Alternativet was a party for the creative class rather than a party for everyone, which immediately resulted in declining support. This conviction was later bolstered when journalists revealed that Alternativet's leading candidate in Copenhagen, now mayor of culture and leisure, had spent almost €20,000 on redecorating his office with contemporary art and expensive furniture. In the immediate wake of the local elections, Alternativet fell from 7.2 to 3.1 per cent in national polls and lost more than 10 per cent of its members.

Action-based inconsistency

As mentioned in the previous chapter, at least three types of cultural inconsistency exist: action based (discrepancy between espoused values and actual practices), symbolic (discrepancy between espoused values and artefacts) and ideological (discrepancy between two or more espoused values). In this section, I will examine each of these three types of inconsistency with regard to Alternativet and unfold how they ignite different kinds of conflict within the party. I will begin with the perhaps most obvious inconsistency.

Cultural researchers primarily use the notion of action-based inconsistency to explore discrepancies between the lofty values that managers espouse and the actual practices they sanction (Martin, 1992). For instance, the management of a company might espouse values like fairness and responsibility, but hide profits in tax havens. This type of inconsistency is easy to detect in the case of Alternativet. After all, the practice of spending upwards of €20,000 of taxpayer money on fancy furniture and expensive art for a private office is difficult to reconcile with values like humility and generosity, which the party itself has defined as a matter of being modest, unassuming and sharing 'all that can be shared' (Alternativet, 2013e). Similarly, the practice of tampering with democratic decision-making processes and silencing critique seems rather inconsistent with the values of transparency and empathy, with the latter being seen as the ability to put oneself in other people's shoes and creating win–win situations for everyone (Alternativet, 2013e).

Action-based inconsistency can also be used to highlight disharmony between accepted norms and real-life practices. A company might, for example, purport to welcome criticism, but shut it down as soon as it surfaces. In many ways, this is precisely what happened in Alternativet at the time of the local elections. At least, this was the experience of many members at that point in time. Other norms were equally disregarded. For instance, the unofficial but nonetheless accepted norm of never marginalizing other members (never 'I am alternative; you are not') was clearly violated when the leading candidate in Copenhagen decided to advance his own personal agenda at the expense of policy agendas promoted by other candidates. In fact, this was one of the main reasons why the resignation email quoted earlier was circulated internally and later leaked to the press.

Symbolic inconsistency

Symbolic inconsistency occurs when there is discrepancy between espoused values and cultural artefacts. For instance, a company might promote values like equality and horizontalism, but equip managers with corner offices on the top floor, clearly signalling a hierarchical relationship between managers and workers. Once again, it is easy to identify this type of inconsistency in Alternativet. After all, fancy furniture and expensive art clearly serve as artefacts that make the party's explicit commitment to the three humanity values (generosity, humility and empathy) appear shallow or even non-credible. Symbolic inconsistency is also visible in relation to a value that is usually highlighted by members as essential to Alternativet, although not necessarily treated as an 'official' value, namely, trust. As one member put it: "It's the only thing that binds us together. You cannot launch a project like this without unconditional trust in each other. It's the belief that trust is what makes us better. Trust in each other. … I've never been to a place where there's this much trust."

In Alternativet, trust thus functions as an 'attributed' value that members generally regard as representative of the organization (Bourne and Jenkins, 2013: 499). However, the party leadership's commitment to trust was repeatedly questioned by members in the months leading up to the local elections in 2017. For instance, one of the issues highlighted in the leaked email was precisely the leadership's lack of trust towards ordinary members and their ability to develop policies that would be strategically sound for the party. This is, clearly, an example of action-based inconsistency, but it also had a symbolic dimension. A few months before the local elections, Alternativet published a political programme called *17 Goals for Copenhagen*, which the leading candidate claimed to be based on input from more than 500 people from all walks of life. That claim appeared untrustworthy to many members who were convinced that the programme had been developed primarily by the political leadership. Hence, as an artefact, the programme came to represent the leadership's lack of commitment to its own values – most importantly, trust (see Husted and Just, 2022).

Evidently, symbolic inconsistency can also occur in relation to accepted norms. One very prominent norm, which was particularly influential in the years following the launch of Alternativet, was, as stated in the manifesto, that the party is for anyone 'who can feel that something new is starting to replace something old' (Alternativet, 2013c). So, Alternativet is for all those who identify with some kind of alternative to the current state of affairs. That norm initially informed many initiatives within the party, including the political laboratories where heterogeneity was celebrated and even encouraged. However, the local elections in 2017 seriously challenged this idea of almost absolute inclusion. Here, Alternativet's local branch in Copenhagen hosted a colourful election party at an LGBTQIA+ bar called Monastic where participants allegedly could experience 'darkrooms' and 'sex swings'. These were eventually removed before the party, but as artefacts, they nonetheless came to represent a sexualized culture that seemed foreign and repulsive to many ordinary members of Alternativet. As such, Alternativet quickly came to be seen as a party for the creative class in the big cities rather than a party for all 'alternativists'.

Ideological inconsistency

Ideological inconsistency occurs when there is disharmony between different espoused values. For instance, a company's management might promote the values of sustainability and biodiversity, but pride itself on contributing to the nation's consumer economic growth. This type of inconsistency is, perhaps ironically, more difficult to detect in political parties because of their strong focus on political regimentation (Rye, 2014). After all, one of the worst things that can happen to a political party is to be accused of ideological inconsistency and political veering. However, Alternativet is not like most parties. In fact, it was in many ways conceived as an organization that could unite 'the people' in the absence of party discipline and political whipping. In that sense, Alternativet could be said to incarnate the very idea of ideological inconsistency because political diversity is seen as a resource rather than a liability. We will return to this point later.

One possible example of ideological inconsistency did happen in 2015, right after Alternativet's parliamentary entry. When the party entered parliament, the MPs suddenly found themselves in a difficult situation where they had to reconcile the original bottom-up approach to policy making with the type of fast-paced decision-making that occurs in parliament. This resulted in a number of troubling incidents where

MPs sponsored bills in parliament that were seen by members as directly antithetical to the Alternativet agenda (see Chapter 3 for examples). This led Elbæk, in an interview with a national newspaper, to characterize Alternativet as a 'visionary-pragmatic party' capable of developing grand visions through bottom-up processes *while also* allowing MPs 'flexibility' to seek influence in parliament (Alternativet, 2015a). The notion of being visionary-pragmatic was seen by several members as an oxymoronic expression that merely concealed the fact that Alternativet, like so many radical parties before them, had surrendered their alternativity at the altar of realpolitik.

This final example points to the existence of at least two subcultures within Alternativet. On the one hand, there is the parliamentary group, which consists of the political leadership and its staff. This group sees Alternativet as a professional party that is capable of exercising influence in parliament on the basis of a coherent and realistic political strategy. On the other hand, there are the ordinary members who believe Alternativet to be a social movement that is capable of representing a wide range of counter-hegemonic ideas and cares less about parliamentary influence. The first group works according to a number of professional norms, such as fast-paced decision-making and cross-party collaboration, and accepts the current conditions of possibility for political organizations. The second group works according to Alternativet's original values and believes in a radically different society where current conditions have been turned upside-down. In an internal organizational report (Alternativet, 2020: 15), the party even recognizes this cultural division:

> An ongoing debate has unfolded throughout most of Alternativet's life about whether we are a movement or a party or both. ... Perhaps the discussions have been carried by individual preferences and ways of working. Those who have a strong desire for freedom and autonomy might find the movement-part most attractive. On the other hand, those who are preoccupied with running for city council or national parliament will find the party-part attractive.

The parliamentary entry in 2015 and the local elections in 2017 exposed the differences between these two subcultures and sparked several internal conflicts. These contributed more or less directly to significant loss of memberships and declining support in opinion polls. Schein (1985) would arguably have characterized these conflicts as a failure of cultural leadership, while scholars committed to the differentiation approach (for example van Maanen, 1991; Kunda, 1992; Alvesson, 2011) would have described the existence of two or more subcultures as an unavoidable premise for complex organizations such as contemporary political parties.

Fragmentation: ambiguity in Alternativet

Things that seem harmonious or neat at a distance are often much more complex and messier upon further inspection (see Martin, 1992; Hasse, 2011). This is also true for Alternativet's cultural configuration. In the first analytical section – following the integration approach – the party's culture was described as a harmonious mix of vision values and humanity values, supported by a dense network of human and non-human actors. In the second section – following the differentiation approach – it was described as consisting of two more or less homogenous subcultures: one that represents the 'movement part' of Alternativet, and one that represents the 'party part'. The fragmentation approach rejects such easy categorizations by focusing on ambiguity as a defining feature of all organizational cultures.

One way of exposing ambiguity in an organization is by talking to its members and asking them to unfold their own individual interpretations of norms, values and artefacts. When doing so, one will often learn that people are genuinely confused about the exact meaning of these elements, or that they perhaps do not attach much importance to things that otherwise seem very significant. We have already encountered one example of the former in this chapter. Recall the member of Alternativet who was asked to define the value 'empathy': "We're supposed to listen to one another, where the other's coming from ... or, I can't really remember how we put it exactly." I do not suggest that this person doesn't know what the word empathy means, merely that he is unsure what it signifies within Alternativet. In other instances, members might be able to define certain norms and values but simultaneously view them as insignificant or at least less important. For instance, one member was asked to reflect on her attitude to the notion of sustainability, which is fundamental to Alternativet, and the prevalent tendency within the party to equate sustainability with veganism. She expressed her view like this:

> 'I'm not one of those eco-hippies. There are quite a few eco-hippies in Alternativet, and that is totally fine by me. I think that the thing about only eating 100 grams of meat a day is ... well, it's fine by me. I like vegetables and all that, so I don't really provide any resistance toward it. But it's one of those cases where I can't follow the logic.'

The final part of this quote is particularly interesting. The member clearly dismisses the juxtapositioning of sustainability and veganism, which she associates with the 'eco-hippies', but she does not 'provide any resistance toward it'. This illustrates the type of individual freedom that exists within Alternativet. One is free to pursue personal agendas and to read one's own preferences into the project, as long as this pursuit does not limit other members' ability to do the same (recall the aim to 'explore the two per cent of truth in what you're saying instead of rejecting things consistently'). However, the quote also illustrates a fundamental point about the fragmentation approach to organizational culture: regardless of how central certain things appear at a distance, they might turn out to be insignificant to the everyday life of individual members. For instance, during interviews and observations, several members would explicitly downplay the importance of Alternativet's six official values and highlight other values that they personally found more fitting – words like love and curiosity were often used in these cases.

Action-based, symbolic and ideological ambiguity

The words inconsistency and ambiguity may appear relatively similar, but, within the cultural perspective, they represent rather different phenomena. While inconsistency points to a deviation from a certain baseline, such as the official values, ambiguity points to polyphony or equivocality – the existence of multiple interpretations or voices – as a more general condition in organizations (see Weick, 1990; Hatch and Erhlich, 1993; Alvesson, 2001). In other words, while inconsistency signifies an episodic occurrence that may or may not transpire, ambiguity represents a fundamental aspect of life as such; inconsistency is avoidable, ambiguity is not. Moreover, while inconsistency relies on a binary logic – consistent vs inconsistent – ambiguity relies on a logic of polyvalence. In a situation characterized as ambiguous, there are not just two but multiple possible interpretations. This is why the two terms belong to different theoretical approaches (Martin, 1992).

Nonetheless, like inconsistency, ambiguity can be observed in relation to actions, symbols and ideology. Action-based ambiguity is particularly visible when there is confusion about the relationship between an organization's espoused values and its actual practices. One of Alternativet's values that seems easy to understand, but often turns out to yield plenty of ambiguity, is transparency. In contemporary society, where consecutive waves of digitalization have afforded an unprecedented level of organizational visibility, transparency is often seen as the primary way of generating legitimacy (see Barros, 2014). Plesner and Husted (2019: 196) note: 'We are witnessing a general rise in expectations regarding how organizations interact legitimately with the surrounding society, and how they disclose information that allows the public to judge whether they act legitimately.' One of the most remarkable transparency initiatives that Alternativet launched in order to generate this kind of legitimacy was to live-stream meetings in the parliamentary group via Facebook. In a press release (Alternativet, 2016b), Elbæk explained the reasoning behind the initiative:

Trust in politicians continues to fall to unprecedented low levels. I believe this tendency is caused by the high degree of closedness that permeates the political space. We try to break down this closedness. This is why we, on several occasions, have invited journalists to observe our group meetings. ... I see the live-streaming of our group meetings as a natural extension of this effort. Obviously, we have thought hard about it and discussed whether it would limit the willingness to debate. However, because we have values like transparency and courage, I believe we should be the ones to open up. If not us, who will?

Many observers heralded this initiative and characterized it as a practical realization of the new political culture. Others, however, were sceptical and described the initiative as little more than strategic window-dressing. Some warned that it would deny the MPs their ability to discuss sensitive matters, while others pointed out that important conversations would simply move to the corridor (see Ringel, 2019, for a similar discussion within the German Pirate Party). In other words, there was no stable consensus on how to interpret the initiative. When the initiative finally launched, few ordinary members had time or energy to sit through hour-long and sometimes rather dull meetings on a regular Tuesday or Thursday morning, and live-streaming was soon discontinued as a consequence. Hence, the live-streamed group meetings are an example of action-based ambiguity because they expose the existence of cultural equivocality. Other elements of Alternativet are clearly also marked by ambiguity, but the visibly equivocal nature of this initiative made it directly observable.

Symbolic ambiguity is particularly visible when there is confusion about the relationship between espoused values and cultural artefacts. As mentioned, one of the most popular values within Alternativet, among both ordinary members as well as the political leadership, is humour. In most cases, humour is not only associated with fun, but also seen as an important source of creativity. This may be the reason why Elbæk was often seen at important events such as party conferences wearing a light green tulle dress while imitating a graceful ballerina. During one party conference in 2017, Elbæk told the press: 'We wish to signal that politics should not be taken too seriously. Politics is so pompous. We use humour to say, yes, politics is serious but let us exercise it in a humane manner' (Alternativet, 2017). Like the transparency initiative, some members applauded Elbæk's attempt to build a humorous approach to politics, and the green dress somehow came to represent the party's critique of the old political culture. However, others, especially young people, saw it as distracting focus from serious political issues and as a violation of the party's core ambitions in relation to issues such as global warming and democratic disengagement. For instance, one media pundit criticized Alternativet's inability to mobilize the 'new angry generation' and characterized Elbæk's political project as having been 'muddled by tulle dresses' (Madsen, 2019).

Ideological ambiguity is particularly visible when there is clear uncertainty about the relationship between different espoused values and their exact meanings. One effective way of exposing ideological ambiguity is by employing the concept of *différance* (Derrida, 1982). This allows the researcher to focus on the 'haunting absences' that add meaning to a particular identity (Del Fa and Vásquez, 2019) and to explore what is silently assumed in descriptions of organizational cultures. In Joanne Martin's (1990) own work, she illustrates the utility of this concept through an analysis of hidden gendered dynamics in a male CEO's story of a female employee who took three months off for the birth of her child because it was 'an important thing for her to do'. As described in the previous chapter, such différance has both a spatial and temporal dimension. On the one hand, it signifies the act of being different or non-identical (spatially); on the other hand, it signifies the act of deferring or postponing meaning into the past or the future (temporally). Both types of absence are easily identified in the case of Alternativet.

The spatial dimension is at the forefront of Alternativet as a political project. The party continuously stresses the flaws of the 'old political culture' and it constructs its identity in a highly oppositional manner by emphasizing how Alternativet is a direct response to the ills of modern-day politics. In fact, opposition and negativity is built directly into the party's name, which in English means *the* alternative. As such, oppositional thinking permeates the organization and its rhetoric. This is further visible in the way the party pictures itself as a direct response to several different crises in contemporary society: the climate crisis, the resource crisis, the empathy crisis, the trust crisis, the system crisis and so on. The successful articulation of such crises provides a fertile ground for alternatives to emerge, as Stavrakakis et al (2018) have shown.

The temporal dimension of différance is similarly easy to detect in Alternativet's political rhetoric. Once again, the manifesto provides the clearest expression of this. Here, the party claims to constitute a 'hope', a 'dream' and a 'yearning for meaning' (Alternativet, 2013b). Such utterances align uncannily well with Derrida's (1994: 65) idea that empty signifiers such as 'democracy' or 'communism' (or 'alternative') must represent a hope that 'cannot be anticipated' to be politically useful. Such signifiers refer back to some idealized past and thrive on a type of political 'potentialization' (Andersen and Pors, 2022) that keeps the future open and invites people to read their own preferences into whatever they represent (Laclau, 1994). Such utterances are part of what initially made Alternativet so appealing to so many, particularly because they are often supplemented by direct appeals to the reader.

The opening line in the original manifesto reads: 'There is always an alternative!' (Alternativet, 2013b). This quickly became a slogan for the party and still figures prominently in campaign material and on the official website. Moreover, the idea of continuously envisioning alternatives to the current state of affairs was initially also ingrained in a number of organizational practices. For instance, the political laboratories were conceived as places where people could deliberate on specific policy issues (tax, education, health and so on), but they always included 'dives' (*slyngelstuer* in Danish) where people who were not particularly interested in the issue(s) at hand could discuss whatever they pleased. As such, the dives provided a space for political dissensus that could challenge provisional stabilizations of Alternativet's political project and breathe new life into the idea that there always is an alternative – even to *the* alternative.

Designed ambiguity as party discipline

As we have just seen, ambiguity is at the centre of Alternativet as a political project. There are multiple reasons why. For one, Alternativet was initially conceived as a bottom-up project with little political direction, which invited many different people to read many different things into the project. In that sense, the party might even be characterized as purposefully ambivalent in terms of its ideological commitments. However, as I have tried to show, ambiguity also permeates other parts of the organization. The organizational values are, for instance, incredibly ambiguous, and their moral exhortations are clearly open to numerous interpretations. What exactly does it mean to be transparent, courageous and humorous? What does it mean to be empathetic, humble and generous? What does it mean to show trust, and how is curiosity best enacted? Furthermore, how do these values assist members in realizing the new political culture? The answers to these questions are blowing in the wind, partly because the values remain somewhat empty, but also because freedom is 'the right to imagine everything being different', as Elbæk explains in his own manifesto *The Next Denmark* (Alternativet, 2018a).

As such, one might say that Alternativet's organizational culture is founded on what Kunda (1992: 18) calls 'designed ambiguity'; that is, a cultural set-up deprived of consistency, clarity and consensus – all the things that characterize harmonious monocultures – but something that nonetheless 'sucks people in'. In Kunda's analysis, the ambiguous cultural set-up indirectly encourages employees at Tech to work tirelessly to satisfy essentially insatiable demands. Since they do not know what is expected of them (other than 'do what is right'), the employees look to each other for confirmation on how to structure their work lives, and since the norm at Tech is to work around the clock, this is what most people end up doing.

But how does cultural ambiguity work in Alternativet? My argument is that ambiguity, although seemingly liberating, functions as a subtle type of party discipline that serves to keep members on board and in line. The high level of ideological ambiguity is not only incredibly effective in terms of political mobilization, it also deprives members of the ability to demarcate the party politically (see Husted, 2018). By refusing to be pigeonholed on a traditional left/right-scale ('we are based on values, not ideology'), and by constantly deferring the question of political direction ('freedom is the right to imagine everything being different'), Alternativet was initially able to attract members from across the spectrum. Since no one had the authority to decide Alternativet's ideological position, anyone could potentially interpret the party's official stance as aligned with their own political views. When asked about how one recognizes a true 'Alternativist', one member put it like this:

> 'Who's an Alternativist? Well, at the most fundamental level, I would say that everyone is. Then, of course, there will always be some hardcore business dude with grey hair that needs a bit more persuading. But then again, in the end, I bet he too once had dreams and visions.'

In other words, cultural ambiguity is an effective tool for attracting political support, since it appeals to anyone with 'dreams and visions'. This is clearly also why so many political projects are based on empty signifiers like 'freedom', 'solidarity' or 'sustainability' (Laclau, 1994). But there is another aspect of the type of ambiguity that characterizes Alternativet's cultural set-up. It not only *attracts* people, it also *limits* people's ability and willingness to exclude or marginalize fellow party members with diverging views. I keep returning to the idea that the antithesis to being alternative within Alternativet is to say, 'I am alternative; you are not'. This norm of non-marginalization, which is clearly fuelled by cultural ambiguity, serves as an excellent tool for disciplining members. Instead of policing the party through explicit regimentation, whipping or 'wire-pulling', as Ostrogorski (1902) calls it, the political leadership can safely count on members being inclusive towards each other. No one can delimitate the party politically, which means that everyone is potentially welcome.

The flip side of this somewhat laissez-faire type of party discipline is that it may give rise to a 'tyranny of structurelessness', in which 'the strong or the lucky [can establish] unquestioned hegemony over others' (Freeman, 1972: 232). In many ways, this is precisely what happened during the local elections in 2017. Coincidentally, this event is what marks the beginning of Alternativet's downfall. Designed ambiguity is, in that sense, a potentially dangerous strategy for political parties. It is, however, one of the ways in which parties can respond to the need for keeping members in line and on board, while falling back on 'traditional notions of command and discipline' (Rye, 2015: 1053).

10

Towards an Eclectic Framework

> We may imagine a way of enhancing the compensation of blind
> spots in a different direction. The inspiration might be: two
> diametrically contradictory theories, each, however, resting
> exactly on the other's blind spot, so that they cannot be integrated
> into a synthesis. ... Neither theory is 'right'; it is the conflict
> between them that makes both 'right'. Constant 'switching' from
> one to the other gives an almost simultaneous observation from
> two contradictory but complementary perspectives. But there
> is a strict condition for complementarity: that each be able to
> illuminate the other's blind spot.
>
> Gunther Teubner (2006: 60): 'In the blind spot'

Focus and blind spots

The previous chapters have been concerned with the description and
application of four distinct perspectives on party organization: classical,
configurational, comparative and cultural. As mentioned, the exact
demarcation of these four ways of approaching the study of party organization
is in no way God-given. Lines could easily have been drawn elsewhere; a
fifth perspective should perhaps have been added to make the discussion
more nuanced; or two perspectives might have been merged to make it
simpler. The distinctions between the four perspectives represent my way of
ordering the literature on party organization, and it could have been done
very differently. It is, furthermore, important for me to stress that this book
in no way pretends to paint an exhaustive picture of contemporary party
organization research. I have selected a number of key contributions that
I believe are central to each of the four perspectives and then used these as
examples of particular ways of observing and thinking about political parties.

Each perspective focuses on something particular and uses this 'something'
as a point of departure for talking about political parties in general. With

focus, however, comes blind spots. 'The eye that sees everything is no longer able to see anything', as Gunther Teubner (2006: 58), the author behind this final chapter's epigraph, rightly asserts. When we look for something particular in the empirical world, we automatically exclude other things from consideration. This may be because we are simply not interested in that which is excluded, but it might also have something to do with the theoretical and methodological assumptions that guide our analytical gaze. Clarifying the connection between focus and blind spots is at the heart of any proper analytical strategy (Andersen, 2003), but such considerations nonetheless remain surprisingly hidden in much academic work, where arguments are often phrased as impeccable truths rather than as the product of contingent and sometimes arbitrary choices.

This also goes for the literature on party organization, especially perhaps to the body of research that I have called 'the comparative perspective'. Because of its undeniable scholarly dominance, it sometimes fails to account for the analytical and methodological choices that are fundamental to its mode of operation. For instance, why is it 'riskier' for researchers to enter 'too far into the analysis of each case' than to construct 'an overly superficial analysis of the different case studies' (Panebianco, 1988: xiv)? In other words, why is analytical depth less important than analytical width? Similarly, why is the otherwise well-established conviction that researchers should not rely too heavily on official material produced by the parties themselves 'fundamentally wrong in its emphasis' (Katz and Mair, 1992: 8)? In other words, why is

Table 10.1: Focus, assumptions and blind spots of the four perspectives

	Classical	Configurational	Comparative	Cultural
Focus	Authority and democracy	Structures and systems	Genetics and contingencies	Norms and values
Core assumptions	The individual is the locus of democracy, and power is always employed to restrict individual action.	Organizations are determined by their own anatomy, but can have effects on surrounding institutions.	Organizations are contingent upon their history and environment, and official data reflects actual power dynamics.	Humans are governed mostly by the informal aspects of organizations, and cultures can be fragmented.
Blind spots	The absence of 'organization' is not always liberating, and power is not necessarily conservative.	Formalities do not always guide practice, and organizations rarely live an autonomous existence.	Many things that matter *cannot* be quantified and compared, and official data only represents one version of reality.	Many things that matter *can* be quantified and compared, and formal rules significantly impact practice.

it safe to assume that actual power struggles will automatically materialize in sanctioned rules and regulations, when plenty of classical studies tell us otherwise? Finally, why is the only viable alternative to relying on official material to 'collect expert judgements' (Scarrow and Webb, 2017: 13)? In other words, why are ethnographic observations and other qualitative methods not an option when it comes to understanding how parties organize, especially given the fact that so much party activity takes place 'in an ill-defined domain, often deliberately out of public eye' (Noel, 2010: 63)? There are probably many reasonable answers to these questions, but they are often blowing in the wind. In Table 10.1, I have listed what I believe are the most important focuses, assumptions and blind spots for each perspective.

An eclectic framework for the study of party organization

As shown here, all four perspectives rest on a number of core assumptions and blind spots. There is nothing surprising or invidious in that. All analytical strategies have blind spots. The task is to be transparent about these and to clarify the boundary conditions for the argument that one is advancing. What can we actually say something about, and what assumptions are necessary for the argument to be valid? Once the boundary conditions have been established, we could leave it at that, which again is perfectly fine. But we can also push further, in an attempt to illuminate that which we cannot otherwise see. Doing so, however, requires a commitment to what might be called 'eclecticism'; that is, the combination of elements from seemingly incommensurable theoretical perspectives, in order to observe things that might otherwise remain hidden 'in the blind spot' (Teubner, 2006). According to Rudra Sil and Peter Katzenstein (2010: 2), who argue in favour of what they call 'analytic eclecticism', the point is 'to resist the temptation to assume that one or another research tradition is inherently superior for posing and solving all problems', while maintaining 'that we can and should do a better job of recognizing and delineating relationships between concepts, observations, and causal stories originally constructed in different analytic perspectives'.

A couple of years ago, I edited a Danish textbook on eclecticism with Justine Grønbæk Pors. In the introductory chapter, we outline two approaches to the combination of otherwise distinct theoretical perspectives (see Husted and Pors, 2021). The first approach is called *integration*. The point of the integration approach is to combine elements from theoretical perspectives that rely on somewhat similar assumptions but which have diverging analytical interests. Doing so may help us explore a range of empirical phenomena that do not fall naturally within one particular perspective. For instance, we might combine two perspectives that rely on the same assumptions about power and resistance but focus on relatively different empirical phenomena. This may help us expand the boundary conditions for our argument or bring nuance to academic discussions that have reached some kind of stalemate. The other approach to eclecticism is what we call *friction*. Here, the point is to combine elements from theoretical perspectives that rely on more or less incommensurable assumptions. This may sound like a non-scientific endeavour that might quickly lead to trouble, but it is the approach advocated by Teubner (2006), based on the conviction that new insights can be generated by 'switching' from one perspective to the other. The task is, as also highlighted by Sil and Katzenstein (2010), not to view one perspective as superior to the other, but to use them as analytical resources that complement each other. However, as Teubner (2006: 60) notes, there is one crucial condition for combining elements from two incommensurable perspectives: 'that each be able to illuminate the other's blind spot'.

The main difference between the two types of eclecticism is that the integration approach, true to its name, seeks to construct one *integrated* analytical framework, while the friction approach oscillates between two diverging frameworks. In the former, the ambition is to integrate disparate elements into one coherent synthesis. In the latter, the point is to keep these elements apart, because they simply cannot be integrated into a single analytical strategy, and to use this incompatibility to expose blind spots. That which cannot be seen by one perspective might be at the heart of another perspective, and to use this difference strategically is the overall ambition of the friction approach to eclecticism.

Based on the preceding chapters, it seems to me that some of the four perspectives can be combined according to the integration approach, while others can be combined in line with the friction approach. As we have seen, the configurational perspective relies on many of the same assumptions as the comparative perspective. This may have something to do with their shared relationship to contingency theory. In fact, some might even argue that they should be merged into one single point of observation. For reasons I cannot revisit here, I disagree with that proposition (see Chapter 4), but I certainly believe that the two perspectives can be easily integrated. For instance, we might wish to use Duverger's concept of 'basic elements' to explore the prevalence of these across national contexts or at different levels of the same national context. We might also wish to explore how certain internal contingencies, such as organizational size, financing or participatory structures, give rise to particular configurations, or how certain external contingencies, such as party systems, technological inventions or voter demographics, limit the emergence of other configurations.

In a similar fashion, I believe the classical perspective and the cultural perspective can be integrated without too much trouble. In fact, some might argue that the cultural perspective represents a return to some of the research interests that were central to the classical perspective, such as the relationship between power and democracy, and that the two perspectives overlap with respect to their methodological dispositions, including the preference for participant observation. That said, some elements, such as the conceptualization of power and the prescriptive line of inquiry that we find in the classical perspective, clearly set the two apart. Nonetheless, interesting research could no doubt be conducted based on a fusion of the two perspectives. For instance, we might wish to understand how oligarchy emerges on a micro-sociological level: how is elite rule justified in everyday interactions, and what cultural artefacts support the assumption that the few should rule the many? Conversely, we might wish to explore how certain cultural norms and values serve democratic ends while others pull in the opposite direction, and how members disagree on the meaning of these norms and values.

The most novel research might be produced by combining perspectives that appear incommensurable. The perhaps most colourful combination includes the comparative perspective and the cultural perspective since these are diametrically opposed theoretically as well as methodologically. For instance, we might explore how certain environmental conditions give rise to a particular type of party, and then subsequently ponder how that party constructs its own organizational culture and identity in practice. Such a combined research interest is valuable because the two sub-analyses rest precisely on each other's blind spot. While the cultural perspective can say very little about the contingencies that impact an organization in a causal manner, the comparative perspective can. And while the comparative perspective can say very little about the inner life of the party, the cultural perspective can. The two perspectives cannot be integrated because they rest of diverging assumptions about organizational reality and scientific inquiry, but we can indeed switch between them and make productive use of the friction that occurs.

Four perspectives on an alternative party

In a sense, this is precisely what I have been trying to do throughout this book. By repeatedly applying the four perspectives to the case of Alternativet, I have tried to show how seemingly incommensurable perspectives can be combined in a productive manner, and how these combinations allow us to see things that we might not otherwise have seen.

In Chapter 3, I analysed Alternativet based on insights from the classical perspective. I showed how the party emerged as a result of a problematization process where the status quo was challenged through appeals to 'something new' and where voters were encouraged to read their own preferences into this new project. I also showed how this very open articulation attracted support from across the political spectrum, which quickly caused problems associated with the ideological particularization of Alternativet as a political party. To manage such problems, Alternativet introduced a new organizational unit called *political forum* as the executive body of the bottom-up process of policy making. This marked the beginning of an oligarchization process, in which the super-democratic set-up of Alternativet was compromised, in order for the party leadership to prepare the organization for election. Finally, I analysed the way in which Alternativet's political goals have transformed as a consequence of the parliamentary entry in 2015. Against the common assumption that goals become increasingly conservative when a party enters parliament, I concluded that moments of re-radicalization have indeed occurred, and that some of these moments have been instigated by the party leadership rather than grassroots activists.

In Chapter 5, I analysed Alternativet based on insights from the configurational perspective. First, I showed how the party's official creation myth paints an overly idyllic and heroic picture of Uffe Elbæk as the founding father who single-handedly conceived the idea of Alternativet. Having moderated this narrative, I went on to outline the configuration of the party. My argument was that Alternativet is a branch-based party with a somewhat weak articulation, which makes it possible for caucuses within the organization to exercise disproportional influence on internal affairs. Furthermore, while Alternativet is indeed a decentralized organization, it is not horizontal in the Duvergerian sense, meaning that local branches are granted some decision-making power, such as candidate selection, but that collaborative ties primarily run between centre and periphery. Finally, I worked with some of the ideal typical configurations that have emerged from the post-Duvergerian literature to assess the extent to which Alternativet fits these abstractions. Here, I concluded that Alternativet can be described as a combination of a mass party, a movement party and a digital party.

In Chapter 7, I compared Alternativet with two other movement parties in contemporary Europe, namely Podemos in Spain and Píratar in Iceland. The overall purpose of this analysis was to understand whether similar parties that emerged at the same point in time have matured in the same way as Alternativet. To that end, I focused on three different themes: voters and members, income and spending and participation and representation. In terms of votes, I showed that all three parties have gone through an inverted U-curve in terms of electoral support. They all peaked around 2016 and have since lost significant ground to new contenders on both sides of the political spectrum. Meanwhile, both Podemos and Alternativet have lost the majority of their (active) members since the heyday in 2016. Píratar, on the other hand, has managed to continuously add members throughout its years of existence. In terms of income, all parties are increasingly relying on public funds. While Píratar has always received most of its funding from state and municipal sources, Podemos and Alternativet have become much more reliant on public funding in recent years due to the dramatic loss of members. Finally, in terms of participatory structures, I concluded that the super-democratic set-ups that initially made both Podemos and Alternativet famous have been compromised in both cases, but that Píratar remains committed to an open-source process of policy making. In short, Alternativet and Podemos have followed similar trajectories, although they operate in very different institutional environments. The main difference is that Podemos has managed to enter a governmental coalition, whereas Alternativet has always lived a life on the margins of governmental affairs.

In Chapter 9, I analysed the organizational culture of Alternativet based primarily on the work of Joanne Martin (1992). Here, I opted for a multifaceted approach that allowed me to explore integrative, differential and fragmentary elements of the party's culture(s). In terms of the first, I analysed how Alternativet's official commitment to certain norms and values have worked surprisingly well in terms of managing the difficult process of ideological particularization. In particular, the combination of 'vision values' and 'humanity values' has allowed Alternativet to enrol and maintain members with very different political views. In terms of differentiation, I showed how internal conflicts arose in relation to the local elections in 2017, and how aspects of these conflicts can be explained with reference to different interpretations of Alternativet's norms and values. Finally, in terms of fragmentation, I explored how the party's culture is based on a type of designed ambiguity that allows members and supporters to construct their own personal visions of the political project that is called Alternativet. Towards the end of the chapter, I explored how cultural manifestations discipline members into being morally inclusive towards people with different views and objectives. In that sense, fragmentation has worked (and continues to work) as a means of cohesion rather than a source of disintegration.

In sum, the story of Alternativet is a story of a challenger party's rise, fall and possible rebirth. It is the story of a party that, despite earnest efforts, could not resist the oligarchic tendencies of the formal political system, but still managed to push Danish politics in a more sustainable and democratic direction (Chapter 3). It is also the story of a digitalized movement party that adopted many of the configurational characteristics associated with mass parties in order to weather the consequences of running for parliament, but which nonetheless maintained a certain level of structurelessness to keep things informal and negotiable (Chapter 5). It is, furthermore, the story of a movement party that resembles other European movement parties in terms of its organizational development, despite the fact that it operates in a stable and friendly environment (Chapter 7). And then, it is the story of a party that chose to work consciously with its own organizational culture in an attempt to turn itself into a microcosm of democratic debate and to create a level of commitment and engagement rarely seen in contemporary electoral politics (Chapter 9). The story of Alternativet is the story of a small party that made a big difference in a small country. Hopefully, this book can help keep that story alive and spread it to other parts of the world.

Concluding remarks

Taken together, the four analytical chapters show something that one single analysis could not. They show that a political party can be approached from a multiplicity of perspectives, regardless of the fact that some of these perspectives are incommensurable theoretically as well as methodologically. As such, the chapters hopefully serve to break down the otherwise tall boundaries that separate disciplines from one another. There is, in my view, no reason why political scientists and organization scholars could not leave differences aside and enter a productive dialogue about party organization. Approximately 100 years ago, organization scholars and political scientists parted ways and a division of labour was decided. Organization scholars would study seemingly non-political organizations, and political scientists would stick to the political organizations. Recently, the two disciplines have gradually begun to approach each other, with organization scholars studying social movements and activist networks, and political scientists taking an interest in the workings of 'normal' enterprises.

The political party, however, has been forgotten in that process. Political scientists study parties like never before, but they tend to do so in a way that few organization scholars would recognize as truly organizational, and organization scholars themselves still have not rediscovered the value of studying parties as organizations. This book has been an attempt to remedy this shortcoming; an attempt to start a conversation that hopefully will give rise to many rewarding accounts of party organization.

Notes

Chapter 7

[1]   I am particularly indebted to Andreu Paneque, Davide Vittori, Viktor Valgarðsson and Oddný Helgadóttir for their invaluable insights on Podemos and Píratar.

Chapter 8

[1]   In Schein's later work, he clearly recognizes the existence of subcultures. Hence, this proposition primarily relates to the 1985 edition of his book.

[2]   Patronizing descriptions of 'the deep psychological identification of Balinese men with their cocks' are telling in this regard (Geertz, 1973, quoted in Crapanzano, 1986: 70–71).

References

Abbott, GN, White, FA and Charles, MA (2005) Linking values and organizational commitment: A correlational and experimental investigation in two organizations, *Journal of Occupational and Organizational Psychology*, 78(4): 531–551.

Adler, PS (ed) (2009) *The Oxford Handbook of Sociology and Organization Studies*, Oxford: Oxford University Press.

Adler, PS, Forbes, LC and Willmott, H (2007) Critical management studies, *The Academy of Management Annals*, 1(1): 119–179.

Almqvist, FM (2016) Pirate politics between protest movement and parliament, *ephemera*, 16(2): 97–114.

Alternativet (2013a) *Overordnede værdimæssige og konceptuelle betragtninger om Alternativet – The Alternative: Et internationalt parti, en bevægelse og en kulturel stemme*, working paper: 1–7.

Alternativet (2013b) Video: Uffe Elbæk præsenterede sit nye parti, *DR*, 27 November.

Alternativet (2013c) *Manifesto: There is always an Alternative*, available at: alternativet.dk/en/politics/manifesto.

Alternativet (2013d) *Debate Principles*, available at: alternativet.dk/en/politics/debate-principles.

Alternativet (2013e) *Our Values*, available at: alternativet.dk/en/politics/our-values.

Alternativet (2014a) *Party Programme*, available at: alternativet.dk/en/politics/party-programme.

Alternativet (2014b) Alternativet klar med ombudsmandsråd, press release, nd.

Alternativet (2015a) Elbæk: Vi er et visionært pragmatisk parti [interview article by Kim Kristensen], *Information*, 23 June.

Alternativet (2015b) Klaus Riskær Pedersen ekskluderet som medlem af Alternativet efter mislykket mæglingsforsøg, press release, 13 March.

Alternativet (2016a) Uffe Elbæk er lutter øren [interview article by Amalie Hypolit], *Retorikforlaget*, 7 June.

Alternativet (2016b) Nu begynder streaming fra gruppemøder, press release, 10 October.

Alternativet (Uffe Elbæk) (2016c) Lessons from abroad: There is always an alternative, in L Nandy, C Lucas and C Bowers (eds) *The Alternative*, Hull: Biteback, pp 237–252.

Alternativet (2016d) Uffe Elbæk indleder venlig revolution ud af empatikrisen, Jyllands-Posten, 16 June.

Alternativet (2017) Mindfulness og tyldskørter: Alternativet holder årsmøde, Jyllands-Posten, 27 May.

Alternativet (2018a) *The Next Denmark: Freedom and Community – A Narrative*, Copenhagen: Alternativet.

Alternativet (2018b) *Evaluering af Politikudviklingsprocesser i Alternativet*, Copenhagen: Alternativet.

Alternativet (2020) *Anbefalinger til fremtidig organisering og principper for beslutningsprocesser i Alternativet* [report by Kathrine Lauritzen and Mark Desholm], Copenhagen: Alternativet.

Alternativet (2023a) *Vores historie*, available at: alternativet.dk/om-os/alternativets-historie.

Alternativet (2023b) Bliv medlem, available at: alternativet.dk/blivmedlem.

Alternativet's Ombudsman's Council (2015) Første notat fra Alternativets Ombudsmandsråd, 1 May.

Alvesson, M (2001) Knowledge work: Ambiguity, image and identity, *Human Relations*, 54(7): 863–886.

Alvesson, M (2011) *Understanding Organizational Culture*, London: Sage.

Alvesson, M and Willmott, H (2002) Identity regulation as organizational control: Producing the appropriate individual, *Journal of Management Studies*, 39(5): 619–644.

Anastasiadis, V (1999) Political 'parties' in Athenian democracy: A modernising topos, *Arethusa*, 32(3): 313–335.

Andersen, JG (2017) Portræt af vælgernes socio-demografi, in KM Hansen and R Stubager (eds) *Oprør Fra Udkanten*, København: Jurist-og Økonomiforbundets Forlag, pp 41–68.

Andersen, NÅ (2003) *Discursive Analytical Strategies: Understanding Foucault, Koselleck, Laclau, Luhmann*, Bristol: Policy Press.

Andersen, NÅ (2015) Lay-offs in the name of love: The Danish example, *International Journal of Work Organisation and Emotion*, 7(1): 16.

Andersen, NÅ and Pors, JG (2022) Transformation and potentialization: how to extend the present and produce possibilities?, Kybernetes (online first): 1–16.

Anderson, B (1991) *Imagined Communities: Reflections on the Origin and Spread of Nationalism*, London: Verso.

Andrews, JT and Jackman, RW (2008) If winning isn't everything, why do they keep score? Consequences of electoral performance for party leaders, *British Journal of Political Science*, 38(4): 657–675.

Anria, S (2019) *When Movements Become Parties: The Bolivian MAS in Comparative Perspective*, Cambridge: Cambridge University Press.

Ansell, C (2009) Mary Parker Follett and pragmatist organization, in PS Adler (ed) *The Oxford Handbook of Sociology and Organization Studies*, Oxford: Oxford University Press, pp 464–485.

Antentas, JM (2022) The 15M, Podemos and the Long Crisis in Spain: Gramscian perspectives, *Journal of Iberian and Latin American Research*, 28(3): 365–380.

Argyris, C and Schön, D (1978) *Organizational Learning: A Theory of Action Perspective*, Reading: Addison-Wesley.

Aronoff, MJ (1977) *Power and Ritual in the Israel Labor Party: A Study in Political Anthropology*, New York: Routledge.

Aronoff, MJ (1993) *Power and Ritual in the Israel Labor Party: A Study in Political Anthropology* (2nd edn), New York: Routledge.

Arter, D and Kestilä-Kekkonen, E (2014) Measuring the extent of party institutionalisation: The case of a populist entrepreneur party, *West European Politics*, 37(5): 932–956.

Bachrach, P and Baratz, MS (1962) Two faces of power, *American Political Science Review*, 56(04): 947–952.

Bakardjieva, M (2009) Subactivism: Lifeworld and politics in the age of the internet, *The Information Society*, 25(2): 91–104.

Bale, T, Webb, PD and Poletti, M (2019) *Footsoldiers: Political Party Membership in the 21st Century*, London: Routledge.

Bardi, L, Calossi, E and Pizzimenti, E (2017) Which face comes first? The ascendancy of the party in public office, in SE Scarrow, PD Webb and T Poguntke (eds) *Organizing Political Parties*, Oxford: Oxford University Press, pp 62–83.

Barker, JR (1993) Tightening the iron cage: Concertive control in self-managing teams, *Administrative Science Quarterly*, 38(3): 408–437.

Barker, R and Howard-Johnston, X (1975) The politics and political ideas of Moisei Ostrogorski, *Political Studies*, 23(4): 415–429.

Barnard, C (1938) *The Functions of the Executive*, Cambridge, MA: Harvard University Press.

Barrling, K (2013) Exploring the inner life of the party: A framework for analysing elite party culture, *Scandinavian Political Studies*, 36(2): 177–199.

Barros, M (2014) Tools of legitimacy: The case of the Petrobras corporate blog, *Organization Studies*, 35(8): 1211–1230.

Beck, U and Beck-Gernsheim, E (2002) *Individualization: Institutionalized Individualism and Its Social and Political Consequences*. London: Sage.

Bennett, WL and Segerberg, A (2011) Digital media and the personalization of collective action: Social technology and the organization of protests against the global economic crisis, *Information Communication & Society*, 14(6): 770–799.

Bennett, WL and Segerberg, A (2012) The logic of connective action, *Information, Communication & Society* 15(5): 739–768.

Biancalana, C and Vittori, D (2021) Cyber-parties' membership between empowerment and pseudo-participation: The cases of Podemos and the Five Star Movement, in O Barberà, G Sandri, P Correa et al (eds) *Digital Parties*, Cham: Springer, pp 109–126.

Bickerton, CJ and Accetti, CI (2018) 'Techno-populism' as a new party family: The case of the Five Star Movement and Podemos, *Contemporary Italian Politics*, 10(2): 132–150.

Bille, L (1994) Denmark: The decline of the membership party, in: RS Katz and P Mair (eds) *How Parties Organize*, London: Sage, pp 134–157.

Blau, P and Schnoenherr, R (1971) *The Structure of Organizations*, New York: Basic Books.

Bolin, N, Aylott, N, von dem Berge, B, et al (2017) Patterns of intra-party democracy across the world, in SE Scarrow, PD Webb and T Poguntke (eds) *Organizing Political Parties*, Oxford: Oxford University Press, pp 158–186.

Boltanski, L and Chiapello, E (2005) *The New Spirit of Capitalism*, London: Verso.

Bormann, NC and Golder, M (2022) Democratic electoral systems around the world, 1946–2020, *Electoral Studies*, 78: 1–7.

Borz, G and Janda, K (2020) Contemporary trends in party organization: Revisiting intra-party democracy, *Party Politics*, 26(1): 3–8.

Bosch, A (2020) The Spanish electoral system, in D Muro and I Lago (eds) *The Oxford Handbook of Spanish Politics*, Oxford: Oxford University Press, pp 389–409.

Bourdieu, P and Passeron, J-C (1977) *Reproduction in Education, Society and Culture*, London: Sage.

Bourne, H and Jenkins, M (2013) Organizational values: A dynamic perspective, *Organization Studies*, 34(4): 495–514.

Breines, W (1980) Community and organization: The New Left and Michels' 'iron law', *Social Problems*, 27(4): 419–429.

Brinton, C (1961) *The Jacobins: An Essay in the New History*, New York: Macmillan.

Broomfield, M (2016) Iceland's Pirate Party secures more election funding than all its rivals as it continues to top polls, The Independent, 13 May.

Brown, L (1998) How totalitarian is Plato's Republic, in E Ostenfeld (ed) *Essays on Plato's Republic*, Aarhus: Aarhus University Press, pp 13–27.

Bryce, J (1888) *The American Commonwealth*, London: Macmillan.

Bryce, J (1921) *Modern Democracies*, London: Macmillan and Company.

Buchanan, B (1974) Building organizational commitment: The socialization of managers in work organizations, *Administrative Science Quarterly*, 19(4): 533–546.

Burnham, J (1943) *The Machiavellians: Defenders of Freedom*, New York: John Day Company.

Burns, T and Stalker, G (1961) *The Management of Innovation*, London: Tavistock.

Butler, N, Delaney, H, Hesselbo, E et al (2020) Beyond measure, *ephemera*, 20(3): 1–16.

Butler, N, Hoedemaeker, C and Russell, D (2015) The comic organization, *ephemera*, 15(3): 497–512.

Cabantous, L, Gond, J-P, Harding, N et al (2016) Critical essay: Reconsidering critical performativity, *Human Relations*, 69(2): 197–213.

Caiani, M, Padoan, E and Marino, B (2022) Candidate selection, personalization and different logics of centralization in new Southern European populism: The cases of Podemos and the M5S, *Government and Opposition*, 57(3): 404–427.

Caiden, GE (1989) The value of comparative analysis, *International Journal of Public Administration*, 12(3): 459–475.

Carvajal, Á and Sanz, L (2017) Vistalegre II: Pablo Iglesias arrasa a Íñigo Errejón e impone la línea dura en Podemos, El Mundo, 12 February.

Casey, C (1999) 'Come, Join Our Family': Discipline and integration in corporate organizational culture, *Human Relations*, 52(1): 155–178.

Castells, M (2012) *Networks of Outrage and Hope: Social Movements in the Internet Age*, Cambridge: Polity Press.

Chandler, A (1962) *Strategy and Structure: Chapters in the History of American Enterprise*, Boston: MIT Press.

Chatman, JA and O'Reilly, CA (2016) Paradigm lost: Reinvigorating the study of organizational culture, *Research in Organizational Behavior*, 36: 199–224.

Chironi, D and Fittipaldi, R (2017) Social movements and new forms of political organization: Podemos as a hybrid party, *Partecipazione e Conflitto*, 10(1): 275–305.

Christensen, LT, Morsing, M and Thyssen, O (2013) CSR as aspirational talk, *Organization*, 20(3): 372–393.

Clift, B and Fisher, J (2004) Comparative party finance reform: The cases of France and Britain, *Party Politics*, 10(6): 677–699.

Contu, A (2019) Conflict and organization studies, *Organization Studies*, 40(10): 1445–1462.

Contu, A and Willmott, H (2003) Re-embedding situatedness: The importance of power relations in Learning Theory, *Organization Science*, 14(3): 283–296.

Cook, PJ (1971) Robert Michels's *Political Parties* in perspective, *The Journal of Politics*, 33(3): 773–796.

Costas, J (2012) 'We are all friends here': Reinforcing paradoxes of normative control in a culture of friendship, *Journal of Management Inquiry*, 21(4): 377–395.

Courpasson, D and Clegg, S (2006) Dissolving the iron cages? Tocqueville, Michels, bureaucracy and the perpetuation of elite power, *Organization*, 13(3): 319–343.

Crapanzano, V (1986) Hermes' dilemma, in J Clifford and G Marcus (eds) *Writing Culture*, Berkeley: University of California Press, pp 51–76.

Crewe, E (2015) *The House of Commons: An Anthropology of MPs at Work*, London: Routledge.

Cross, W and Katz, RS (2013) *The Challenges of Intra-Party Democracy*, Oxford: Oxford University Press.

Crozier, M (1964) *The Bureaucratic Phenomenon*, Chicago: Chicago University Press.

Czarniawska-Joerges, B (1988) *Ideological Control in Nonideological Organizations*, New York: Praeger.

Dahlman, S, Mygind du Plessis, E, Husted, E et al (2022) Alternativity as freedom: Exploring tactics of emergence in alternative forms of organizing, *Human Relations*, 75(10): 1961–1985.

Dalton, RJ and Wattenberg, MP (2002) *Parties Without Partisans: Political Change in Advanced Industrial Democracies*, Oxford: Oxford University Press.

Day, R (2005) *Gramsci is Dead: Anarchist Currents in the Newest Social Movements*, London: Pluto Press.

Deal, T and Kennedy, A (2000) *Corporate Cultures: The Rites and Rituals of Corporate Life* (2nd edn), New York: Basic Books.

Dean, J (2016) *Crowds and Party*, London: Verso.

DeGama, N, Elias, S and Peticca-Harris, A (2019) The good academic: Re-imagining good research in organization and management studies, *Qualitative Research in Organizations and Management*, 14(1): 2–9.

Del Fa, S and Vásquez, C (2019) Existing through differantiation: A Derridean approach to alternative organizations, *M@n@gement*, 22(4): 559–583.

Della Porta, D (2007) The global justice movement: An introduction, in D della Porta (ed) *Global Justice Movement*, New York: Paradigm.

Della Porta, D (2013) *Can Democracy Be Saved? Participation, Deliberation and Social Movements*, Cambridge: Polity Press.

Della Porta, D (2021) Communication in progressive movement parties: Against populism and beyond digitalism, *Information, Communication and Society*, 24(10): 1344–1360.

Della Porta, D, Fernández, J, Kouki, H and Mosca, L (2017) *Movement Parties Against Austerity*, Cambridge: Polity Press.

Derrida, J (1982) *Différance*, Copenhagen: Hans Reitzels Forlag.

Derrida, J (1994) *Specters of Marx*, London: Routledge.

Deseriis, M (2020) Digital movement parties: A comparative analysis of the technopolitical cultures and the participation platforms of the Movimento 5 Stelle and the Piratenpartei, *Information Communication and Society*, 23(12): 1770–1786.

Deseriis, M and Vittori, D (2019) The impact of online participation platforms on the internal democracy of two southern European parties: Podemos and the Five Star Movement, *International Journal of Communication*, 13: 5696–5714.

de Tocqueville, A (1838) *Democracy in America*, New York: George Dearborn & Co.

Detterbeck, K. (2005) Cartel parties in Western Europe? *Party Politics*, 11(2): 173–191.

De Vries, C and Hobolt, S (2020) The rise of challenger parties, *Political Insight*, 11(3): 16–19.

Diefenbach, T (2019) Why Michels' 'iron law of oligarchy' is not an iron law – and how democratic organisations can stay 'oligarchy-free', *Organization Studies*, 40(4): 545–562.

Donaldson, L (2001) *The Contingency Theory of Organizations*, London: Sage.

Douglas, M (1987) *How Institutions Think*, London: Routledge.

Downs, A (1957) *An Economic Theory of Democracy*, New York: Harper and Row.

Drory, A and Romm, T (1990) The definition of organizational politics: A review, *Human Relations*, 43(11): 1133–1154.

Du Gay, P and Vikkelsø, S (2016) *For Formal Organization: The Past in the Present and Future of Organization Theory*, Oxford: Oxford University Press.

Du Plessis, EM and Husted, E (2022) Five challenges for prefiguration research: A sympathetic polemic, in L Monticelli (ed) *The Future Is Now*, Bristol: Bristol University Press, pp 217–229.

Duverger, M (1954) *Political Parties: Their Organization and Activity in the Modern State*, London: Methuen.

Duverger, M (1977) *L'autre Côté des Choses*, Paris: Albin Michel.

Duverger, M (1980) A new political system model: Semi-presidential government, *European Journal of Political Research*, 8(2): 165–187.

Dyck, B and Silvestre, BS (2019) A novel NGO approach to facilitate the adoption of sustainable innovations in low-income countries: Lessons from small-scale farms in Nicaragua, *Organization Studies*, 40(3): 443–461.

Eagleton, T (2007) *Ideology: An Introduction*, London: Verso.

Eisenstadt, SN (1990) Functional analysis in anthropology and sociology: An interpretative essay, *Annual Review of Anthropology*, 19(1): 243–260.

Elbæk, U (2012) *Valgkamp på Kanten*, unpublished working paper.

Elbæk, U (2014a) Ja, politik er en teaterforestilling, BT, 29 December.

Elbæk, U (2014b) Christiansborg-kulturen fremmer sladder og store egoer, Information, 6 December.

Elbæk, U (2016a) Jeg vil ikke være bange. Jeg vil være fucking modig. Politiken, 31 December.

Elbæk, U (2016b) Nytårstale med højdeskræk – Spring ud i det, *Facebook video*, available at: https://www.facebook.com/watch/?v=139954667 3412879

Elbæk, U and Lawson, N (2014) *The Bridge: How the Politics of the Future Will Link the Vertical to the Horizontal*, available at: compassonline.org.uk/publications/the-bridge.

Eldersveld, SJ (1964) *Political Parties: A Behavioral Analysis*, Chicago: Rand McNally and Company.

Eldersveld, SJ (1982) *Political Parties in American Society*, New York: Basic Books.

Elgie, R (2011) Maurice Duverger: A law, a hypothesis and a paradox, in G Campus D, Pasquino and M Bull (eds) *Maestri of Political Science, Volume 2*, Colchester: ECPR Press, pp 75–92.

Eliassen, K and Svaasand, L (1975) The formation of mass political organizations: An analytical framework, *Scandinavian Political Studies*, 10(1): 95–121.

Epstein, LD (1967) *Political Parties in Western Democracies*, New York: Frederick A Praeger.

Eriksen, TH (2021) Ethnography in all the right places, in D Podjed, M Gorup, P Borecký et al (eds) *Why the World Needs Anthropologists*, London: Routledge, pp 17–31.

Errejón, Í and Mouffe, C (2016) *Podemos: In the Name of the People*, London: Lawrence & Wishart.

Etzioni, A (1964) *Modern Organizations*, Englewood Cliffs: Prentice-Hall.

Falguera, E, Jones, S and Ohman, M (eds) (2014) *Funding of Political Parties and Election Campaigns: A Handbook on Political Finance*, Stockholm: International IDEA.

Faucher, F (1999) Party organisation and democracy: A comparison of Les Verts and the British Green Party, *GeoJournal*, 47(3): 487–496.

Faucher, F (2021) An anthropology of contemporary political parties: Reflexions on methods and theory, *ephemera*, 21(2): 53–75.

Faucher-King, F (2005) *Changing Parties: An Anthropology of British Political Conferences*, Basingstoke: Palgrave MacMillan.

Finegan, JE (2000) The impact of person and organizational values on organizational commitment, *Journal of Occupational and Organizational Psychology*, 73(2): 149–169.

Fisher, J, Denver, D and Hands, G (2006) The relative electoral impact of central party co-ordination and size of party membership at constituency level, *Electoral Studies*, 25(4): 664–676.

Fleming, P (2005) 'Kindergarten cop': Paternalism and resistance in a high-commitment workplace, *Journal of Management Studies*, 42(7): 1469–1489.

Fleming, P and Banerjee, SB (2016) When performativity fails: Implications for Critical Management Studies, *Human Relations*, 69(2): 257–276.

Fleming, P and Spicer, A (2003) Working at a cynical distance: Implications for power, subjectivity and resistance, *Organization*, 10(1): 157–179.

Fleming, P and Spicer, A (2007) *Contesting the Corporation: Struggle, Power and Resistance in Organizations*, Cambridge: Cambridge University Press.

Fleming, P and Spicer, A (2014) Power in management and organization science, *The Academy of Management Annals*, 8(1): 237–298.

Fleming, P and Sturdy, A (2009) 'Just be yourself!': Towards neo-normative control in organisations?, *Employee Relations*, 31(6): 569–583.

Fleming, P and Sturdy, A (2011) 'Being yourself' in the electronic sweatshop: New forms of normative control, *Human Relations*, 64(2): 177–200.

Flyvbjerg, B (2006) Five misunderstandings about case-study research, *Qualitative Inquiry*, 12(2): 219–245.

Follett, MP (1918) *The New State: Group Organization the Solution to of Popular Government*, University Park: Pennsylvania State University Press.

Fominaya, CF (2020) *Democracy Reloaded: Inside Spain's Political Laboratory from 15-M to Podemos*, Oxford: Oxford University Press.

Fournier, V and Grey, C (2000) At the critical moment: Conditions and prospects for critical management studies, *Human Relations*, 53(1): 7–32.

Freeden, M (2006) Ideology and political theory, *Journal of Political Ideologies*, 11(1): 3–22.

Freeman, J (1972) The tyranny of structurelessness, *Berkeley Journal of Sociology*, 17: 151–164.

Funke, PN and Wolfson, T (2017) From Global Justice to Occupy and Podemos: Mapping three stages of contemporary activism, *triple*, 15(2): 393–403.

Gallagher, M and Marsh, M (1988) *Candidate Selection in Comparative Perspective: The Secret Garden of Politics*, London: Sage.

Gamson, WA (1975) *The Strategy of Social Protest*, Homewood: Dorsey Press.

Gauja, A (2015) The construction of party membership, *European Journal of Political Research*, 54(2): 232–248.

Gauja, A and Kosiara-Pedersen, K (2021a) The comparative study of political party organization: Changing perspectives and prospects, *ephemera*, 21(2): 19–52.

Gauja, A and Kosiara-Pedersen, K (2021b) Decline, adaptation and relevance: Political parties and their researchers in the twentieth century, *European Political Science*, 20(1): 123–138.

Geertz, C (1973) *The Interpretation of Cultures*, New York: Basic Books.

Gerbaudo, P (2012) *Tweets and the Streets: Social Media and Contemporary Activism*, London: Pluto Press.

Gerbaudo, P (2019) *The Digital Party: Political Organisation and Online Democracy*, London: Pluto Press.

Gerbaudo, P (2021a) Digital parties and their organizational challenges, *ephemera*, 21(2): 177–186.

Gerbaudo, P (2021b) *The Great Recoil: Politics After Populism and Pandemic*, London: Verso.

Gerbaudo, P (2021c) To recapture the spirit of the Indignados, Podemos has to speak to working people, *Jacobin*, 15 May.

Gerbaudo, P (2021d) Are digital parties more democratic than traditional parties? Evaluating Podemos and Movimento 5 Stelle's online decision-making platforms, *Party Politics*, 27(4): 730–742.

Gienapp, WE (1987) *The Origins of the Republican Party, 1852–1856*, Oxford: Oxford University Press.

GRECO (2008) *Evaluation Report on Iceland: Transparency of Party Funding*, Strasbourg: Council of Europe.

GRECO (2009) *Evaluation Report on Spain: Transparency of Party Funding*, Strasbourg: Council of Europe.

Green-Pedersen, C and Kosiara-Pedersen, K (2020) The party system: Open yet stable, in PM Christiansen (ed) *The Oxford Handbook of Danish Politics*, Oxford: Oxford University Press, pp 212–229.

Gulowsen, J (1985) Hearocracy: The deterioration of democracy in a Norwegian trade union, *Organization Studies*, 6(4): 349–365.

Hammond, N (1988) The expedition of Xerxes, in J Boardman, N Hammond, D Lewis et al (eds) *Cambridge Ancient History, Vol. IV*, Cambridge: Cambridge University Press, pp 518–592.

Hansen, KM (2020) Electoral turnout: Strong social norms of voting, in PM Christiansen (ed) *The Oxford Handbook of Danish Politics*, Oxford: Oxford University Press, pp 76–87.

Hansen, KM and Stubager, R (2017) Folketingsvalget 2015: Oprør fra udkanten, in KM Hansen and R Stubager (eds) *Oprør Fra Udkanten*, Copenhagen: Jurist-og Økonomiforbundets Forlag, pp 21–40.

Hansen, M (2014) Political parties in democratic Athens?, *Greek, Roman, and Byzantine Studies*, 54: 379–403.

Hardt, M and Negri, A (2017) *Assembly*, Oxford: Oxford University Press.

Harmel, R and Janda, K (1982) *Parties and Their Environment: Limits to Reform?*, London: Longman.

Hasse, C (2011) *Kulturanalyse i Organisationer: Begreber, Metoder Og Forbløffende Læreprocesser*, Frederiksberg: Samfundslitteratur.

Hatch, MJ and Erhlich, SB (1993) Spontaneous humour as an indicator of paradox and ambiguity in organizations, *Organization Studies*, 14(4): 505–526.

Hazan, R and Rahat, G (2010) *Democracy Within Parties: Candidate Selection Methods and Their Political Consequences*, Oxford: Oxford University Press.

Heidar, K (2020) Book review: *Organizing Political Parties: Representation, Participation and Power, Party Politics*, 26(1): 82–83.

Heidar, K and Koole, R (eds) (1999) *Parliamentary Party Groups in European Democracies: Political Parties Behind Closed Doors*, London: Routledge.

Helgason, T (2010) Apportionment of Seats to Althingi, the Icelandic Parliament. Reykjavik: The National Electoral Commission of Iceland.

Helles, SB (2017) Leaked email to Alternativet's leadership, available at: https://legacy.altinget.dk/misc/Stine%20Berdeleben%20Helles%20mail%20til%20partitoppen%20i%20Alternativet.pdf

Hernes, T (2014) *A Process Theory of Organization*, Oxford: Oxford University Press.

Herzberg, F, Mausner, B and Snyderman, B (1959) *The Motivation to Work*, New Brunswick: Transaction Publishers.

Hjorth, F (2017) Emneejerskab – Hvilke partier ejer hvilke emner?, in KM Hansen and R Stubager (eds) *Oprør Fra Udkanten*, Copenhagen: Djøf Forlag, pp 193–206.

Hochschild, AR (1983) *The Managed Heart: Commercialization of Human Feeling*, Berkeley: University of California Press.

Hoffmann-Martinot, V (2005) A short biography of Maurice Duverger, *French Politics*, 3(3): 304–309.

Hofstede, G (1980) *Culture's Consequences*, Beverly Hills: Sage.

Holloway, J (2002) *Change the World without Taking Power: The Meaning of Revolution Today*, London: Pluto Press.

Hopkin, J (2004) The problem with party finance: Theoretical perspectives on the funding of party politics, *Party Politics*, 10(6): 627–651.

Hopkin, J and Paolucci, C (1999) The business firm model of party organisation: Cases from Spain and Italy, *European Journal of Political Research*, 35(3): 307–339.

Hotho, J and Saka-Helmhout, A (2017) In and between societies: Reconnecting comparative institutionalism and organization theory, *Organization Studies*, 38(5): 647–666.

Hume, D (1742/2002) Of parties in general, in SE Scarrow (ed) *Perspectives on Political Parties: Classic Readings*, New York: Palgrave, pp 33–36.

Husted, E (2018) Mobilizing 'the Alternativist': Exploring the management of subjectivity in a radical political party, *ephemera*, 18(4): 737–765.

Husted, E (2019) Party organization in the digital age, *ephemera*, 19(3): 651–662.

Husted, E (2020) 'Some have ideologies, we have values': The relationship between organizational values and commitment in a political party, *Culture and Organization*, 26(3): 175–195.

Husted, E (2021) Alternative organization and neo-normative control: Notes on a British town council, *Culture and Organization*, 27(2): 132–151.

Husted, E and Hansen, AD (2017) The alternative to occupy? Radical politics between protest and parliament, *tripleC*, 15(2): 459–477.

Husted, E and Just, SN (2022) The politics of trust: How trust reconciles autonomy and solidarity in alternative organizations, *Organization Theory*, 3(2): 1–19.

Husted, E and Mac, M (2022) Instituting deliberation: Three stages of bottom-up policymaking in Denmark's alternative party, in J Brichzin and J Siri (eds) *Soziologie der Parteien*, Cham: Springer, pp 59–80.

Husted, E and Plesner, U (2017) Spaces of open-source politics: Physical and digital conditions for political organization, *Organization*, 24(5): 648–670.

Husted, E and Pors, JG (2021) *Eklektiske Analysestrategier*, Frederiksberg: Nyt fra Samfundsvidenskaberne.

Husted, E, Moufahim, M and Frederiksson, M (2021) Welcome to the party, *ephemera*, 21(2): 1–17.

Husted, E, Moufahim, M and Frederiksson, M (2022) Political parties and organization studies: The party as a critical case of organizing, *Organization Studies*, 43(8): 1327–1341.

Iglesias, P (2015) *Politics in a Time of Crisis: Podemos and the Future of a Democratic Europe*, London: Verso.

Ignazi, P (2017) *Party and Democracy: The Uneven Road to Party Legitimacy*, Oxford: Oxford University Press.

Ignazi, P (2020) The four knights of intra-party democracy: A rescue for party delegitimation, *Party Politics*, 26(1): 9–20.

Jaakson, K (2010) Management by values: Are some values better than others?, *Journal of Management Development*, 29(9): 795–806.

Janda, K (1980) *Political Parties: A Cross-National Survey*, New York: Free Press.

Janda, K and King, D (1985) Formalizing and testing Duverger's theories on political parties, *Comparative Political Studies*, 18(2): 139–169.

Jenkins, JC (1977) Radical transformation of organizational goals, *Administrative Science Quarterly*, 22(4): 568–586.

Jensen, MC and Meckling, WH (1976) Theory of the firm: Managerial behavior, agency costs and ownership structure, *Journal of Financial Economics*, 3(4): 305–360.

Jímenez, F and Villoria, M (2018) Party funding in Spain, in J Mendilow and E Phélippeau (eds) *Handbook of Political Party Funding*, Cheltenham: Edward Elgar Publishing, pp 349–364.

Jupskås, AR (2016) The Norwegian Progress Party: Between a business firm and a mass party, in R Heinisch and O Mazzoleni (eds) *Understanding Populist Party Organization*, Basingstoke: Palgrave Macmillan, pp 159–188.

Justesen, L and Mik-Meyer, N (2012) *Qualitative Research Methods in Organization Studies*, Copenhagen: Hans Reitzels Forlag.

Kahan, M (1978) *Power and Ritual in the Israel Labor Party: A Study in Political Anthropology*. By M. J. Aronoff, *American Political Science Review*, 72(4): 1444–1445.

Kanter, MR (1972) *Commitment and Community: Communes and Utopias in Sociological Perspective*, Cambridge, MA: Harvard University Press.

Karlsen, MP and Villadsen, K (2015) Laughing for real? Humour, management power and subversion, *ephemera*, 15(3): 513–535.

Kärreman, D and Alvesson, M (2004) Cages in tandem: Management control, social identity, and identification in a knowledge-intensive firm, *Organization*, 11(1): 149–175.

Karthikeyan, SI, Jonsson, S and Wezel, FC (2016) The travails of identity change: Competitor claims and distinctiveness of British political parties, 1970–1992, *Organization Science*, 27(1): 106–122.

Katz, RS and Mair, P (eds) (1992) *Party Organizations: A Data Handbook on Party Organizations in Western Democracies, 1960–90*, London: Sage.

Katz, RS and Mair, P (1993) The evolution of party organizations in Europe: The three faces of party organization, *American Review of Politics*, 14(winter): 593–617.

Katz, RS and Mair, P (eds) (1994) *How Parties Organize: Change and Adaption in Party Organizations in Western Democracies*, London: Sage.

Katz, RS and Mair, P (1995) Changing models of party organization and party democracy: The emergence of the cartel party, *Party Politics*, 1(1): 5–28.

Katz, RS and Mair, P (1996) Cadre, catch-all or cartel?, *Party Politics*, 2(4): 525–534.

Katz, RS and Mair, P (2009) The cartel party thesis: A restatement, *Perspectives on Politics*, 7(4): 753–766.

Keane, J (2009) *The Life and Death of Democracy*, New York: WW Norton & Company.

Kelly, C (1990) Social identity and intergroup perceptions in minority-majority contexts, *Human Relations*, 43(6): 583–599.

Kertzer, DI (1996) *Politics and Symbols: The Italian Communist Party and the Fall of Communism*, New Haven: Yale University Press.

Key, VO (1942) *Politics, Parties, and Pressure Groups*, New York: Thomas Y Crowell.

Kioupkiolis, A (2016) Podemos: The ambiguous promises of left-wing populism in contemporary Spain, *Journal of Political Ideologies*, 21(2): 99–120.

Kirchheimer, O (1966) The transformation of the Western European party systems, in J LaPalombara and W Myron (eds) *Political Parties and Political Development*, Princeton: Princeton University Press, pp 177–200.

Kitschelt, H (2006) Movement parties, in R Katz and W Crotty (eds) *Handbook of Party Politics*, London: SAGE, pp 178–290.

Knudsen, C and Tsoukas, H (eds) (2005) *The Oxford Handbook of Organization Theory: Meta-Theoretical Perspectives*, Oxford: Oxford University Press.

Knudsen, M (2017) Conditions for critical performativity in a polycontextural society, *M@n@gement*, 20(1): 9–27.

Knudsen, T (2016) Pirater overtager Island med direkte demokrati og Robin Hood-magt, *Berlingske,* 8 April.

Kokkinidis, G (2015) Spaces of possibilities: Workers' self-management in Greece, *Organization*, 22(6): 847–871.

Kölln, AK (2016) Party membership in Europe: Testing party-level explanations of decline, *Party Politics*, 22(4): 465–477.

Kondo, D (1990) *Crafting Selves: Power, Gender, and Discourses of Identity in a Japanese Workplace*, Chicago: University of Chicago Press.

Kopeček, L (2016) 'I'm paying, so I decide': Czech ANO as an extreme form of a business-firm party, *East European Politics and Societies*, 30(4): 725–749.

Korte, RF (2009) How newcomers learn the social norms of an organization: A case study of the socialization of newly hired engineers, *Human Resource Development Quarterly*, 20(3): 285–306.

Kosiara-Pedersen, K (2017) *Demokratiets Ildsjæle: Partimedlemmer i Danmark*, Copenhagen: Djøf Forlag.

Koß, M (2010) *The Politics of Party Funding: State Funding to Political Parties and Party Competition in Western Europe*, Oxford: Oxford University Press.

Kristensen, FB (2015) Alternativet om håndværkerfradrag: 'Hvis vi havde 90 mandater, var det ikke den her vej, vi var gået', Politiken, 26 August.

Kristensen, M (2017) Ny optælling: Se hvilke partier der er størst på sociale medier, *Politisk-analyse.dk,* 23 March.

Krogsholm, MF (2015) Data-analyse: Alternativet stormer frem på sociale medier, *Altinget,* 23 June.

Krouwel, A (2003) Otto Kirchheimer and the catch-all party, *West European Politics*, 26(2): 23–40.

Krouwel, A (2006) Party models, in RS Katz and W Crotty (eds) *Handbook of Party Politics*, London: SAGE, pp 249–269.

Kunda, G (1992) *Engineering Culture: Control and Commitment in a High-Tech Corporation*, Philadelphia: Temple University Press.

Laclau, E (1994) Why do empty signifiers matter to politics?, in J Weeks (ed) *The Lesser Evil and the Greater Good*, London: Rivers Oram Press, pp 167–178.

Laclau, E (1997) The death and resurrection of the theory of ideology, *MLN*, 112(3, German issue): 297–321.

Laclau, E (2005) *On Populist Reason*, London: Verso.

Lago, MM (2020) Parties and party systems, in D Muro and I Lago (eds) *The Oxford Handbook of Spanish Politics*, Oxford: Oxford University Press, pp 331–348.

Lassman, P and Speirs, R (1994) Introduction, in P Lassman and R Speirs (eds) *Weber: Political Writings*, Cambridge: Cambridge University Press, pp vii–xxv.

Lawrence, PR and Lorsch, JW (1967) Differentiation and integration in complex organizations, *Administrative Science Quarterly*, 12(1): 1–47.

Lawson, K (1994) *How Parties Work: Perspectives from Within*, Westport: Praeger.

Lawson, K and Merkl, PH (1988) *How Parties Fail: Emerging Alternative Organizations*, Princeton: Princeton University Press.

Lefebvre, H (1991) *The Production of Space*, Oxford: Blackwell Publishing.

Linz, JJ (2006) *Robert Michels, Political Sociology, and the Future of Democracy*, Abingdon: Routledge.

Lipset, SM (1964) Introduction: Ostrogorski and the analytical approach to the comparative study of political parties, in M Ostrogorski, *Democracy and the Organization of Political Parties*, New York: Anchor Books, pp ix–lxv.

Lipset, SM, Trow, MA and Coleman, JS (1956) *Union Democracy: The Internal Politics of the International Typographical Union*, New York: The Free Press.

Lisi, M (2019) Party innovation, hybridization and the crisis: The case of Podemos, *Italian Political Science Review / Rivista Italiana di Scienza Politica*, 49(3): 245–262.

Lolle, H and Borre, O (2007) Kernevælgere og marginalvælgere, in JG Andersen, J Andersen, O Borre et al (eds) *Det Nye Politiske Landskab*, Aarhus: Systeme Academic, pp 275–288.

Lopdrup-Hjorth, T (2015) Object and objective lost?: Organization-phobia in organization theory, *Journal of Cultural Economy*, 8(4): 439–461.

Lowell, L (1908) *The Government of England*, vol 2. London: Macmillan.

Loxbo, K (2011) The fate of intra-party democracy: Leadership autonomy and activist influence in the mass party and the cartel party, *Party Politics*, 19(4): 537–554.

Lubinski, C (2018) From 'history as told' to 'history as experienced': Contextualizing the uses of the past, *Organization Studies*, 39(12): 1785–1809.

Luhmann, N (2018) *Organization and Decision*, Cambridge: Cambridge University Press.

Lupato, FG, Jerez, A and Meloni, M (2023) Digital innovation in electoral campaigns: The case of microcredit in Podemos, *Policy Studies* (online first): 1–19.

Madsen, K (2019) Elbæk skrev historie, men kunne ikke nå en ny vred generation, Politiken, 16 December.

Maeckelbergh, M (2009) *The Will of the Many: How the Alterglobalization Movement is Changing the Face of Democracy*, London: Pluto Press.

Mair, P (1994) Party organizations: From civil society to the state, in RS Katz and P Mair (eds) *How Parties Organize*, London: Sage, pp 1–22.

Mair, P (2003) Political parties and democracy: What sort of future?, available at: foresightfordevelopment.org/%0Asobipro/54/661-political-parties-and-democracy-what-sort-of-future.

Malone, C and Fredericks, V (2013) OWS and US electoral politics: An early critical assessment, in E Welty, M Bolton, M Nayak et al (eds) *Occupying Political Science*, New York: Palgrave Macmillan, pp 191–223.

Mansbridge, J (1980) *Beyond Adversary Democracy*, Chicago: University of Chicago Press.

Mansø, RG and Svendsen, AB (2022) Ét emne topper 'overraskende stort' danskernes liste over, hvad de vil have politikerne til at løse, DR, 4 September.

Margetts, HZ (2001) The cyber party: The causes and consequences of organisational innovation in European political parties, *European Consortium of Political Research (ECPR) Joint Sessions of Workshops*, Grenoble, 6–11 April.

Margolis, M and Resnick, D (2000) *Politics as Usual: The Cyberspace 'Revolution'*, Thousand Oaks: Sage.

Merriam-Webster (2023) Cadre, available at: https://www.merriam-webster.com/dictionary/cadre

Martin, J (1990) Deconstructing organizational taboos: The suppression of gender conflict in organizations, *Organization Science*, 1(4): 339–359.

Martin, J (1992) *Cultures in Organizations: Three Perspectives*, Oxford: Oxford University Press.

Martin, J and Frost, P (1996) The organizational culture war games: A struggle for intellectual dominance, in SR Clegg, C Hardy and W Nord (eds) *Handbook of Organization Studies*, London: Sage, pp 599–621.

Martin, J, Frost, P and O'Neill, O (2004) *Organisational Culture: Beyond Struggles for Intellectual Dominance*, working paper 1864, Stanford: Stanford Graduate School of Business.

Mayer, M and Ely, J (1998) Success and dilemmas of green party politics, in M Mayer and J Ely (eds) *The German Greens: Paradox Between Movement and Party*, Philadelphia: Temple University Press, pp 3–28.

Mayes, BT and Allen, RW (1977) Toward a definition of organizational politics, *The Academy of Management Review*, 2(4): 672–678.

Mazmanian, M and Beckman, CM (2018) 'Making' your numbers: Engendering organizational control through a ritual of quantification, *Organization Science*, 29(3): 357–379.

Mazzoleni, O and Voerman, G (2017) Memberless parties: Beyond the business-firm model?, *Party Politics*, 23(6): 783–792.

McCulloch, A (1983) The Ecology Party and constituency politics: The anatomy of a grassroots party, Political Studies Association Annual Conference, Newcastle, April: 1–32.

McKenzie, R (1955) *British Political Parties: The Distribution of Power within the Conservative and Labour Parties*, London: William Heinemann.

Messinger, SL (1955) Organizational transformation: A case study of a declining social movement, *American Sociological Review*, 20(1): 3–10.

Michels, R (1915) *Political Parties: A Sociological Study of the Oligarchical Tendencies of Modern Democracy*, New York: Dover Publications.

Miegel, F and Olsson, T (2008) From pirates to politicians: The story of the Swedish file sharers who became a political party, in N Carpentier, P Pruulmann-Vengerfeldt, K Nordenstreng et al (eds) *Democracy, Journalism and Technology*, Tartu: Tartu University Press, pp 203–217.

Mills, TL, Boylstein, CA and Lorean, S (2001) 'Doing' organizational culture in the Saturn Corporation, *Organization Studies*, 22(1): 117–143.

Mintzberg, H (1980) Structure in 5s: A synthesis of the research on organization design, *Management Science*, 26(3): 322–341.

Mintzberg, H (1979) *The Structuring of Organizations: A Synthesis of the Research*, Englewood Cliffs: Prentice Hall.

Mondon, A and Winter, A (2020) *Reactionary Democracy: How Racism and the Populist Far Right Became Mainstream*, London: Verso.

Monticelli, L (ed) (2022) *The Future is Now: An Introduction to Prefigurative Politics*, Bristol: Bristol University Press.

Moufahim, M, Reedy, P and Humphreys, M (2015) The Vlaams Belang: The rhetoric of organizational identity, *Organization Studies*, 36(1): 91–111.

Muhr, SL, Holck, L and Just, SN (2022) Ambiguous culture in Greenland police: Proposing a multi-dimensional framework of organizational culture for Human Resource Management theory and practice, *Human Resource Management Journal*, 32(4): 826–843.

Muldoon, J (2012) The Hawthorne legacy: A reassessment of the impact of the Hawthorne studies on management scholarship, 1930–1958, *Journal of Management History*, 18(1): 105–119.

Müller, M (2017) 'Brand-centred control': A study of internal branding and normative control, *Organization Studies*, 38(7): 895–915.

Müller, W and Strøm, K (eds) (1999) *Policy, Office, or Votes? How Political Parties in Western Europe Make Hard Decisions*, Cambridge: Cambridge University Press.

Neumann, S (1956) *Modern Political Parties*, Chicago: Chicago University Press.

Newton, K, Stolle, D and Zmerli, S (2018) Social and political trust, in E Uslaner (ed) *The Oxford Handbook of Social and Political Trust*, Oxford: Oxford University Press, pp 37–56.

Noel, H (2010) Methodological issues in the study of political parties, in SL Maisel, JM Berry and GC Edwards (eds) *The Oxford Handbook of American Political Parties and Interest Groups*, Oxford: Oxford University Press, pp 57–76.

Ómarsdóttir, SB and Valgarðsson, VO (2020) Anarchy in Iceland? The global left, pirates and socialists in post-crash Icelandic politics, *Globalizations*, 17(5): 840–853.

Önnudóttir, EH, Helgason, AF, Harðarson, ÓT et al (2022) *Electoral Politics in Crisis after the Great Recession: Change, Fluctuations and Stability in Iceland*, London: Routledge.

O'Reilly, CA and Chatman, JA (1996) Culture as social control: Corporations, cults, and commitment, *Research in Organizational Behavior*, 18: 157–200.

Osborne, R (2010) *Athens and Athenian Democracy*, Cambridge: Cambridge University Press.

Østergaard, J (2017) Ballade hos Elbæks tropper: Storsponsors søn smidt på porten, *Ekstra Bladet*, 18 May.

Osterman, P (2006) Overcoming oligarchy: Culture and agency in social movement organizations, *Administrative Science Quarterly*, 51(4): 622–649.

Ostrogorski, M (1902) *Democracy and the Organization of Political Parties*, New York: Macmillan.

O'Toole, M and Grey, C (2016) 'We can tell them to get lost, but we won't do that': Cultural control and resistance in voluntary work, *Organization Studies*, 37(1): 55–75.

Panebianco, A (1988) *Political Parties: Organization and Power*, Cambridge: Cambridge University Press.

Paneque, A (2023) *Podemos, Still a Movement Party? The Effect of Institutionalisation on a Political Party*, working paper, Barcelona: Universitat Pompeu Fabra.

Paolucci, C (1996) *A firm masquerading as a party transforms Italy: Berlusconi's Forza Italia*, ECPR Joint Session, Nicosia, April.

Parker, M (2000) *Organizational Culture and Identity*, London: Sage.

Parker, M (2021) The romance of prefiguration and the task of organization, *Journal of Marketing Management*, 39(9–10): 901–909.

Parker, S and Parker, M (2017) Antagonism, accommodation and agonism in critical management studies: Alternative organizations as allies, *Human Relations*, 70(11): 1366–1387.

Passarelli, G (ed) (2015) *The Presidentialization of Political Parties: Organizations, Institutions and Leaders*, Basingstoke: Palgrave Macmillan.

Pavía, JM, Bodoque, A and Martín, J (2016) The birth of a new party: Podemos, a hurricane in the Spanish crisis of trust, *Open Journal of Social Sciences*, 4(9): 67–86.

Pedersen, HH and Schumacher, G (2015) Do leadership changes improve electoral performance?, in W Cross and J-B Pilet (eds) *The Politics of Party Leadership*, Oxford: Oxford University Press, pp 149–164.

Pedersen, K and Saglie, J (2005) New technology in ageing parties, *Party Politics*, 11(3): 359–377.

Perrow, C (1967) A framework for the comparative analysis of organizations, *American Sociological Review*, 32(2): 194–208.

Peters, T and Waterman, R (1982) *In Search of Excellence: Lessons from America's Best-Run Companies*, New York: Harper & Row.

Petersen, LM, Just, SN and Husted, E (2022) Redistributive solidarity? Exploring the utopian potential of unconditional basic income, *Critical Sociology*, 49(3): 495–513.

Peterson, MF and Søndergaard, M (2011) Traditions and transitions in quantitative societal culture research in organization studies, *Organization Studies*, 32(11): 1539–1558.

Pilkington, E (2013) Icelandic MP who released WikiLeaks video plans US visit despite legal threat, *The Guardian*, 11 February.

Piven, F and Cloward, R (1977) *Poor People's Movement: Why They Succeed, Why They Fail*, New York: Vintage.

Plesner, U and Husted E (2019) *Digital Organizing: Revisiting Themes in Organization Studies*, London: Red Globe Press.

Poguntke, T and Webb, PD (2005) *The Presidentialization of Politics: A Comparative Study of Modern Democracies*, Oxford: Oxford University Press.

Polletta, F (2002) *Freedom Is an Endless Meeting: Democracy in American Social Movements*, Chicago: University of Chicago Press.

Podemos (2023) Transparencia Podemos, available at: https://transparencia.podemos.info/

Pombeni, P (1994) Starting in reason, ending in passion: Bryce, Lowell, Ostrogorski and the problem of democracy, *The Historical Journal*, 37(2): 319–341.

Popescu, D and Loveland, M (2022) Judging Deliberation: An assessment of the crowdsourced Icelandic constitutional project, *Journal of Deliberative Democracy*, 18(1): 1–14.

Prentoulis, M and Thomassen, L (2013) Political theory in the square: Protest, representation and subjectification, *Contemporary Political Theory*, 12(3): 166–184.

Pullen, A, Helin, J and Harding, N (eds) (2020) *Writing Differently*, Bingley: Emerald Publishing.

Quagliariello, G (1996) *Politics Without Parties: Moisei Ostrogorski and the Debate on Political Parties on the Eve of the Twentieth Century*, Brookfield: Ashgate.

Redding, SG (1994) Comparative management theory: Jungle, zoo or fossil bed?, *Organization Studies*, 15(3): 323–359.

Reedy, P, King, D and Coupland, C (2016) Organizing for individuation: Alternative organizing, politics and new identities, *Organization Studies*, 37(11): 1553–1573.

Reinecke, J (2018) Social movements and prefigurative organizing: Confronting entrenched inequalities in Occupy London, *Organization Studies*, 39(9): 1299–1321.

Reischauer, G and Ringel, L (2023) Unmanaged transparency in a digital society: Swiss army knife or double-edged sword?, *Organization Studies*, 44(1): 77–104.

Rhodes, RAW (2011) *Everyday Life in British Government*, Oxford: Oxford University Press.

Ringel, L (2019) Unpacking the transparency-secrecy nexus: Frontstage and backstage behaviour in a political party, *Organization Studies*, 40(5): 705–723.

Ringel, L and Brichzin, J (2021) Getting 'sucked into parliament': Tracing the process of professional political socialization, *ephemera*, 21(2): 77–107.

Robinson, M (2020) Corbyn's 'toxic culture' of chaos, Daily Mail, 19 June.

Robinson, K and Merrow, W (2020) The Arab Spring at ten years: What's the legacy of the uprisings?, Council on Foreign Affairs, 3 December.

Rodríguez-Teruel, J, Barrio, A and Barberà, O (2016) Fast and furious: Podemos' quest for power in multi-level Spain, *South European Society and Politics*, 21(4): 561–585.

Roethlisberger, FJ and Dickson, WJ (1939) *Management and the Worker*, Cambridge, MA: Harvard University Press.

Rosanvallon, P (2008) *Counter-Democracy: Politics in the Age of Distrust*, Cambridge: Cambridge University Press.

Rosenblum, N (2008) *On the Side of the Angels: An Appreciation of Parties and Partisanship*, Princeton: Princeton University Press.

Rothschild-Whitt, J (1979) The collectivist organization: An alternative to rational-bureaucratic models, *American Sociological Review*, 44(4): 509–527.

Roy, R (1967) Factionalism and 'stratarchy': The experience of the Congress Party, *Asian Survey*, 7(12): 896–908.

Rye, D (2014) *Political Parties and the Concept of Power*, Basingstoke: Palgrave Macmillan.

Rye, D (2015) Political parties and power: A new framework for analysis, *Political Studies*, 63(5): 1052–1069.

Samuels, D and Shugart, M (2010) *Presidents, Parties, and Prime Ministers: How the Separation of Powers Affects Party Organization and Behavior*, Cambridge: Cambridge University Press.

Sanches, ER, Lisi, M, Razzuoli, I and do Espírito Santo, P (2018) Intra-party democracy from members' viewpoint: The case of left-wing parties in Portugal, *Acta Politica*, 53(3): 391–408.

Sartori, G (1969) From the sociology of politics to political sociology, *Government and Opposition*, 4(2): 195–214.

Sartori, G (1976) *Parties and Party Systems: A Framework for Analysis, Volume I*, Cambridge: Cambridge University Press.

Scaff, LA (1981) Max Weber and Robert Michels, *American Journal of Sociology*, 86(6): 1269–1286.

Scarrow, SE (2002) Parties without members: Party organization in a changing electoral environment, in RJ Dalton and M Wattenberg (eds) *Parties without Partisans*, Oxford: Oxford University Press.

Scarrow, SE (2007) Political finance in comparative perspective, *Annual Review of Political Science*, 10: 193–210.

Scarrow, SE (2015) *Beyond Party Members: Changing Approaches to Partisan Mobilization*, Oxford: Oxford University Press.

Scarrow, SE and Webb, PD (2017) Investigating party organization: Structures, resources, and representative strategies, in S Scarrow, P Webb and T Poguntke (eds) *Organizing Political Parties*, Oxford: Oxford University Press, pp 1–28.

Scarrow, SE, Webb, PD and Poguntke, T (eds) (2017) *Organizing Political Parties: Representation, Participation, and Power*, Oxford: Oxford University Press.

Schattschneider, EE (1942) *Party Government*, New York: Holt, Rinehart and Winston.

Schatz, E (2009) *Political Ethnography: What Immersion Contributes to the Study of Power*, Chicago: University of Chicago Press.

Schein, EH (1985) *Organizational Culture and Leadership*, San Francisco: Jossey-Bass.

Schlesinger, JA (1984) On the theory of party organization, *The Journal of Politics*, 46(2): 369–400.

Schreyögg, G (1980) Contingency and choice in organization theory, *Organization Studies*, 1(4): 305–326.

Schultz, M (1995) *On Studying Organizational Cultures: Diagnosis and Understanding*, Berlin: Walter de Gruyter.

Schumacher, G and Giger, N (2017) Who leads the party? On membership size, selectorates and party oligarchy, *Political Studies*, 65(1): 162–181.

Schwartz, SH (2007) Universalism values and the inclusiveness of our moral universe, *Journal of Cross-Cultural Psychology*, 38(6): 711–728.

Selznick, P (1949) *TVA and the Grass Roots: A Study of Politics and Organization*, Berkeley: University of California Press.

Selznick, P (1952) *The Organizational Weapon: A Study of Bolshevik Strategy and Tactics*, New York: McGraw-Hill.

Selznick, P (1957) *Leadership in Administration*, New York: Harper & Row.

Seyd, P (2020) Corbyn's Labour Party: Managing the membership surge, *British Politics*, 15(1): 1–24.

Sheingate, AD (2003) Political entrepreneurship, institutional change, and American political development, *Studies in American Political Development*, 17(2): 185–203.

Sigurdarson, HT (2021) Reboot and repeat: Political entrepreneurship in the Icelandic Pirate Party, *ephemera*, 21(2): 139–175.

Sil, R and Katzenstein, PJ (2010) Analytic eclecticism in the study of world politics: Reconfiguring problems and mechanisms across research traditions, *Perspectives on Politics*, 8(2): 411–431.

Sinha, P, Smolović Jones, O and Carroll, B (2021) Theorizing dramaturgical resistance leadership from the leadership campaigns of Jeremy Corbyn, *Human Relations*, 74(3): 354–382.

Smith, JK (2009) Campaigning and the catch-all party: The process of party transformation in Britain, *Party Politics*, 15(5): 555–572.

Smolović Jones, O, Carroll, B and Sinha, P (2021) Resources of history and hope: Studying left-wing political parties through loss, *ephemera*, 21(2): 199–215.

Solebello, N, Tschirhart, M and Leiter, J (2016) The paradox of inclusion and exclusion in membership associations, *Human Relations*, 69(2): 439–460.

Solijonov, A (2016) *Voter Turnout Trends around the World*, Stockholm: International IDEA.

Southwell, P and Pirch, K (2021) Iceland's Pirate Party (Píratar) – In permanent opposition?, *Review of European Studies*, 13(3): 57–62.

Spicer, A (2014) Organization studies, sociology, and the quest for a public organization theory, in PS, Adler, P du Gay, G Morgan et al (eds) *The Oxford Handbook of Sociology, Social Theory, and Organization Studies*, Oxford: Oxford University Press.

Spicer, A, Alvesson, M and Kärreman, D (2009) Critical performativity: The unfinished business of critical management studies, *Human Relations*, 62(4): 537–560.

Spicer, A, Alvesson, M and Kärreman, D (2016) Extending critical performativity, *Human Relations*, 69(2): 225–249.

Spoelstra, S and Svensson, P (2015) Critical performativity: The happy end of critical management studies?, in A Prasad, P Prasad, AJ Mills et al (eds) *The Routledge Companion to Critical Management Studies*, Abingdon: Routledge, pp 69–79.

Stablein, R (2003) Data in organization studies, in SR Clegg, C Hardy and WR Nord (eds) *Handbook of Organization Studies*, London: Sage, pp 509–526.

Staggenborg, S (1988) The consequences of professionalization and formalization in the pro-choice movement, *American Sociological Review*, 53(4): 585–605.

Stavrakakis, Y (1997) Green ideology: A discursive reading, *Journal of Political Ideologies*, 2(3): 259–279.

Stavrakakis, Y, Katsambekis, G, Kioupkiolis, A et al (2018) Populism, anti-populism and crisis, *Contemporary Political Theory*, 17(1): 4–27.

Strøm, K and Müller, W (1999) Political parties and hard choices, in W Müller and K Strøm (eds) *Policy, Office, or Votes?*, Cambridge: Cambridge University Press, pp 1–35.

Suau-Gomila, G, Pont-Sorribes, C and Pedraza-Jiménez, R (2020) Politicians or influencers? Twitter profiles of Pablo Iglesias and Albert Rivera in the Spanish general elections of 20-D and 26-J, *Communication & Society*, 33(2): 209–225.

Sutherland, N, Land, C and Böhm, S (2014) Anti-leaders(hip) in social movement organizations: The case of autonomous grassroots groups, *Organization*, 21(6): 759–781.

Swan, J and Scarbrough, H (2005) The politics of networked innovation, *Human Relations*, 58(7): 913–943.

Swedberg, R (2009) *Tocqueville's Political Economy*, Princeton: Princeton University Press.

Taylor, FW (1911) *The Principles of Scientific Management*, New York: WW Norton & Company.

Teorell, J (1999) A deliberative defence of intra-party democracy, *Party Politics*, 5(3): 363–382.

Teubner, G (2006) In the blind spot: The hybridization of contracting, *Theoretical Inquiries in Law*, 7: 51–71.

Tholfsen, T (1959) The origins of the Birmingham Caucus, *The Historical Journal*, 2(2): 161–184.

Thorarensen, B (2014) Why the making of a crowd-sourced constitution in Iceland failed, *Constitution Making & Constitutional Change,* 26 February.

Thornborrow, T and Brown, AD (2009) 'Being regimented': Aspiration, discipline and identity work in the British parachute regiment, *Organization Studies*, 30(4): 355–376.

Tolbert, PS and Hiatt, SR (2009) On organizations and oligarchies: Michels in the twenty-first century, in PS Adler (ed) *The Oxford Handbook of Sociology and Organization Studies*, Oxford: Oxford University Press, pp 174–199.

Tormey, S (2015) *The End of Representative Politics*, Cambridge: Polity Press.

Tridimas, G (2019) Democracy without political parties: The case of ancient Athens, *Journal of Institutional Economics*, 15(6): 983–998.

Tulinius, K (2012) So what's this Pirate Party I keep hearing about?, Reykjavik Grapevine, 30 June.

Turner, V (1974) *The Ritual Process: Structure and Anti-Structure*, London: Penguin Books.

Van Biezen, I (2008) State intervention in party politics: The public funding and regulation of political parties, *European Review*, 16(3): 337–353.

Van Biezen, I (2012) Constitutionalizing party democracy: The constitutive codification of political parties in post-war Europe, *British Journal of Political Science*, 42(1): 187–212.

Van Biezen, I and Kopecký, P (2017) The paradox of party funding: The limited impact of state subsidies on party membership, in SE Scarrow, PD Webb and T Poguntke (eds) *Organizing Political Parties*, Oxford: Oxford University Press, pp 84–105.

Van Biezen, I and Piccio, D (2013) Shaping intra-party democracy: On the legal regulation of internal party organizations, in: W Cross and R Katz (eds) *The Challenges of Intra-Party Democracy*, Oxford: Oxford University Press.

Van Biezen, I, Mair, P and Poguntke, T (2012) Going, going, … gone? The decline of party membership in contemporary Europe, *European Journal of Political Research*, 51(1): 24–56.

Van Haute, E (2016) *Green Parties in Europe*, London: Routledge.

Van Maanen, J (1991) The Smile Factory: Work at Disneyland, in P Frost, LF Moore, MR Louis et al (eds) *Reframing Organizational Culture*, London: Sage, pp 58–76.

Varman, R and Chakrabarti, M (2004) Contradictions of democracy in a workers' cooperative, *Organization Studies*, 25(2): 183–208.

Vikkelsø, S (2014) Core task and organizational reality, *Journal of Cultural Economy*, 8(4): 418–438.

Vikkelsø, S (2016) Technologies of organizational analysis: Charting 'organization' as a practical and epistemic object, *STS Encounters*, 8(3): 1–24.

Vittori, D (2017) Podemos and the Five Stars Movement: Divergent trajectories in a similar crisis, *Constellations*, 24: 324–338.

Von dem Berge, B and Poguntke, T (2017) Varieties of intra-party democracy: Conceptualization and index construction, in SE Scarrow, PD Webb, and T Poguntke (eds) *Organizing Political Parties*, Oxford: Oxford University Press, pp 136–157.

Webb, PD and Keith, D (2017) Assessing the strength of party organizational resources: A survey of the evidence from the Political Party Database, in SE Scarrow, PD Webb and T Poguntke (eds) *Organizing Political Parties*, Oxford: Oxford University Press, pp 31–61.

Weber, M (1918/1994) Parliament and government in Germany under a new political order, in P Lassman and R Speirs (eds) *Weber: Political Writings*, Cambridge: Cambridge University Press, pp 130–271.

Weber, M (1919/2012) Politics as vocation, in HH Gerth and CW Mills (eds) *From Max Weber: Essays in Sociology*, Oxford: Oxford University Press, pp 396–450.

Weber, M (1922/1968) *Economy and Society: An Outline of Interpretive Sociology*, New York: Bedminster Press.

Weber, M (1949) *Methodology of Social Sciences*, Glencoe: Free Press.

Weick, KE (1969) *The Social Psychology of Organizing*, New York: McGraw-Hill.

Weick, KE (1990) Technology as equivoque: Sensemaking in new technologies, in P Goodman and L Sproull (eds) *Technology and Organizations*, San Francisco: Jossey-Bass, pp 1–44.

Weldon, S (2006) Downsize my polity? The impact of size on party membership and member activism, *Political Studies*, 12(4): 467–481.

Westwood, R and Johnston, A (2012) Reclaiming authentic selves: Control, resistive humour and identity work in the office, *Organization*, 19(6): 787–808.

White, J and Ypi, L (2016) *The Meaning of Partisanship*, Oxford: Oxford University Press.

White, M (2016) *The End of Protest: A Playbook for Revolution*, Toronto: Knopf Canada.

White, PE (1974) Intra- and inter-organizational studies: Do they require separate conceptualizations?, *Administration & Society*, 6(1): 107–152.

Whiteley, PF (2011) Is the party over? The decline of party activism and membership across the democratic world, *Party Politics*, 17(1): 21–44.

Whyte, W (1956) *The Organization Man*, Philadelphia: Simon & Schuster.

Widfeldt, A (2018) The radical right in the Nordic countries, in J Rydgren (ed) *The Oxford Handbook of the Radical Right*, Oxford: Oxford University Press, pp 545–564.

Willmott, H (1993) Strength is ignorance; slavery is freedom: Managing culture in modern organizations, *Journal of Management Studies*, 30(4): 515–552.

Wilson, F (1999) Cultural control within the virtual organization, *The Sociological Review*, 47(4): 672–694.

Wilson, JQ (1974) *Political Organizations*, New York: Basic Books.

Wolinetz, SB (1991) Party system change: The catch-all thesis revisited, *West European Politics*, 14(1): 113–128.

Wolkenstein, F (2016) A deliberative model of intra-party democracy, *Journal of Political Philosophy*, 24(3): 297–320.

Wolkenstein, F (2021) How can parties integrate today?, *ephemera*, 21(2): 217–232.

Woodward, J (1965) *Industrial Organisation: Theory and Practice*, Oxford: Oxford University Press.

Wright, C, Nyberg, D and Grant, D (2012) 'Hippies on the third floor': Climate change, narrative identity and the micro-politics of corporate environmentalism, *Organization Studies*, 33(11): 1451–1475.

Yanow, D, Ybema, S and van Hulst, V (2012) Practising organizational ethnography, in G Symon and C Cassell (eds) *Qualitative Organizational Research*, London: Sage, pp 331–350.

Zald, MN and Ash, R (1966) Social movement organizations: growth, decay and change, *Social Forces*, 44(3): 327–341.

Zald, MN and Denton, P (1963) From evangelism to general service: The transformation of the YMCA, *Administrative Science Quarterly*, 8(2): 214–234.

Zenner, W (1978) *Power and Ritual in the Israel Labor Party: A Study in Political Anthropology* by M. J. Aronoff, *American Ethnologist*, 5(2): 375–379.

Žižek, S (1989) *The Sublime Object of Ideology*, London: Verso.

Index

References to figures appear in *italic* type; those in **bold** refer to tables.

militias 14, 71
minority clause 27, 32
Mintzberg, Henry 91, 189–190
Momentum *see* United Kingdom
moral commitment 190
moral inclusiveness 207, 211–212
Moufahim, Mona 8
movement party 42, 67, 85–87, 114, 140
  see also European movement parties; parties
Movimento 5 Stelle 3, 78, 88, 148, 165
multifaceted cultural approach 179, 187–189,
  200, 206
Mussolini 72

N

National Council of Churches (NCC) 41
national culture and party culture 194
National Liberal Party (Germany) 4
neighbourhood-based groups 39
Netherlands 3, 131, 134, 135
  Dutch Freedom Party 140
Neumann, Sigmund 80
New Left 42
new/old parties, new ways 3, 49, 52, 80, 115
NGOs 5, 109, 122, 144, 153, 192
Noel, Hans 197
Nordic green party 20
Nordqvist, Rasmus 62, 97
norms 178, 198, 201, 220
  normative control mechanisms 10, 29–30,
    189–192
  normative power 189–190
Norwegian Progress Party 85

O

Occhetto, Achille 195
Occupy Wall street 3, 147–148
office redecoration expense 216
official story 5, 16–17, 118, 142
  election of leaders 44
  the hegemony of 128–138, 198
old ways 201–202, 223
oligarchy
  and Alternativet's political forum 56–60
  countering oligarchy 39–40
  iron law of 12, 23, 33–43
  process of oligarchization 36, 38, 43, 58
  'radical oligarchy' 63
organizational culture 31
  Alternativet 187–189
  cultural control 189–192
  differentiation 183–185
  fragmentation 185–187
  integration 180–183
  and leaders 180
  party cultures 192–197
  Schein's model *182*
  three approaches to 179–187
organizational sociology 30

organizational structure 15
  of Alternativet 103–105
  radical politics and formality 42
  types of party organizations 79–91
organizational studies 23–24
  anti-imperial stance 93–94
  and comparative perspective 141–145
  and the configurational perspective 91–94
  environmental contingencies *126*
  institutionalization of parties 126–128
  new parties, new ways 3–4
  organization of politics 4–6
  party organization 16, 119, 228–230
  power and stability 120–123
origin stories 69–70, 158
  Alternativet 96–99
Osterman, Paul 42
Ostrogorski, Moisei 4, 23, 34–36, 43, 56
  abolition of parties 30, 33
  and the corruption of democracy 24–33
  *Democracy and the Organization of Political
    Parties* 12–13, 24
  functional analysis 31
  life of 24
  and organization studies 30–33

P

Panama Papers 149, 168
Panebianco, Angelo 5, 8, 152, 161
  comparative-history theory 118–128
  Political Parties 15, 119
  uncertainty zones **121**
Parker, Martin 179, 186
ParlGov Project 145
Parson, Talcott 31
participation 87, 171
  and digital parties 89
  modes of 75, 109–112
  of movement parties 172–174
  and New Left movement 42
  observation research 44
particularization, problem of 108, 115, 214
parties 3, 17, 66, 131, 140, 187, 228–230
  abolition of parties 2, 30, 33
  basic anatomy of 69–73
  business firm party 67, 84–85
  cartel party 2, 8, 38, 67, 82–84, 132
  catch-all party 14–15, 67, 80–82
  caucus party 14, 26–29, 43, 60, 70–71
  and democracy 32, 39
  designed ambiguity 224–225
  Duverger's configurations *74*
  Duverger's theory of 68–78
  European movement parties 147–151
  history of 6–8, 26–28, 123
  income and spending 133–138
  institutionalization of 126–128
  mass party to cartel *83*
  members and staff 130–133